Phyllis Thompson
July 1986

◖◗◖◗◖◗◖◗◖◗◖◗◖◗◖◗◖◗◖◗◖◗◖◗◖◗◖◗◖◗◖◗◖◗◖◗

Facilitating
Education
for Older Learners

◯◖◗◯

David A. Peterson

Facilitating
Education
for Older Learners

Jossey-Bass Publishers

San Francisco • Washington • London • 1983

FACILITATING EDUCATION FOR OLDER LEARNERS
by David A. Peterson

Copyright © 1983 by: Jossey-Bass Inc., Publishers
433 California Street
San Francisco, California 94104
&
Jossey-Bass Limited
28 Banner Street
London EC1Y 8QE

Library of Congress Cataloging in Publication Data

Peterson, David Alan, 1937–
Facilitating education for older learners.

Bibliography: p. 307
Includes index.
1. Life skills—Study and teaching—United States.
2. Education of the aged. I. Title.
HQ2039.U6P47   1983   362.6'3   82-49041
ISBN 0-87589-565-4

Manufactured in the United States of America

The paper in this book meets the guidelines for permanence and durability of the Committee on Production Guidelines for Book Longevity of the Council on Library Resources.

JACKET DESIGN BY WILLI BAUM

FIRST EDITION

Code 8313

CI

A joint publication in
The Jossey-Bass Higher Education Series
and
The Jossey-Bass
Social and Behavioral Sciences Series

Preface

The older population is the fastest-growing segment of American society. This diverse group includes people who are experiencing good health, income, and social involvement as well as people who are struggling to maintain minimal control over their environment. Concern for this latter group has resulted in the development of numerous health and social programs. During the past few years, another trend has emerged to augment social services with programs designed to assist older persons in developing the skills they need to help themselves rather than rely on government or private agencies. These programs include intact, healthy, financially solvent persons as well as people who are seeking assistance with major problems. The emphasis and sponsorship of these offerings differ, but generally all fall under the rubric of education.

Educational programs can be used to diminish the dependence of middle-aged and older people, help them identify and solve their own problems, and facilitate psychological and social growth. Education, almost universally provided to youth, has been extensively available to older adults only in the last decade. Educational and community institutions, however, now realizing the potential of serving this clientele, are expanding their offerings. A wide range of programs has been developed that includes such topics as second-career preparation, preretirement education, planning for use of leisure, diploma and degree completion, personal growth, recreation, coping with change, retraining, and advocacy skills.

The demand for educational programs for older learners is running high, and institutional providers have found that recruiting large numbers of older students may be very worthwhile. However, institutions are also discovering that older students will not accept the same methods, materials, and curricula that served a younger clientele. Students from the older population groups demand substantial modification of admission procedures, content emphases, evaluation processes, course scheduling, and instructor behaviors.

In discussing the learning needs and interests of older persons, it is necessary to specify the persons who comprise this group. It is common to try to categorize older persons as individuals over 75 or 65 or 55 or some other age. However, chronological age is not a very accurate measure of oldness. Some persons are old at 55, while others are not at 75. The distinction is more accurately based on physical and psychological characteristics as well as social expectations, but because these are difficult to determine readily, chronological age is typically used. In this book, *older people* refers to persons who are over 55 and to those who are younger but who are experiencing difficulties caused by age-related factors. Thus, a person of 40 to 55 who cannot find a job, maintain a role, or undertake an activity because of age is considered an older person. Such individuals have difficulties that can be assisted through education, but the mode of instruction may need to be modified in order to best serve them.

As educational institutions, community organizations, and corporations have recognized the older person's urgent need for information and skills, programs designed to meet the instructional needs of older people have grown rapidly. *Facilitating Education for Older Learners* provides a comprehensive review of this area; identifies and traces the developing themes, showing how these are likely to affect the future; provides help to program developers and instructors on the best instructional procedures; and suggests knowledge and actions that will be needed if the field is to continue to grow in size and stature.

Facilitating Education for Older Learners brings together relevant research and experience concerning problems that confront instructors and program planners. In the process, it identifies the implications and applications of that research. It provides the basic knowledge necessary to achieve a consistent approach to high-quality instruction for older people. This is the essential purpose of the book—to help teachers and program planners understand the educational needs, wants, and characteristics of older learners so that appealing, valuable, and efficient instruction can be developed.

This book is directed toward people who are most likely to interact with older adults in a learning setting: professionals in continuing education programs; employees of agencies serving older people; program planners in community and nonprofit agencies; in-service trainers; personnel and training staff in business and industry; faculty members in the fields of psychology, counseling, education, or administration; and students in such areas as adult education, educational psychology, higher education, psychology, sociology, nursing, allied health, gerontology, and community development.

Organization and Content

The book is divided into fifteen chapters. Chapter One identifies the challenges posed to society now that increasing numbers of persons are living longer and spending greater amounts of time outside the typical work role. This growing population of retired but active people is causing major economic difficulties for the nation because we are failing to use its great talents and skills in productive work, both paid and voluntary. Current social norms support extended retirement, and the slow economy has caused much unemployment, but in the future we will need more workers. Educational institutions and community organizations are in a position to provide the updating and encouragement necessary for these millions of persons to reenter the economic marketplace and to continue their social contributions.

Chapter Two provides a brief history of education for older people. Although older adults have been involved in education for centuries, it is only in the last twenty or thirty years that learning programs have been specifically designed for them. To date, their participation has been somewhat limited, but as Chapter Three points out, it is rapidly changing. Indeed, older adult learning is one of the fastest-growing and most exciting areas of education, in part because of the large number of well-educated people in this age group.

However, stereotypes about older persons' ability to learn detract from the quality and scope of instructional programs. As Chapter Four indicates, early studies which concluded that intelligence declines throughout adulthood gave rise to inaccurate impressions that persist today. More recent studies have shown that one form of intelligence, crystallized intelligence, is maintained until very late in life and that with some compensation older persons can learn nearly as efficiently as young adults. Chapter Five describes adjustments that can be made to increase the learning performance of older people. These include slower pacing, increasing the meaningfulness of the content, making provisions for declines in vision and hearing, and reducing interference. When these accommodations are made by the instructor, older people can learn very well.

The physical and perceptual changes of aging are presented in Chapter Six. As a backdrop to designing educational programs, instructors and program administrators must recognize the typical physical changes that occur with aging.

Chapter Seven begins the discussion of the learning needs and wants of middle-aged and older persons. By considering the physical, psychological, and sociocultural changes that occur across the life span, it is possible to identify typical teachable moments. Content can then be developed that will more accurately address the interests and needs of older students. Specific content areas are discussed in Chapter Eight. Needs and wants are not necessarily the same, and program planners are cautioned against focusing exclusively on either.

Building on the foregoing discussions, Chapter Nine describes instructional methods that appear to be most effective for, and best received by, older learners. Many of the methodological suggestions are based on the concept of andragogy, but as is shown, this approach is not appropriate for all settings. Chapter Ten, on teaching and learning styles, expands the position that there is no one best way to instruct all older people. By considering the concept of cognitive style, teachers can begin to see distinctions among the learners and design instruction to fit the type of person they are teaching.

Chapter Eleven deals with one specific content area, that of retraining middle-aged and older workers. This is a part of the developing field of industrial gerontology and is one place where educational institutions and private-sector employers are jointly undertaking programs. Chapter Twelve deals with another area of instruction—preparation for retirement, which is one of the few content areas currently encompassing a large body of literature and practice. Since retirement preparation is such a vital area today, its content, process, and results are described in some detail.

Other aspects of the instructional delivery system are described in Chapter Thirteen. Since the field of senior adult education is relatively new and since it has not developed exclusively from any one institutional base, the variety of programs and sponsors is truly diverse. This is both a strength, because programs are available in many forms and from many organizations, and a weakness, because coordination at the community level has yet to be achieved.

Since so many organizations and individuals are interested in developing instructional programs for older persons, Chapter Fourteen provides an overview of the program development process. It suggests the steps that can be used and identifies some pitfalls which should be avoided. Chapter Fifteen concludes the book with some comments on the future of learning programs for older people and the challenges that face instructors and program developers in the coming years.

Acknowledgments

This book includes some parts that I have written for other works. The first draft of Chapter Two is to be included in a forthcoming book that D. B. Lumsden is editing for Hemisphere Publications. Parts of Chapter Three were published in the September-October 1981 issue of *Educational Gerontology*. Chapter Ten was originally written as an article with Donna Eden and published in the July 1981 issue of *Educational Gerontology*, and parts of Chapter Fifteen were included in a chapter of the Summer 1982 issue of *New Directions for Continuing Education* titled *Older Adult Learning*, edited by Morris Okun.

I would like to express my appreciation to May Ng, Tally Mintie, and Maiysha Myshere, who typed the manuscript; to Berit Burton and Karen Horwich, research assistants; to Jean Rarig, who edited much of the manuscript; to Helen Dennis, who provided much of the material for Chapter Twelve; and to Rosemary Orgren, who helped develop Chapter Fifteen. They and the supportive staff of the Leonard Davis School of Gerontology have provided encouragement and advice throughout the writing process.

Los Angeles, California   David A. Peterson
February 1983

Contents

jc/

Part Three   Developing Instructional Programs for Older Learners

The Author

David A. Peterson is professor of gerontology and director of the Leonard Davis School of Gerontology, Andrus Gerontology Center, University of Southern California, Los Angeles. He received his B.A. degree in history and education from Albion College (1959), his M.A. degree in teaching of social science from Western Michigan University (1964), and his Ph.D. degree in adult and continuing education from the University of Michigan (1969).

Peterson served as training director for the Institute of Gerontology and as assistant professor in the School of Education at the University of Michigan from 1969 to 1972. He moved to Omaha where he was director of the gerontology program and chairman of the University of Nebraska Center on Aging from 1972 to 1978. Since 1978, he has been at the University of Southern California.

His interest in the design and conduct of educational programs led to the publication in 1980 of *Gerontology Instruction in Higher Education,* a book he coauthored with Christopher Bolton. Peterson has published a number of articles and chapters on gerontology as a profession as well as works on the value of education for older persons. His teaching includes courses on professional issues in gerontology, retirement preparation, and educational gerontology.

Facilitating
Education
for Older Learners

1

Changing Social
and Economic Roles

We are living in an aging society. The United States has changed during this century from a nation in which most of our citizens were predominantly children and adolescents to one in which an increasingly large percentage are middle-aged and older. This has occurred because widespread application of medical care, public health, and consumer protection has made it possible for virtually everyone to avoid the illnesses and traumas of infancy and to live a healthy and productive life. This is the triumph of aging—the successful culmination of the search for extended, healthy life. Almost every person can count on living well into his or her seventies, and many will reach 80 to 85. Health concerns, though multiplying during the later years, can be controlled to such an extent that an active social, family, volunteer, and work life will be possible for nearly everyone.

And yet, the extension of life and the increasing numbers of older people are also a curse facing us, because the growing older population has brought with it massive new problems for this nation and increasingly for others around the world. An aging society has large numbers of persons who make costly demands on the health care system, who are dependent, and who

1

are kept from contributing to society by the social convention of retirement, which encourages withdrawal from productive employment.

At most points in the history of this nation, there have been few older, retired persons, and they presented limited problems, because they continued to work and live in circumstances similar to those of middle-aged persons. With the dissolution of the three-generation family, residential mobility, smaller houses, lengthened life expectancy, and retirement, older persons have become a greater concern. They frequently face income, health, housing, and transportation problems that tax their personal resources and require the assistance of families, the local community, and the government.

People are living longer, maintaining good health, and expecting that early retirement will provide for their "golden years." However, the costs of these developments to both the individuals and society are very large. To divert sufficient resources from the production sector of society to older people who are outside the work force is proving to be very costly and will become more so. The aging of America, then, poses serious challenges—ones that must be thoughtfully and innovatively addressed if both the nation and the older persons are to prosper.

This book is designed to address the learning needs and values of "older adults." *Old*, however, is a difficult concept to pinpoint. The U.S. Department of Labor defines older workers as those over 40; many social service and recreation programs for "seniors" use age 50 or 55 as a criterion; and the Social Security Administration uses age 65 for full retirement benefits. Any of these could be used as the definition of the term *old*. Here, however, *older persons* refers to those who by virtue of age require modification of the educational process; thus, persons who are perceived by others as old and are subtly discriminated against or expected to fail; persons with accumulated age-related decrements that modify perceptions or behaviors; or persons who have interests related to retirement, old age, or chronic health conditions—all these will be considered "older persons." These characteristics begin to occur most frequently around the age of 50 to 55.

Growth of the Older Population

In 1900 approximately 7 million persons in the United States were over age 55 (10 percent of the population). Both the absolute number and the percentage have increased throughout the century, so that by 1980 there were 45.5 million older people, nearly 23 percent of the population. Their numbers will continue to grow, and by 2000 we can expect 55 million persons in this category. However, the major impact of the aging society will not be felt until after the year 2010, when the baby boom of the 1950s and 1960s reaches retirement age. By 2040 we can expect up to 91 million persons in this age group (U.S. Bureau of the Census, 1979).

Human beings, like all other species, have a finite life span—probably about 110 years (Rockstein, Chesky, and Sussman, 1977). Throughout history, people have seldom approached that length of life, dying earlier because of disease, accidents, wars, starvation, or other environmental causes. Average life expectancy, 49 years at the beginning of this century, has steadily increased until today it approaches 78 for women and 70 for men (U.S. Bureau of the Census, 1979). It is still increasing and may be expected to reach approximately 85 years with assistance from the health community and appropriate personal life patterns (Fries and Crapo, 1981). By improving diet, getting sufficient exercise, eliminating smoking, and reducing alcohol consumption, the individual can retard the onset of debilitating diseases and extend healthy, vigorous life until at least age 85.

At the turn of the century, retirement and death were closely associated. People tended to work until health problems caused them to retire, typically only a short time before death. Today this is not the usual pattern. The period of healthy functioning has been extended, and people are retiring earlier. In 1900, 63 percent of men over 65 remained in the work force. Today, only 20 percent of men in this age group are employed (U.S. Bureau of the Census, 1979). This means that a whole new period of life has been created, a time after the employment years but before debilitating health conditions require reductions in mobility, activities, and involvement. This period is often called "later maturity" and is characterized by persons between the ages of 60 and 75 who are capable of continuing all their middle-age activities but have chosen to remain outside the work force. They are the persons seen at volunteer programs, senior centers, travel programs, golf courses, retirement communities, shopping centers, and hobby shows. They are a growing group whose personal and economic resources make them a new force in the economy and the community.

The successful achievement of the golden years for so many, however, is tarnished by the realization that a large older population is accompanied by huge economic and social responsibilities. When people live outside the work force, their financial needs must be met through someone else's productivity. For most retirees this occurs through social programs supported by government funds. Social Security, Medicare, and civil service and military pensions are examples of areas in which the federal government has accepted sole responsibility. In other programs, such as disability and Medicaid, state and federal government share the costs of services to the poor, the disabled, or those with specific health conditions. The government's responsibility to provide this type of support has grown since the inception of such programs in 1935 and was not seriously questioned until recently, when the size of the older population combined with difficult economic times to make the burden too heavy for government.

This burden may be seen in the current commitments of the federal government to service and income programs for the elderly. In 1978 the federal government's expenditure for the elderly was $112 billion, or 24 percent of the total federal budget; it is expected to reach $635 billion, 40 percent of the federal budget, by 2025 (Califano, 1978). This occurs because Social Security and pensions are linked to the cost of living, and the number of retired persons continues to grow. Unchecked, the total federal expenditure for older persons could ultimately demand the entire federal budget. This is obviously an intolerable situation. It is now receiving close scrutiny and must be dealt with in the near future.

Similarly, state and local government and private employers are facing a problematic future. They have made pension commitments to current employees but have not set aside funds to cover these. As the number of retirees rises and the length of time in retirement increases, a greater and greater proportion of current income must be devoted to pension payments. The disproportion has become so serious that some corporations have greater unfunded pension debt than the total value of the company. This may not pose a problem in the immediate future, but the long-range implications are tremendously serious.

The financial situation for older persons has improved over the decades of this century. The percentage of older people living in poverty has steadily declined until it is now only 15 percent. This remains too large a group, but substantial progress has been made. The quality of life for many retirees has become reasonably good, and they have come to enjoy the fruits of their later years.

Older persons, however, are increasingly being asked to contribute to their own welfare. Some are able to do this very easily through savings and acquired wealth. Others, however, are finding that to maintain the standard of living that they previously enjoyed, they must seek part-time employment or find some other means of supplementing their income. The contributions expected from older people are not limited to personal finances. They are being asked to contribute to the nation through volunteer and philanthropic roles. In the past, homemakers were a major source of volunteer labor for nonprofit community organizations. Their increased numbers in the labor market have resulted in vacant volunteer positions, which are being taken by older persons who have the time, vitality, and energy to complete these roles. This level of commitment will be necessary in the future if these organizations are to continue their critical role in health, social service, and recreational areas. Thus, older people will be expected to contribute to the welfare of the nation, whether in a voluntary or paid role.

Orientation Toward Older Persons

At the turn of the century, older persons typically fell into two categories: those who were healthy and still employed and thus not substantially different from middle-aged persons and those who were ill or disabled and outside the work force. People in the former category were not thought of as old and were treated no differently from those in their fifties or sixties. Families and communities accepted the responsibility of supporting and caring for those in the latter category, who were perceived to be unable to care for themselves.

As retirement became more common, persons who were not disabled or seriously ill left the work force, but our collective attitude remained one of providing assistance to them. Moody (1976) described this approach as a social service orientation that is common to many contemporary human service professionals and educators. Based on the belief that the unmet needs of older people must be ameliorated by changes in public policy, a social service orientation leads to the implementation of transfer payments or social programs provided by professionals, generally at government expense. The projects are based on contemporary society's liberalism and the belief in a welfare state where social justice and equality are highly valued. Too often the emphasis is placed on attacking the symptoms rather than correcting the causes of the social problems faced by the elderly. Older people often become passive recipients of services rather than honing the skills that could enable them to initiate their own more effective programs. In addition, social service programs may lead to segregation of persons of different ages and disengagement of these older individuals from their traditional roles and relationships. Programs may become mere activities rather than providing older persons with knowledge and skill that will ultimately enable them to improve their own lives.

The costs of the social service orientation have become extreme and within the near future will become unbearable. Consequently, some other orientation is likely to replace it. Moody suggested a second type of orientation, which he termed *participation*. This orientation contends that older people should continue to participate in the mainstream of society because they have skills and abilities that may help overcome some of the societal problems facing the nation.

Under this orientation, education is directed at normalizing the roles of the elderly and preserving individual dignity.

These are largely political values and can be realized through activity that is meaningful to the individual and the society. Educational programs in this area would encourage and facilitate such activity by assisting in the development of increased societal participation, by preparing individuals for second careers, and by expanding volunteer roles for those persons who are outside the work force. Through meaningful participation, older people can improve the quality of life in the country generally and at the same time assist themselves and their age mates to adjust to their changing circumstances.

Since many older persons are likely to maintain their health and energy resources and contribute through volunteer and paid roles in society, and since many are likely to desire the stimulation, involvement, and financial remuneration that result, the time seems appropriate to explore means by which this transition can be facilitated. This is not to suggest that a transition is not already beginning to occur; the changed retirement role is successfully acquired by a modest percentage of the older population, but the total numbers could be expanded quickly if policy and programs encouraged this development.

The Learning Society

Role change, employment, prevention of obsolescence, personal growth, and knowledge of opportunities can all be encouraged through education. In a society where the needs for change are great, and the group seeking change is outside the normal educational age, it is necessary to create alternative approaches to knowledge, attitude, and skill development. Fortunately, the United States is currently undergoing a basic and pervasive change in its educational system. We are entering what has been called the "learning society" (Cross, 1974). This is a society where lifelong learning is encouraged and implemented to some degree in order to meet the needs of all for learning from birth to death (Hoffman, 1980). In the United States today, as many as 58 million adults participate in educational activities. More than 5 million adults are studying for degrees; 10 million are enrolled in noncredit courses; 4 million are involved in company-sponsored training programs; and millions more participate in educational activities of churches, museums, libraries, and voluntary associations (Hoffman, 1980).

This learning society is characterized by three attributes that distinguish it from the more traditional relationships of education to the population. First, educational opportunities in a learning society are open to as many people as possible, rather than limited to a select group that is exclusively allowed to pursue more than rudimentary education. Second, educational institutions have begun to reach out to the community through off-campus courses, involvement in community affairs and problems, and the involvement of laypersons in instructional and policy-making roles. This movement has led to an openness toward teacher qualifications and a willingness to have as teachers people who are knowledgeable and skilled regardless of their formal academic preparation. Third, a learning society is likely to use teaching and learning resources wherever they are found, not restrict instruction solely to educational institutions. Clearly, many associations, businesses, libraries, museums, corporations, publishers, voluntary groups, churches, and hospitals are heavily involved in instruction.

In a learning society, change is continuous, and so must education be. Because people find it necessary to adjust and to succeed, they are almost compelled to discover means by which they can deal with the realities of change and personal growth. These means are increasingly available, and the diversity of providers allows much choice in terms of format, price, emphasis, and content. Education is no longer restricted to educational institutions, with the result that people of all ages are continuing their planned learning through a wide variety of means.

Older adults, who have not been the first clientele of these instructional programs, are now becoming increasingly visible in educational settings. Some programs are designed specifically for older persons, and these are growing in number, quality, and content breadth. They include courses at public schools, community colleges, liberal arts colleges, and universities as well as those offered by senior centers, community agencies, business and industry, and voluntary organizations. Older people also participate in educational experiences offered to persons of all ages and so are found in age-integrated programs in many types of educational, corporate, and service organizations. The learning society, however, includes not only those persons who choose to enroll in formal educational activities but also those who cultivate their personal growth and professional development by pursuing interests and solving their problems through conscious, planned learning. These people may never see an educational institution or an instructor, but through the development of their personal plan they are able to continue their learning throughout life. Older people, as one portion of this total audience, continue to be involved, and it is expected that they will provide an increasing proportion of the learning market in the years ahead. They are likely to be involved in educational experiences that differ greatly in content and purpose. For instance, they may participate in adult basic education, upgrading of job skills, retraining for second careers, group discussion for volunteer roles, development of leisure skills, development of health and consumer skills, or training for new roles or responsibilities.

Value of Education for Older People

The learning society is making formal education and individual learning available to increasing numbers of persons—older persons being one major group. Educational programs for older people encompass multiple delivery systems and lead to multiple outcomes. For instance, education may be designed to help the older person to understand the changes occurring within society, to be able to anticipate changes, and to prepare for them. Likewise, education may help to clarify the physical and psychological changes occurring within the individual that may cause concern if they are not differentiated from pathological conditions that occasionally occur in later life. Education may help the individual to develop coping skills for the new roles that may accompany retirement, widowhood, or relocation. It may help middle-aged persons prepare for these situations and maintain integration with both individuals and organizations. Education may be helpful in other ways. It may deepen lifelong interests by aiding in understanding the complexity of a subject matter area and by identifying persons with similar interests who can share the enjoyment and exploration of the area. It can be remedial, helping to overcome knowledge or skill deficiencies remaining from the years of formal schooling during childhood. However, education need not be limited to remedial or preventive functions; it can also be additive and growth-providing. Through instruction, people can undertake continuing personal growth and life enrichment, explore their ultimate potential, and expand the horizons their past lives and expectations have set for them. They can grow and contribute to others in ways that are both socially helpful and personally rewarding.

Although many types of education are of value and will continue to expand, there are three major areas in which social need and collective preference encourage educational development today. These are the areas of financial independence, health maintenance, and community involvement.

Financial Security. Increasingly, older adults need to continue working beyond normal retirement age to maintain their standard of living, and society needs the productive capacity that this large group offers. The linear life plan (education—work—retirement) is no longer universal as adults move into and out of education, work, and leisure. Retirement is becoming blurred as part-time work, temporary employment, paid volunteerism, seasonal employment, and phased retirement become common. In adulthood and later life, a blended life plan that intersperses education, work, and leisure is needed to provide financial resources, knowledge development, and revitalization.

Although it is true that interest in career information and training declines markedly after the age of 55 or 60, DeCrow (1978, p. 7) points out that "there is a reservoir of older people, several million, who are able, willing, in many cases eager to work—to improve or maintain income, to continue personal development, or to contribute to the social welfare as they always have over the long decades." In a recent survey conducted by the National Retired Teachers Association/American Association of Retired Persons (1980), 49 percent of those interested in enrolling in educational programs indicated that acquiring job skills was one of their most important reasons for participation.

Among retired males, 20 percent indicate an interest in returning to the labor force (Parnes and others, 1979), and of persons approaching retirement, fully 46 percent are interested in continuing their employment if appropriate alternative work designs are available (McConnell and others, 1979). This means that between 5 million and 12 million older adults currently have an interest in remaining employed.

Health Maintenance. Learning about health maintenance practices is important at every age but has particular significance for older adults. First, although illness is certainly not an inevitable part of normal aging, older adults are more vulnerable to it, they are more likely to require hospitalization, and they take longer to recover. It is important that they learn both preventive measures and new strategies for coping with the chronic conditions that occur in 80 percent of the older population. Second, as medical knowledge increases, so does the complexity of the health care system. While future cohorts of older adults can expect to enjoy increasing years of good health as diseases are eliminated or their effects minimized, they can also expect to face a bewildering array of choices about the best medical care, problems in gaining access to the medical care system, and the need to seek out a variety of medical specialists each interested in one bodily system or disease, but none concerned with the whole person. Older adults can reduce their own health care costs and lengthen their healthy years by taking an active role in their health care through relating more effectively to medical practitioners, asking pertinent questions, and making informed decisions.

Personal Development. Later adulthood is a dynamic time of life, offering each individual the opportunity to grow or decline. Changing roles, changing social needs, physical decline, and economic conditions present older persons with a continuing challenge to grow and adapt.

Prior experiences play a major role in how individuals develop, although "during adulthood, the meanings of past experiences and the influence they have on how a person perceives and responds to new events continually changes" (Knox, 1977, p. 11). For older adults, past experience has particular significance; there is a need to integrate and interpret it so that it gives meaning and continuity to one's life. Erikson (1963) refers to this period of life as one of the major developmental stages, "Ego Integrity vs. Despair."

The role of education in personal development, as in health development or financial security, is proactive, that is, it offers a means by which the initiative can be taken to help older learners both to optimize their potential for continued growth and to prevent psychosocial decline. Courses that help students learn how to learn, develop as whole persons, assess their values, and overcome psychological barriers to growth are among those that contribute to growth and integration. Courses that help older persons to "recover knowledge from their own life experiences" (Moody, 1978, p. 40) through life review, autobiographical exercises, and other techniques are particularly useful in helping them free their own potential for growth. Through such courses older learners will maintain growth that can be applied in various productive areas.

Benefits to Society. Older persons are not the only beneficiaries of their educational participation. Their families, friends, communities, and society as a whole reap positive rewards and avoid numerous ills that might have accompanied the increased age of the American population. Family and friends are the immediate beneficiaries of increased independence of older persons, as they need offer substantially less service and support when such persons can determine and carry out plans for their own welfare. Friends and relatives may also be indirect recipients of the information provided and the insights gained from instructional involvement. With increased numbers of educated older persons, family and friends have immediate access to role models for their own future and are able to observe the opportunities and enthusiasm that can be encouraged by education.

Communities benefit through the added contributions of older persons in voluntary activities, leadership positions, and paid employment. These involvements increase the older person's value in the community and lead the community to view the older person more favorably. They also provide increased opportunities for intergenerational contact, resulting in reduced isolation, greater cross-age understanding, and improved relationships among age groups in the community.

Society as a whole benefits from increased education of older people through increased numbers of persons who can continue productive employment, reduced pension and Social Security benefits for those outside the work force, healthier persons who need fewer services, and informed citizens who contribute through volunteer and community service roles.

Equalizing Educational Opportunity

Education is widely accepted as contributing to individuals' development and productivity. In this nation we annually invest huge sums of money for the education of children and young people, but we have not yet done the same for middle-aged and older adults. This inequity needs to be eliminated. Its removal will result in a major improvement in the lives of individuals and future prospects for society.

At the present stage of development, one of the most pressing concerns of education for older persons is its accessibility to older learners who, for reasons related in large part to their poorer educational backgrounds and their age, are seriously underrepresented.

Present Participation. Examination of the demographic characteristics of participants in continuing and adult education activities reveals a pattern that is already too familiar in the more traditional forms of education: The majority are relatively well educated, financially secure, and younger than nonparticipants. Of these attributes, the amount of formal schooling has the greatest influence (Cross, 1981). Persons with lower levels of formal education are far less likely to participate.

The second most powerful predictor of participation is age. Only 4.5 percent of adults 55 and over participated in some form of organized adult education in 1975; statistically, the older the person, the less likely he or she was to participate (National

Center for Education Statistics, 1978). One important reason for lower participation rates among older adults is undoubtedly their lower level of formal education, but age appears to act independently of other socioeconomic indicators in its influence on participation.

Other factors shown to influence participation are proximity and availability of opportunities. Studies comparing different regions of the country find greater participation in the western states, particularly in California, than elsewhere. This is attributed largely to the availability of educational opportunities that are offered without charge (Cross, 1981). The greater visibility of such programs appears to have created a climate of acceptance and interest not seen elsewhere.

What participation statistics do not reveal is the number of persons who are interested in further learning but do not take advantage of available programs. Cross (1978) notes that needs-assessment surveys typically find a large number of such persons, whom she terms "potential" or "would-be" learners; nearly three quarters of the adult population expresses interest in further learning, but only one third actually participates. Some nonparticipators identify themselves as self-directed learners, but even those persons express interest in having outside help at some time during their learning projects. Lack of interest, then, does not appear to be the main reason for the unequal participation rates among different groups.

Barriers to Participation. As important as the issue of accessibility is an understanding of what inhibits participation—the barriers, real or perceived, that prevent people from engaging in educational activities.

To date, the most comprehensive discussion of barriers to participation in education has been provided by K. Patricia Cross (1978), who classifies them under three headings: situational, dispositional, and institutional. Situational barriers are those that are related to one's life situation at a particular time. For older adults situational barriers include lack of mobility and lack of knowledge about available opportunities. Because older adults are outside the educational mainstream, they typically are unaware of community opportunities unless a concerted public information effort has been made by sponsoring organizations or institutions.

The cost of programs is also reported as a deterrent to participation. Cross has suggested that this apparently situational barrier may reflect unwillingness to pay certain costs more than inability to pay them, implying in such cases that program offerings are not seen as significant in value or relevance.

Dispositional barriers are those related to the ways one perceives oneself as a learner. For older adults, one such barrier is poor self-image, including the belief that one is too old to learn (a negative stereotype internalized by many older persons). Self-awareness as a learner may be distorted or subdued by such feelings. The educational background of older persons, which is more limited than that of younger persons, often engenders lack of interest in further learning, insecurity about the capacity to learn, and an inability to see the relevance of education to one's life.

Institutional barriers are organizational practices or procedures that exclude or discourage participation. These include inflexibility in scheduling, fee structures, inappropriate course offerings, unnecessarily complicated application and registration procedures, buildings and sites that are physically inaccessible, and poor dissemination of information about educational opportunities.

The barriers mentioned most often by adults are lack of time and cost. Other barriers frequently mentioned, in descending order, are scheduling problems, institutional requirements (red tape), lack of information about opportunities, problems with child care or transportation, lack of confidence, and lack of interest. The relative importance of such barriers may differ for persons of various ages and socioeconomic backgrounds. Older adults, for instance, cite being "too old" as a barrier more often. Furthermore, the real significance of such barriers as lack of confidence may be masked. It is probably more acceptable socially to cite lack of time as a barrier than lack of confidence.

Overcoming Barriers to Participation. In the future, the gap between educational participants and nonparticipants may widen. Those who have higher levels of education are likely to select adult education activities, while others may not, thus accentuating the existing inequity. Clearly, efforts to reach and serve the educationally disadvantaged will be critically needed.

Many strategies for making educational programs more accessible to older adults have been developed and successfully demonstrated. Institutions have reduced or waived tuition, expanded their continuing education curricula, and in some cases offered a distinct and cohesive program of courses designed specifically for older adults (Florio, 1978). Sometimes support services are available, and benefits such as use of campus facilities, a special meeting place, or reduced admission fees to campus events may be offered. The form that these efforts take has often been directly suggested by the existing barriers: cutting red tape in registration procedures, scheduling short-term courses that meet during the day, or including orientation workshops and counseling as a regular part of the program (Florio, 1978). Other efforts—networking and using outreach strategies to find older adults and assure them of their capabilities, for instance— are suggested by an analysis of current literature (Cross, 1981; Spencer, 1980; Van Dusen, Miller, and Pokorny, 1978).

In sum, educational programs for older persons are increasing and enrollments are growing. This growth can be attributed both to the larger numbers of older persons in our society and to the fact that educational institutions and community organizations have consciously developed programs to serve this population. The problem of equity (equal access) remains, however. Older persons, especially those who have experienced limited access to educational opportunities over a lifetime, are still underrepresented in the organized learning activities that could improve their lives in important ways. Barriers to educational participation that older persons face are not universally understood, and efforts to overcome them are scattered.

Quality of Instruction

Quality of instruction is essentially concerned with two concepts: effectiveness and efficiency. High-quality instructional activities accomplish their objectives using a minimum of resources and time. This requires good planning and careful selection of materials, methods, and faculty to fit different course objectives and learner abilities. Although most instructors are adept in handling these variables when teaching typical students, they are less experienced at tailoring instruction to the learning styles and desires of older adults.

It is sometimes argued that education is fundamentally the same for all ages (Houle, 1972) and that basic differences between learners, not age groups, have the greatest influence on selection of instructional strategies (Richardson, 1981). For example, learners with the greatest educational experience and self-motivation require quite different instructional strategies than less sophisticated learners. These differences exist among learners of all ages; instructors of older persons unquestionably face many of the same challenges as instructors of younger persons.

Recent research, however, suggests that older adults can profit from the use of strategies and techniques designed to address their unique abilities and learning needs (Botwinick, 1978; Arenberg and Robertson-Tchabo, 1977). For older learners, slower pacing, use of advance organizers (see Chapter Five), positive feedback, reducing diversity and interaction of tasks, and building on previous experience and knowledge are effective techniques. Teaching older adults requires not only knowledge of the content and appropriate methodology but also understanding of the real potential of the older learner and the unique limitations that members of this group typically bring to the learning experience.

Although educational programs for older adults are growing in number, no parallel increase in training for the educators employed in these programs has occurred. It is not surprising to find that many instructors share popularly held but inaccurate beliefs about the aged and their learning abilities and know little of strategies and techniques that would improve their teaching.

Intelligence. The popular notion that older persons are not able to learn can be traced to early studies of intelligence that indicated that learning potential peaked at age 16 to 22, remained stable for some time, and then declined throughout the remainder of life. These early studies used a cross-sectional approach, which compared people of various ages. When older persons achieved lower scores, the conclusion was that their intellectual capacity had declined. Such comparisons did not account for the many other possible explanations: cohort differences, historical variations, or age-related differences in educational attainment, occupational status, health status, or social environment. Subsequent longitudinal and sequential research (which combined cross-sectional and longitudinal measurement) has yielded a far more positive picture of intelligence in old age (Schaie and Parr, 1981).

It is now recognized that intelligence does not universally decline after young adulthood and that verbal and information skills may even continue to increase in later life. Although biological structure may determine psychological function in childhood, factors other than one's biological makeup have greater influence on intellectual development in maturity. Furthermore, mental ability is not unitary; it has many aspects, which develop at different rates. Some may decline in later life while others improve; for each individual the process is a little different. Summarizing research from 1883 through 1979, Schaie (1980) concluded that "it is clear that reliable decrement until very old age (and by that I mean late eighties) cannot be found for all abilities or for all individuals" (p. 70). Decrements that do occur involve abilities that require speed of response, and such decrements are more likely to be found in persons living in socially deprived environments. "In healthy, well-educated populations ontogenetic change on intellectual-ability variables is proportionally small" (Schaie, 1980, p. 71).

Despite such research, the belief that intelligence declines in old age persists, even appearing in such journals as *Nation's Schools and Colleges*; one author maintained that "after middle-age our brains begin to die . . . the large reserve of mental capacity enjoyed in younger years begins to disappear so that at 70, say, we must either function at the limits of our intellects or face senility" (Downey, 1974, p. 36). This belief needs to be countered by widely distributing statements such as the following: "Cognitive tests that assess an individual's accumulation of verbal skills and general information, or tasks of learning, memory and problem solving that are well imbedded in a matrix of meaning, are those typically found to improve throughout adulthood and well into old age. On the other hand, tests relating to the perception of relationships among abstract symbols (for example, geometric shapes), to the integration of new and complex material, or to the effective use of information under conditions of time restriction and in highly abstract contexts are the kinds of tests on which older adults tend to do much more poorly than their younger counterparts" (Labouvie-Vief, 1978, p. 233).

Learning Skills. Other writers (E. B. Bolton, 1978; Moody, 1978) have focused on the special problems older adults face because of physical and perceptual deterioration. Physical changes occur throughout adulthood, and in later life their cumulative effects may influence efficiency of learning (included are slowed reactions, substantial decline in visual and auditory perception, and reduced levels of energy and physical stamina). These physical elements, along with other noncognitive factors (heightened anxiety in a learning experience, increased susceptibility to interference, motivation to learn), substantially affect the way older people learn.

Conclusions

Studies of intelligence and learning performance indicate a high level of cognitive capacity throughout the life span. Older people are able to learn and adapt their behavior in order to remain useful in both paid employment and volunteer roles. This productivity will be imperative in the future, as economic and demographic changes are forcing this nation to use all resources efficiently in order to maintain the current quality of life. To date, contributive demands have seldom been made on the older segment of our population. Both older workers and employers have looked toward early retirement rather than an extended work life. Education has the responsibility of reversing the negative biases that support this viewpoint and providing the skills necessary to successfully incorporate the contributions of this substantial group. This is the challenge facing our nation today (and much of the rest of the world); it is the topic that is addressed in this book.

2

⊙I⊙I⊙I⊙I⊙I⊙I⊙I⊙I⊙I⊙I⊙I⊙I⊙I⊙I⊙I⊙I⊙I⊙I⊙I⊙I⊙I⊙I

Trends in Educational Programs

Older people have participated in instructional activities as long as such programs have existed. Historically, education was directed primarily toward adults, and participants were persons with available time and interest. Older people were part of this group, involved both as learners and as teachers. Education, then, is not foreign to older people, but in the United States only recently have conscious attempts been made to recruit older participants and to design educational experiences specially for persons in this age group.

Florio (n.d.) has suggested that there are three main categories of education for older people. They are based mainly on the emphasis of the instructional offerings and the way these offerings are designed. The categories are (1) programs in which special privileges for seniors are provided. These consist of nothing more than the regular course offerings of an organization or institution but are provided to older people at a reduced cost, with lower admission criteria, or without credit. (2) Programs in which a few courses have been modified so that they fit the special interests of older adults. These offerings may be specially designed for the older participant, or they may be typical courses

Higher Ed.

with a new title or time assignment made to attract a few more older students. (3) Programs in which new courses are designed, packaged, and offered specifically and often exclusively for older persons. Frequently, these offerings exist apart from other curricula of the institution and are presented in a manner and at a time when they are most appealing to older persons.

Education, then, can include older people in an indirect way, or it can be designed specifically for their unique interests and capabilities. Over the history of this nation, a variety of programmatic developments have involved older people, initially as a part of the general clientele and later as a primary audience.

Development of Adult Education in the United States

Education of older people developed primarily from the adult education movement of the United States. This movement is as old as the nation itself and has its roots in the social, cultural, and political concerns of the time. Our earliest leaders believed that American democracy rested on the informed participation of its citizens, that public decisions could be improved through the widespread use of education. Thus, education became a citizen's right, and discussion of it dealt not with whether the general public should be educated but with how this education could be most effectively provided.

Early adult education, then, had an underlying concern for the development of good citizenship; the capacity to read and write was cultivated so that the individual could participate in the decisions of the nation. Literacy was often associated with a religious emphasis because the ability to read was closely tied to an understanding of the Bible and the desire to gain salvation. Thus, much of religious education had a decidedly political/civic orientation, and much of the political discussion had close ties to Christianity, if not a specific denomination. Political and religious leaders took an active interest in education, and the elementary and secondary school system reflected this concern.

Benjamin Franklin played a key role in developing one of

the first adult education activities in this nation. In 1727 he formed a small study and discussion society, later called the Junto, which lasted for thirty years (Grattan, 1955). It was composed of twelve persons and met weekly to discuss community and social considerations. The group clearly had an intellectual orientation, but its discussions often concerned current problems or issues in Philadelphia. The Junto led to the formation of local lending libraries that made a variety of books available to all citizens and greatly expanded the accessibility of printed material. The Junto also served as the stimulus for the establishment of a national organization, later called the American Philosophical Society. However, the local discussion group in which each member took responsibility for the preparation and presentation of materials was Franklin's major contribution to American adult education.

A hundred years after the creation of the Junto, another adult education innovation began to grow to popular acceptance. This was the Lyceum, a lecture series that provided adult citizens, especially those in small and rural towns, with an introduction to scholarly knowledge, generally in an applied orientation. The Lyceums sought to raise the education level of adults who had not had the opportunity to complete an elementary education, and the movement's adherents became strong supporters of common schools in each community. Much of the Lyceum program was provided by traveling lecturers who dispensed both enlightenment and inspiration through the well-prepared and delivered oration. The Lyceum movement lasted over 100 years and was the means for bringing some intellectual stimulation into many of the rural areas of the nation, especially in the Midwest.

The Chautauqua movement followed the development of the Lyceum by fifty years and provided a combination of religious orientation, liberal education, and the performing arts. Founded as a summer assembly on the shores of Lake Chautauqua, New York, in 1874, it provided training for Sunday school teachers, enlightenment for church members, and the basis for a national outreach of tent performances over several decades. Initially established by the Methodist Episcopal Church, the summer assembly became basically nondenominational and drew audiences from a wide range of religious and cultural backgrounds. Music, drama, lectures, discussions, and individual study were encouraged in a pleasant and relaxed atmosphere that proved to be appealing to many people. The "tent chautauquas" provided similar programs across the nation, although they did not include the residential aspect of the original New York setting. Tent chautauquas continue to be held to this day, and the summer assembly grounds in New York remain a popular setting for education of older people (see Watkins, 1981).

There is little reason to believe that the Junto, Lyceum, and Chautauqua were designed or operated mainly for older learners. The Lyceum was oriented principally toward younger people, and the Junto included persons of all ages. The Chautauqua may have appealed more to older people, since it was a summer resort where people typically stayed a few days to several weeks. At least today, one finds that many of the persons in attendance are of retirement age, although this may be a recent phenomenon. These programs, however, provide the basic orientation of most of the current programs for older adults— liberal education, religious education, vocational/personal education, and civic/community education.

Educational Programs for Older Adults

Educational programs for older persons today reflect the history and heritage of the adult education movement. They include a variety of program types, and the purposes are extremely broad. Many have been in existence for several years and have developed distinctive formats and extensive offerings. It is surprising, then, that these programs are so difficult to characterize and that their history has been reviewed so infrequently. The diversity of programs makes them very troublesome to describe, and the lack of a formal history offers the reviewer limited clues to their collective genesis. There are several reasons that description is difficult:

Problems

- The lack of definition as to what constitutes education.

- The diversity of agencies and institutions that offer these programs.
- The current nonexistence of a national association that would coordinate and facilitate these programs.
- The variety of funding sources that support programs.
- The lack of a continuing collection and presentation of data on program content, enrollment, and budget.

The weakness of the field in these five areas clearly indicates the limited institutionalization that has occurred in this type of instruction. Educational offerings for older people are heterogeneous in sponsors, program types, audiences, and content. There is no central system of support or of monitoring these activities, and so they develop in idiosyncratic patterns depending on the preferences of administrators and the needs of local communities. This often makes them very responsive to the wishes of the constituent clientele but does not facilitate development of easily described program categories, nor does it provide much assistance in replicating a program with other sites and sponsors.

An additional reason for lack of clarity in this developing area is the unevenness of program reporting. Those few fortunate organizations that have received financial support from a federal agency or foundation have frequently been required or encouraged to report their results in monographs or journal articles. Many of these are available and form the best source for assessing the state of the field. Most programs, however, have been built on local funding without the expectation or requirement to disseminate information about their progress. Consequently, descriptions are not likely to be found in the literature. These programs are less likely to be visible beyond their own boundaries and may be overlooked in any summary of activities in this general area.

Early Programs. A number of surveys have been conducted to provide insight into the extent and type of instructional programming for older people (Hendrickson and Barnes, 1964; American Association of State Colleges and Universities, 1974; Korim, 1974; Glickman, Hersey, and Goldenberg, 1975;

Sarno, 1975; Edelson, 1976; Sprouse, 1976; DeCrow, 1978, n.d.; Rappole, 1978; Institute of Law and Aging, 1978; Scanlon, 1978; Chelsvig and Timmermann, 1979). Although each of these reports some of the data collected, most emphasize that the response rate was too small to be generalizable. Accordingly, the researchers resort to the method of describing selected programs as models of what can be done in specific settings and content areas. Such descriptions provide extensive understanding of the history and operation of an individual institution's project but offer little insight into the comparative aspects of program development or the general extent of educational programming for older adults. Hence, we are left with a very partial view of the programs, both historically and currently. We must be guided both by what is said and by what is not said and balance it with general knowledge and personal experience, hoping that the true pattern of development is not too far from what the literature describes.

Educational experiences for older people developed as an extension of other community-based adult education programs. One of the earliest comprehensive surveys of such activities (Donahue, 1955) indicated that a wide variety of instructional programs were underway by the mid 1950s but that many of these began by simply including older people in the organization's or agency's existing educational programs. As in Florio's first category of educational programs, older people were not the primary audience but were included in programs designed originally for other age groups. Later these programs were modified to make them more appealing to, and more specifically oriented toward, older people.

The breadth of institutional sponsorship twenty-five years ago is truly surprising, for adult education activities then, as today, were diverse in both content and sponsorship. Donahue's summary described programs in public schools, colleges, university extension, agricultural extension, correspondence, libraries, state agencies, federal agencies, employment agencies, institutions, business and industry, government, and unions. Each of these sponsors was offering instruction and reported good receptivity by older participants.

Few of these programs included a separate administrative structure for their operations. Most were sponsored by an organization or agency designed for some purpose other than education for older people. Older adult education was an adjunct to the organization's primary mission, and although there was major commitment to the programs that were operating, there was little commitment to developing the separate organizational structure that would assure program visibility and long-range maintenance of the activities.

It is not surprising that the number of participants in early programs was reported to be very small. Often programs attracted a few dozen people and would succeed or fail depending on the ability of the program planner to accurately gauge participant interests. The 1950s, then, were the time when program development began, with the first correspondence course at the University of Chicago, the first preretirement education program, the first community-needs survey by the University of Michigan, and numerous other beginning events that led to later expansion and refinement.

The 1960s involved the spread of programs into a greater number of agencies and institutions. Although the type of programs changed little, it became relatively easy to locate educational programs for older people in any part of the country. Thus, the extent and pervasiveness of programs grew rapidly as interest in the problems of older people expanded. Since the 1960s were the time of social concern for many underprivileged groups, it is not surprising that instructional efforts for older people adopted, in Moody's terms, a social service orientation. Educational programs emphasized the crisis of adjustment to retirement and the need for outside assistance to overcome the trauma of role change. Program rationales emphasized the needs of older people and the responsibility of social institutions to meet these needs through service programs.

One example of this type of instructional program can be seen in the series on preparation for retirement developed at the University of Chicago and the University of Michigan. Within both industry and higher education, counseling and instructional programs developed to provide assistance to the older worker who was considering retirement. Woodrow Hunter's work at Michigan was the most visible of these activities, and his surveys of programs as well as his longitudinal research on program outcomes provided much of the literature available at the time (Brahce and Hunter, 1978). This area has continued to develop and has rapidly expanded with the passage of the 1978 Amendments to the Age Discrimination in Employment Act.

The amendments (which eliminated mandatory retirement before age 70) have also encouraged the development of retraining programs for older workers in business and industry. Although such projects have been underway for many years and have been described and refined by Belbin and Belbin (1972), interest in them has been especially high since the passage of the recent legislation. It is likely that retraining activities will make up a major part of the instruction of older people in the years ahead.

A shift from Moody's social service orientation can be noted in the background paper for the 1971 White House Conference on Aging. In it Howard McClusky accurately reflected the new orientation of the 1970s when he changed the emphasis by pointing out the positive nature of education and the potential that every person, regardless of age, has. His statement that education was an affirmative enterprise that resulted in positive outcomes has been quoted on numerous occasions and has proved to be the orientation of the field through much of the decade (McClusky, 1971).

The development of educational programming for older adults continued during the 1960s and was encouraged through a variety of conferences and workshops for those considering involvement. Florida State University was an early entrant into this area, offering annual conferences in the late 1960s and early 1970s designed to train leaders who were interested in education of the aging. It is interesting that each of these early conferences had a heavy dosage of introductory gerontology, including an overview of the physiological, psychological, and social aspects of the aging process. Other content included the educational interests of the elderly, program planning, and experiences of other programs. These conferences often resulted in a publication of the presentations, which was widely circulated for later reference and use.

The New England Gerontology Center held similar conferences in 1974 and 1975, which brought together many educators and program planners from that part of the country and gave impetus to the developing programs in the Northeast. Other conferences (University of Michigan, 1968; University of Southern California, 1972; and Virginia Beach, 1975) have added to the visibility of the area of older adult education and have stimulated its continuing growth.

Regional and national meetings of gerontological and adult education associations have also helped the process. The Western Gerontological Society has made education of older people a major part of its annual conferences for several years. Since the organization is oriented primarily toward the practitioner, workshops and symposia have dealt with program design and operation rather than any research on the topic. The Gerontological Society, through the auspices of its Education Committee, held several symposia on education and training in aging at its annual meetings in the early 1970s. These drew large audiences and tended to focus on conceptualization of program purposes, national policy issues, and funding for these programs.

The Adult Education Association of the U.S.A. (AEA) has had a Section on Aging since its establishment in 1951 and has generally included some sessions on older participants in its annual conferences. The AEA has also been active in developing publications in the area of education for the aging. Donahue's (1955) book was the product of the AEA project, as were Grabowski and Mason's volume *Education for the Aging* (n.d.) and Jacobs, Mason, and Kauffman's summary of the field and bibliography (1970). There were few other major publications before the middle 1970s. Thus, AEA and its Aging Section may be given credit for developing publications that provided much of our knowledge of activities before 1970.

The conferences and workshops, as well as individual project reports, provided a number of guides for the development of instruction of older people. Most of these included an overview of the changing demographic nature of the U.S. popu-

was osh
of until '67

lation, some rationale for the development of such programs, and recommendations for program development (Hixson, 1968; Hendrickson and Aker, 1969; *Adventures in Learning*, 1969; Hendrickson, 1973; Academy for Educational Development, 1974; Glickman, Hersey, and Goldenberg, 1975; Claeys, 1976; Edelson, 1976; Myhr, 1976; Cross and Florio, 1978; Scanlon, 1978; DeCrow, n.d.). Most of these reports were published in paperback and generally have had limited distribution. It is interesting that so few volumes have been offered through regular publishers that provided the "how to" of educational programming for older people.

A recent book that approaches this role is *Introduction to Educational Gerontology*, edited by Ronald Sherron and Barry Lumsden (1978). The book was prepared from a series of papers presented at the First International Congress of Educational Gerontology. (No second conference has been held.) The book includes background material on educational philosophy and psychology as well as on program planning, instructional methods, evaluation, and intergenerational programming. It has been widely used and provides an overview of the field from the perspective of several authors.

Lumsden made another substantial contribution to the field by establishing the journal *Educational Gerontology: An International Quarterly*. Although the international orientation is not often in evidence, the journal has provided an enormous service to researchers and practitioners who wish to share their results, insights, and thoughts regarding the design and operation of education for older people. Since its beginning in 1976, the journal has consistently published high-quality papers covering the subject from a variety of perspectives. Its special issues on old age and literature (1977), training (1978), and reading (1979) have provided comprehensive and useful treatments of these areas, and its regular feature of learning resources in the field is a relevant and helpful summary of recent publications and materials. The journal, though not the product of a scholarly organization, has done more than any other single source during the decade to make the field of research and practice of education for the aging visible and respected.

The most recent volume dealing with older adult instruction is titled *Programs for Older Adults* (1982a), edited by Morris Okun of Arizona State University. As part of the *New Directions for Continuing Education* series, this short volume provides a good survey of the field and includes in-depth descriptions of programs offered by a church, school district, community college, and county commission on aging.

Recent Developments. In 1970, community colleges became the focus of the expanding instructional network in aging when the Administration on Aging provided a grant to the American Association of Community and Junior Colleges (AACJC) to encourage that organization "to develop an awareness of the needs of older Americans and to explore ways in which these community-oriented institutions might contribute to an improvement in the quality of life in the nation's elderly population" (Korim, 1974, p. 5). This project involved a survey of current activities, conduct of several conferences and workshops, and the publication of several documents designed to help community college program planners understand the needs of the older person and educational approaches to fulfilling them.

It is impossible to determine the specific effects of this project, but it is fair to say that the mid 1970s saw the development of many new programs for older people by community and junior colleges. These were not all educational in nature, but they did show the increasing willingness of the community college system to include older people in existing programs and to give them special consideration in designing new instructional and service undertakings. Some of this development would have come without the AACJC project, but its activities were initiated at an ideal time, and the dynamic leadership given by Andrew Korim provided a major impetus to the development of programs in two-year colleges across the nation.

Another major development during the 1970s was the rapid growth of residential education of older persons. Through the Elderhostel program, week-long programs of instruction, discussion, and entertainment for older people are provided by colleges and universities across the nation. These programs have grown rapidly during the past five years and have attracted thousands of persons to learning activities that are reminiscent of the Chautauqua movement. There are few other examples of residential education for older people, but the response to this offering has proved once again that a combination of stimulating atmosphere, congenial company, and varied activities is both desired and appreciated by older people. Its future growth may prove to be one of the most significant movements in senior adult education, for it is basically a return to the liberal arts programs of the past, with a sprinkling of civic instruction. It is a start toward reaching Moody's category of self-actualization and a clear step beyond the social service mentality.

Financial Support. The growth of educational programming for older people did not occur because any single government agency or foundation supplied funding. Most of the activity occurred under the sponsorship of local agencies and institutions, deriving its support from their regular program budget. That is, program developers and administrators initiated these new programs for older adults while continuing whatever other responsibilities they had. Thus, the individual staff member subsidized the planning and development until the organization could be convinced that the program was worthwhile. There is no way of knowing how frequently this happened, but local leadership appears to be the key in developing programs, and so it was undoubtedly very often.

From the national point of view, two funding sources must be highlighted that added substantially to program growth. The federal government has supported educational programs for the aging from several sources. Title I of the Higher Education Act of 1965 has been used by colleges and universities to direct their resources and staff into program development for older people. Although many additional types of community programs were funded under this title, programs for the aging have been developed in many parts of the country and have become a major part of the overall education pattern. The Administration on Aging has also funded many educational programs. Initially under Title III and later as part of the Nutrition Program and Model Projects, numerous education components of other projects and specific instructional programs were supported.

There has been no continuing or national strategy in these
grants; they have stimulated much action and interest but have
resulted in relatively little insight into the most effective means
of designing, implementing, or conducting education for older
people.

Private foundations have also supported educational programs for the aged. Although many foundations have given local
awards, only the Edna McConnell Clark Foundation has devoted large amounts of money to this area and continued the
support over several years. That foundation has chosen to support a few projects, especially those involving the design of volunteer and employment opportunities for older persons. Through
the Academy for Educational Development and several local
projects, the foundation has tried to show what can be done by
consistent support. Although several of its publications indicate
the value of educational programs and describe the steps in developing them, the information does not provide much insight
into the best means of developing such a project. This is disap-
pointing, since the original plan offered the possibility that the
projects would substantially increase our knowledge on the effects of various developmental strategies.

The Contributions of Howard Y. McClusky. An understanding of the development of education for older persons is
not possible without at least a mention of the impact of one
individual on the area. Although many people have contributed,
there is one person who stands out so clearly that his involvement must be dealt with separately. That person is Howard Y.
McClusky, Emeritus Professor of Education from the University
of Michigan. In reviewing conferences, symposia, workshops,
and papers on education for the aging, his name inevitably
emerges as one of the major speakers and conceptualizers of the
field. His background paper for the 1971 White House Conference on Aging has already been mentioned, and his articles and
papers are widely used. However, his influence came about
through his personal assistance as well as his writing and speaking. No one else so consistently and tirelessly helped others to
develop programs for older people.

At conferences and meetings, in his office or in his home,

in the classroom or at workshops, he was continually supportive and enthusiastic about the great potential of education for older people as a positive force to be developed and directed in the years ahead. His personal support of program planners and his willingness to listen, share, and compliment led to the establishment of many programs based on his original ideas and continued encouragement. His support of education and individuals was similar to his belief in the ultimate success of education in changing the social patterns of the nation and in improving the quality of life for older people. He contributed to the field the notion of education as an affirmative enterprise, one that builds on the possibilities and potential of older persons, but he contributed to hundreds and hundreds of individuals the belief that they can succeed and that, through their faith in education and themselves, they can make the world a better place to live.

Implications and Conclusions

Educational programs for older people have developed to such a point that we can now begin to gain some perspective on their growth and to identify several implications for the future. Four of these will be discussed.

First, there now seems to be general acceptance that we are living in a learning society, one in which persons of every age will be required to continue to expand their knowledge and skills in order to survive and prosper. This realization has been reached over the past twenty-five years and provides a firm foundation for the support of instructional programs for older people. Although major needs remain in terms of financial resources for this activity, hesitation about the involvement of older people in programs of educational and community institutions and agencies is rapidly declining. The discussions are more likely to center on whether age-segregated or age-integrated education is preferable rather than whether including older people in educational programs has value.

This change is especially clear in the nation's community colleges, where thousands of older people register each semester. It is apparent to most community college administrators that their close relationship with the local community will require them to serve all the residents of that community, many of whom are old. Some colleges are now enrolling 25 to 50 percent of their total student body in classes especially for older people. In California, where community colleges charge no tuition, older people are finding themselves courted on all sides by colleges trying to maintain their growth rates and replace the diminishing number of younger students. Since the state funds the local college on the basis of enrollment, the expanding older-student enrollment has allowed community colleges to expand both programs and facilities. Other agencies—public schools, universities, libraries, museums, recreation centers, and so on— are likewise seeking older participants, since they provide a consistent and receptive clientele.

The era has passed when gerontologists and leaders of older persons' organizations must advocate for institutions and agencies to provide some services to older people. The sponsors are now seeking out opportunities on their own and developing programs without demands from outsiders. We have been successful in extending recognition of the needs and wants of the older group and now face a period when concern for quality will replace concern for program existence.

Second, there is now general acceptance that a multipurpose rationale for the conduct of educational programs for older people exists. No longer do the introductory statements deal only with the difficulties and crises of old age; more frequently now they deal with people's ability to grow and develop throughout their lives. Thus, older persons are seen as individuals with potential who can contribute and serve as well as cope and survive. This change in orientation has led to many more programs oriented toward self-actualization and growth. Liberal studies, psychological growth, and broadening experience are becoming a greater part of the programs, and lifelong planning is replacing adjustment to retirement.

Third, education for older people is no longer a modest undertaking rating little time or interest and relegated to the smallest division of the institution. Higher-level administrators are realizing its potential and are increasingly involved in this development, which may be of major importance in years ahead. As increasing numbers of older people enroll, the staff and budget will increase, and so will the influence in the organization. To date, this has not happened in many institutions. Although the number of participants is high, budget is still very limited. Those directly administering the programs are doing so with minimal staff, and only through their own extensive commitment do the programs succeed. However, the size of the enrollment is beginning to have an effect, and increases in financial support and staff are starting to occur.

Finally, as the enrollment of older persons increases, institutions that have simply encouraged older people to participate in their regular programs are beginning to develop special offerings exclusively for them. These new programs fall into categories two and three of Florio's conceptualization and are resulting in separate administration, program, and budget. As this occurs, recognition of the other needs of older people has developed. That is, when older people are included in the regular courses or programs of the institution, they are often treated like everyone else. It is now apparent that they will often not condone the indignities and bureaucratic procedures of admission, advisement, and registration that others have tolerated. They need adaptations that will streamline and abbreviate these administrative processes. As this realization reaches through the institution, major modifications of the usual procedures will occur.

Likewise, persons teaching courses that include older people will discover the need for special knowledge of them as students. Adjustments must be made for changes in vision and hearing, and instructors will need to understand the role of experience for older learners, their view of "schooling," their self-image, their desire for relevance, and their need for slower pacing. Ideally, awareness of these special needs will lead to in-service education of faculty and to a continuing development of knowledge about the older person as a student and learner.

3

OIOIOIOIOIOIOIOIOIOIOIOIOIOIOIOIOIOIOIOIOIOIOIO

Patterns of
Participation in
Educational Programs

Educational participation varies across age cohorts, both currently and historically. This variation occurs because of changes in the social climate at different times in our history, either strongly supporting education or relegating it to a less important position. Differences also result from individual developmental stages, psychological disposition toward education, and willingness to make a commitment to it at different ages. The first part of this chapter deals with the social history of education for the current older cohort; the latter half examines the motivational and psychological factors associated with older people's participation in education.

Education in the Early Twentieth Century

Historically, public education in the United States was an important element in developing and energizing the nation. Common schools were early established in the Colonies, and secondary schools were widespread by the late 1800s. We should not assume, however, that because schooling was widespread, it was analogous to the education that is offered today. Most people who are currently in their seventies or eighties were educated before 1920, and instruction in that day was considerably different than today. A description of some of those differences, taken from Butts and Cremin (1953), can be instructive in understanding the attitudes of current older people toward education.

By 1918, education had just become compulsory in every state, and 75 percent of children aged 5-18 were in school. Although universal attendance for the elementary grades had been common practice for many years in the larger metropolitan areas, some parts of the rural and southern United States still had very limited facilities, and programs and enrollments were irregular. Schools were just beginning to admit handicapped youngsters, and those with emotional or intellectual problems were likely to experience little schooling at all.

Education had not yet become a pervasive influence in the development of the individual. It was important, and students came when they could; but if family responsibilities, farm work, or financial need interfered, the student dropped out and began the real business of life. Literacy was generally accepted as necessary for success because jobs for the illiterate were hard to find. It was a point of national pride that only 6 percent of the population over 10 years of age was unable to read and write by 1920. Still, little education beyond these rudiments was expected for most people; literacy and a well-educated person were quite different outcomes.

By 1920, high schools were generally accepted by the average American. Many people were staying in school after age 16, and the comprehensive high school was developing a more varied curriculum. Classics and ancient languages were being replaced by commercial and vocational subjects, and history and science were entering the curriculum. Thus, the schools were beginning the long transition toward relevance to the lives of their students, but that had not yet completely occurred, and many students found the subject matter of little interest or value.

Religious instruction was still common in the schools. The desire to build good character led to a general religious emphasis in much instruction. Moral principles and Biblical reading received attention as a part of the typical day's activities. Religious schools were widespread. Many catered to the European immigrants in an attempt to help them learn English and accept the culture of this nation. The religious schools continued to be the source of learning for a large part of the younger population.

Schools in the South retained an aristocratic orientation, catering to the well-born and rich. College orientation was often a key element of this instruction. Many of the poor children received little or no instruction; economic necessity required their leaving school after a very few years. Segregated schools were still common throughout much of this region, and those serving minority children were decidedly inferior in staff, resources, and facilities.

Although progress was being made in developing an efficient, universal educational system, there remained great diversity in the quality, relevance, and comprehensiveness of the American school system. Urban schools, in general, had moved toward the progressive education supported by Dewey and other reformers, but rural schools remained much like those of the 1800s: one-room, ill equipped, and taught by persons who had completed little more than high school.

The curriculum and methodology of the schools were in the process of change. The emphasis on the three Rs and the classics was being replaced by vocational subjects that would prepare students for jobs. The curriculum was still viewed as consisting of a body of previously discovered facts and principles that should be communicated to the young; there was little interest in personal discovery, individual experience, or application to local situations.

Courses were beginning to develop in history, science, and some vocational topics. High schools had initiated some commercial courses, especially bookkeeping; government and English had become common. Manual arts, a forerunner of the sophisticated shop and mechanics classes currently available, were established as the high school curriculum expanded. It should be kept in mind, however, that the purpose of the high school was college preparation, and the vocational and applied courses were brought in only hesitantly. Many students who had no collegiate aspirations found little of interest or value.

The methodology consisted of rote learning, memorization of textbooks, and exhaustive drill. A strong belief in the value of discipline as a means of improving the mind supported the instruction. Minimal attention was devoted to outcomes; that is, when tedious drills did not result in student learning, they were continued anyway because they were believed to be beneficial in developing persistence and personal discipline.

Today, elementary and secondary education is substantially different in several other ways from that of the 1920s. During those years, economic barriers excluded many students from high school or forced their premature departure. Most never considered college, since scholarships were not generally available and family support was not possible. Those who attended college were still the children of college graduates who had reached the upper middle class. Others had a difficult time breaking into that elite group. There was no federal support of elementary or secondary education, and so the financial level of most schools was low, individual aid was nonexistent, and the quality of education varied greatly among states and communities.

Progressive education, with its interest in developing a well-rounded child, was just reaching the public consciousness. In general, there was little concern for the child's emotional, physical, or social health and growth. Rote memorization and punitive discipline remained too common. The belief that education could be pleasant, easy, enjoyable, and relevant was yet to have a major impact on the public school system. Students' rights and individual interests were generally ignored.

The 1920s marked a watershed in American education, a time of change when teachers, school boards, and parents still held to the traditional values, when school was of limited importance, when educational expenditures were low, and when reformers were pointing out the weaknesses of the existing system of instruction. The education that the current older cohort received can be summarized in a few points:

1. Education was for overcoming illiteracy; anything beyond that was generally for the elite.
2. Education was hard, painful drudgery; to speak of enjoying education was not an understandable concept.
3. Education was generally irrelevant to students' daily lives; it was likely to be academic, literary, or classical in content.
4. Education was authoritarian; the instructor controlled and dominated the class.
5. Education was of variable quality; differences between rural and urban instruction were great.
6. Education was terminal; it was something to be finished rather than the beginning of a continuing intellectual life.
7. Education did not encourage a continuing relationship between the school and the individual, a desire to keep learning, a commitment to lifelong intellectual growth.

These points are instructive in helping us understand the attitude that the majority of older people today have about continuing their education. As will be pointed out in another chapter, the majority of older people indicate little interest in education, few topics they would like to learn about, and limited capability when formal learning is mentioned. One obvious suggestion about the cause of this disposition is that the formal schools of their childhood convinced them that education was not an activity to be undertaken without compulsion. Because their experience was generally negative, they see no current reason to repeat that punishment when they are not required to do so.

Educational Levels of the Older Population

Older people are less likely to have extensive formal education than their younger counterparts. For a variety of reasons, just cited, current older persons typically left school at an early age. Each succeeding cohort has remained in school somewhat longer, and so older people are currently educationally disadvantaged. As seen in Table 1, the educational level of persons

Table 1. Median Years of School Completed, by Age, March 1979.

Age	Years of School
20–24	12.8
25–29	12.9
30–34	12.9
35–39	12.7
40–44	12.6
45–49	12.5
50–54	12.4
55–59	12.4
60–64	12.2
65–69	11.1
70–74	10.3
75+	8.8

Source: U.S. Bureau of the Census.

currently under age 65 is relatively stable. Therefore, as "new" individuals enter the 65+ category, they will have a higher level of formal education and will, over time, raise the average of the older cohort.

This trend toward increased exposure to formal education has been consistent over the greatest part of this century. In 1940, persons over the age of 55 had a median educational level of 8.2 years; this increased to 8.3 in 1950 and 8.6 in 1962. By 1974 it was 10.4 years (U.S. Bureau of the Census, 1980). Thus, we are witnessing a clear trend toward higher levels of formal education, but a trend that affects the oldest age groups many years after the younger cohorts. It is reasonable, therefore, to anticipate that older people are likely to always be educationally disadvantaged but that this disadvantage will lessen, since adults from age 25 to 64 now have approximately the same amount of formal schooling.

Participation in Adult Education

Older people are not large consumers of adult education. Several studies have found that age, along with several other variables, is inversely related to educational participation. This relationship between age and educational participation may be caused by several factors: poor health, lack of transportation, insecurity in a learning environment, lack of interest in new knowledge, or unfamiliarity with available offerings. Whatever the mix of these factors, older people remain the part of the population least served by continuing and adult education offerings.

In a classic study of adult education participation (Johnstone and Rivera, 1965), the National Opinion Research Center of the University of Chicago conducted a national survey in 1961–1962 that projected that over 17 million American adults (15 percent of the population) were actively engaged in educational activities. In general, adults favored courses that were practically oriented rather than of an academic nature. Fifty-seven percent of the participants were under 40 years of age, and 79 percent were under 50. The typical participant was white, married, employed, white-collar, with above-average income, and from a metropolitan area and had more education than the national mean. There were no differences in participation rates of men and women.

Data from the three surveys by the National Center for Education Statistics generally support these conclusions. Those surveys found that participation in organized instruction by adults was approximately 10 percent of the population in 1969, 11.3 percent in 1972, and 11.6 percent in 1975. Younger adults, whites and other nonblacks, those with higher education levels, those with higher incomes, those who were fully employed, and those in metropolitan areas were more active in education (Cross, 1979).

The level of formal education is generally accepted to be the most important predictor of participation in adult education. At every age, income, and occupation level, persons who had spent more years in school were more likely to participate in adult and continuing education activities. This variable overshadowed all other correlates of participation and can be used by program planners as a major consideration in identifying potential audiences.

Age, however, is not an insignificant variable in determining educational participation. In Johnstone and Rivera's (1965) analysis, age accounted for nearly one third of the variance, while education accounted for two thirds. However, differential participation rates may not reflect age itself so much as the contemporary aged cohort's history. Current older people have less formal education than younger people and tend to exhibit the traits of a less-educated group. Comparisons of adult education participation by age group show that after age 30 each successive cohort is less likely to be involved. Thus, 30-year-olds had a higher participation rate than 40-year-olds. One might conclude that people participate less as they advance in years, and this is probably true. However, some of the cohort differences can be explained more by history than by age.

Johnstone and Rivera found that people were likely to have had their first exposure to adult education before age 30 and that this had most frequently occurred in the vocational area. Those who had participated in adult education were less likely to have had their first exposure during their forties, fifties, or sixties. Only 1 percent of the sample had enrolled in their first course after age 60. Since adult education was not widely available in previous decades, and since their involvement with full-time schooling was less, many members of the current older cohort did not have the opportunity or inclination to begin their adult education career early and were progressively less likely to commence with each succeeding decade. In contrast, people who are currently in young adulthood are much more likely to begin their continuing education today and maintain that involvement throughout adulthood and old age. Thus, the percentage and number of older participants can be expected to increase substantially in the future (Riley and Foner, 1968; Birren and Woodruff, 1973; Hooper and March, 1978).

A recent national survey by Louis Harris and Associates (1975) indicated that the number of older people currently participating in adult education activities was not large. Approximately 2 percent of all individuals 65 and over were enrolled, although the percentage was higher (7 percent) for college graduates and lower (1 percent) for persons without a high school diploma.

Several data sources generally support this conclusion. Cross (1979), who analyzed thirty state and national studies of adult education participation and interest, concluded that no more than 5-10 percent of those 55 and over participated, while Johnstone and Rivera found that 9 percent of the 55+ group were involved. As Anderson and Darkenwald (1979) indicated, participation rates reflect the breadth or narrowness of the wording of questionnaire items.

Data from three studies by the National Center for Education Statistics (1978) indicate a clear trend toward greater educational participation by older people. The studies surveyed educational enrollments in adult education programs by persons who were not full-time students. The original data were collected in 1969, and the survey was replicated in 1972 and 1975. Table 2 shows that the absolute number of participants increased

Table 2. Participation of Persons Aged 55+ in Adult Education in the United States, by Sex.

	1969	1972	1975
Number of persons participating	1,048,000	1,363,000	1,627,000
Percentage of persons participating	2.9	3.5	4.0
Number of males participating	412,000	518,000	642,000
Percentage of males participating	2.5	3.0	3.6
Number of females participating	637,000	845,000	984,000
Percentage of females participating	3.2	3.9	4.3

Source: National Center for Education Statistics, *Participation in Adult Education: Final Report—1975.* Washington, D.C.: U.S. Government Printing Office, 1978.

over this six-year period, as did the percentage of participating persons in this age group. This increase meant that in 1969 persons over 55 made up 7.8 percent of the total adult participants, whereas in 1975 they made up 10 percent. The size of the older population increased by 11.5 percent during this period, while adult education participation by this age group expanded by 55.2 percent.

Data on the sex breakdowns of older participants are unclear. Bynum, Cooper, and Acuff (1978) and Heisel, Darkenwald, and Anderson (1981) reported that the number of older women participating was substantially higher than the number of older men, higher even than the proportion of females in the older population would warrant. Marcus (1978) found that females participated in proportion to their numbers in the older population, and Hooper and March (1978) found a higher proportion of men participating than were represented in the sample in their study. Table 2 indicates that a higher percentage of women 55+ than men are involved in adult education. Since older women make up nearly two thirds of the older population, this finding suggests that, overall, women are more likely than men to be found in adult education courses.

Enrollments by older people were well distributed among educational institutions, but community organizations provided the most education; public schools were next; and community colleges were a third choice (Heisel, Darkenwald, and Anderson, 1981). These data are consistent with those of Johnstone and Rivera, who found that older people were much more likely to study religion than were other age groups and that most of this religious study took place in churches, synagogues, and other religious facilities.

Older persons in the Harris (1975) sample indicated that they took courses for a variety of reasons but that expansion of general knowledge was the predominant motivation. They also wanted to use their time well and to be with others in a stimulating environment. Cross (1979) concluded that the primary motivations were pleasure, their own satisfaction, and the desire to meet other people. This finding, indicating that education was not viewed as a way to solve problems, is consistent with Birren and Woodruff's (1973) category of life enrichment as well as maintenance of social integration through a pleasurable group experience.

Through a reanalysis of the National Center for Education Statistics data, Heisel, Darkenwald, and Anderson (1981) reported that age and education seemed to determine the reasons given for educational participation. Persons in the 60-64 age range were more likely than others to indicate that the course work would be useful in their present job, while those over 70 more frequently cited social and recreational reasons for participation. Personal interest as a motivating force appears to be inversely related to educational attainment. Persons with less than a high school education were likely to cite this reason for participation, while those with a college degree were least likely to. For them, job advancement was a more frequent reason.

Educational participation by both younger and older adults in these surveys has been defined as involvement in "organized learning activities," generally involving several hours of class meetings. Tough (1977) and others have suggested that this is an unnecessarily restrictive definition of education and excludes up to 80 percent of real learning activity. This "invisible learning" is undertaken as independent study projects by people of all ages and is defined as a highly deliberate effort to gain or retain certain definite knowledge and skill or to change in some other way. Although Tough suggests that a total of at least seven hours of learning is necessary in order to qualify as a learning project, he indicates that most projects total approximately 100 hours of reading, discussion, or apprenticeship (Gross, Hebert, and Tough, 1977). He concludes from a variety of surveys that up to 98 percent of American adults participate in at least one learning project a year, and many have seven or eight annually.

Hiemstra (1975) carried out a study of the learning projects of persons 55 and over. He reported that the average person carried out 3.3 learning projects a year, involving a total of 324 hours. This research indicated that formal instructional activity accounted for only a small part of adult learning; consequently, low participation rates by older people mean not that adults are uninterested in learning or have had their learning arrested but that they choose other means of meeting their learning goals.

Educational Participation of Older Adults

Several studies have examined the participation of older people in courses and programs offered by a variety of educational and voluntary organizations and associations. A number of personal characteristics have been identified that appear to predispose older people to participate. These include a higher educational level than the median for the older population, especially some college experience (Graney and Hays, 1976; March, Hooper, and Baum, 1977; Bynum, Cooper, and Acuff, 1978; Hooper and March, 1978; Fisher, 1979; Heisel, Darkenwald, and Anderson, 1981), greater amount of time spent reading (March, Hooper, and Baum, 1977), gregariousness (March, Hooper, and Baum, 1977; Hooper and March, 1978), ownership of a home (March, Hooper, and Baum, 1977; Hooper and March, 1978), being married (Hooper and March, 1978), better perceived health (Bynum, Cooper, and Acuff, 1978), and early retirement (Bynum, Cooper, and Acuff, 1978). It has also been found that current older participants were more likely than others to have participated in adult education activities "ten years ago" and to believe that their most admired friends participated in adult education activities (Robinson, 1972).

The opposite characteristics can be assumed to discourage educational participation in later life. However, in attempting to identify the barriers to educational participation, the findings have resulted in more specific constraints than categories of persons. Cross (1979) suggested three types of barriers to educational participation in the adult years: (1) situational barriers, such as lack of transportation, prohibitive costs, and inability to allocate time to this endeavor; (2) institutional barriers, such as location and scheduling of the course, complexity or rigor of admission and registration, type and level of instruction, lack of awareness of the course offerings, and instructor behaviors and stereotypes; and (3) dispositional barriers, such as learning anxiety, belief that learning is impossible, lack of interest in learning, or belief that learning is not for adults and older people.

Surveys of older persons indicate that lack of interest in learning is the most common dispositional barrier to participation (Graney and Hays, 1976; Wasserman, 1976; March, Hooper, and Baum, 1977), but anxiety about learning is also frequently mentioned (Norton, 1970). Situational barriers (such as cost, health, transportation) are also important (Kaplan, 1960; Goodrow, 1975b; March, Hooper, and Baum, 1977; Fisher, 1979). Institutional barriers such as classes being scheduled at an inconvenient time (Fisher, 1979) or lack of information about the instructional offerings (Graney and Hays, 1976) have been found to be less important barriers to participation.

These correlates of participation do not really explain completely the decision-making process that results in a small percentage of older persons enrolling and the majority rejecting this activity. It appears that the barriers are not sufficient explanation for the behavior. Marcus (1978) suggested that the individual's socioeconomic condition is a major variable in the decision process. His data showed that people who had lower income and status and thus had current, pressing needs were not likely to participate in education to meet these needs. Older people who had high income and status were more likely to engage in education, not to meet any needs, but to continue their personal growth and as an enjoyable experience.

Aslanian and Brickell (1980) suggested that the positive push may be role change. Their studies indicated that when individuals foresee the need to change jobs, family situations, living arrangements, or personal behaviors, they are likely to turn to education as a means of anticipating and preparing for the change. To the extent that this finding is an accurate description of behavior, continuing social and personal change should increase the amount of planned learning. Thus, educational participation can be associated with some specific positive push rather than simply the absence of any of the barriers that have been identified.

It is unclear what these pushes may be, but data are available that indicate five explanations. First, people are likely only to attend courses in an institution or organization with which they have had previous contact; thus, the institution is viewed as accessible. For instance, attendees at a noncredit college course are likely to have attended the college, to have children who attend, or to have friends who brought them for the first time (Hooper and March, 1978). Thus, institutional sponsorship can be an important factor.

A second push may be a tradition of educational participation. Houle (1961) identified three types of lifelong learners. Two of these learned because it was an enjoyable activity or because they sought knowledge for its own sake. They attended classes because they had done so much of their lives and found it a typical and valued thing to do. Consequently, a tradition of educational participation may be a major factor in encouraging or discouraging behavior when a learning opportunity is presented.

Third, social interaction may also be a significant motivating force. As other roles are discarded or withdrawn, some older persons seek out new situations in which they can interact with others and maintain personal and intellectual contacts. Fisher (1979) reported that "being with other people" was the chief reason given by older people for their educational participation, and Boshier and Riddell (1978) used the social variable as one of four factors that accounted for participation.

A fourth factor is the need for some particular information or a general interest in a topic. As Marcus (1978) indicated, older people with the greatest need were not the typical educational participants; rather, enrollments more frequently occurred because of an academic or intellectual interest that might prove useful at some point in the future. Fisher (1979) reported that "usefulness of the subject matter" was the third most important reason given for participation. Consequently, the topic or content of the course and the particular situation of the older person may combine to encourage participation.

A fifth factor motivating participation may be the social support and encouragement that result from membership in the sponsoring organization. For example, if a church group offers a special educational workshop that is open to the community, the group's members are the most likely to attend. They participate because they are part of the sponsoring organization, may have participated in the planning, know the people involved, and often feel a responsibility to support, through attendance, the group in which they hold membership.

Research on Participant Motivation

The relative importance of these motivating variables has not been compared before and was the subject of research undertaken on a group of older persons participating in a lecture-discussion program conducted at the Andrus Gerontology Center of the University of Southern California. Questionnaires asked the subjects to identify the importance of various possible reasons for participating in the lecture series, using a 4-point Likert scale ranging from very important (1.0) to very unimportant (4.0). The most important reasons for attending the program were found to be "I want to know more about aging" (1.2 on the 4-point scale), "The knowledge may help me understand myself" (1.4), "I feel part of the Andrus Gerontology Center" (1.4), "The knowledge may help me to help other people" (1.5), "It was sponsored by the Andrus Gerontology Center" (1.5), and "I had heard that the programs were good" (1.8).

The twenty questions used in this study attempted to measure the extent to which participation in the lecture-discussion series was motivated by (1) a desire for social interaction, (2) a need or interest that could be met by the content, (3) institutional sponsorship and a familiarity with the quality of programs in the past, or (4) membership or friendship with the Andrus Volunteers, one of the sponsors. The scores on individual questions indicated that the topic of aging and its general value for self and others was the most important reason for participation. Sponsorship and quality of the lecture-discussion series were of nearly equal importance to the content. The third most important reason for participation was social interaction (knowledge of other participants, acceptance by the group, and opportunities to make new friends). Finally, membership or close relationships with the Andrus Volunteers, the primary sponsor of the program, was of least importance to the participants.

These findings are somewhat similar to those achieved by Sprouse (1981) in a survey of participants in courses for older persons offered in community settings and of participants who were guest auditors in regular courses at the University of Wisconsin—Madison. She reported that cognitive interest, a desire to know more about a particular subject, was the most powerful motivating factor, followed by social contact (social interaction), social welfare (instrumental results in employment, planning, or citizenship activities), with escape/stimulation being the least strong motivator.

Sprouse's findings are especially interesting because she compared the motivations of those older persons who were involved in age-integrated courses and those who chose to participate in age-segregated settings. The age-integrated were guest students on a space-available basis at the university; the age-segregated were enrolled in new instructional programs established through community planning groups in three areas of Wisconsin. She reported that "age-integrated learners differed from age-segregated learners on all variables tested except race" (p. 24). The differences most likely to influence participation were age (age-integrated learners were younger), educational level (age-integrated learners had more years of formal education), income (age-integrated learners had higher incomes), and educational participation (age-integrated learners had taken more classes from more diverse providers).

Conclusions

The conclusions that can be drawn from current research and practice regarding educational participation by older persons are relatively modest. We know something about the demographic characteristics of those persons who volunteer to learn—younger, better educated, higher income, more active. These characteristics are insufficient to predict who will participate, however. There are barriers and motivations that encourage some people in these categories to become involved and restrain others. Sprouse's research is helpful because it begins the process of indicating which kinds of persons are likely to choose which kinds of educational programs. Sprouse has concluded that age-integrated courses are likely to attract persons who are younger, better educated, and more affluent than persons involved in age-segregated courses. Thus, the characteristics identified can be subdivided so that only those with the most of these attributes will become involved in age-integrated education, those with less may opt for community-based, age-segregated education, and those without these characteristics will not participate at all.

Chapter Ten attempts to differentiate educational participation in another way, through the examination of cognitive

4

Intelligence
and Performance

Many studies have attempted to determine the intelligence of individuals and to ascertain whether change typically occurs in this attribute over the life span. The literature describing these findings offers a massive accumulation of data on the basic questions. However, definitive answers are not yet available, and researchers still differ on some points concerning the relationship of intelligence and age. A review of these studies provides insight into the intellectual potential and performance of middle-aged and older persons as well as indicating several significant implications for those who would provide instruction to persons in these age groups.

The research on intelligence has been approached in a variety of ways, and the components of this construct are defined slightly differently in various instruments. Thus, the findings that have accumulated over the fifty to sixty years during which research has been undertaken differ because of variations in research methods, instruments, and analyses. The final determination of intellectual change over the life span probably depends more on how one chooses to define and operationalize the construct than on what is the "real" relationship of intelligence to age.

This chapter will provide an overview of intelligence in later life by describing the meaning and importance of the concept of intelligence, by indicating some of the models used to describe it, by summarizing the findings of longitudinal and cross-sectional studies, by identifying the noncognitive variables that affect the measurement of intelligence, and by drawing some inferences that may be of use to instructors of older people.

The Meaning of Intelligence

Like most fundamental concepts, intelligence is difficult to explain. It is usually considered to be the cognitive capacity of the individual, the ability to learn, the facility at manipulating and understanding common and unique items. Because this cognitive potential is impossible to measure directly, all research on intelligence has inferred the underlying traits of an individual by measuring performance in a number of settings. Performance and innate ability are not necessarily synonymous, since numerous factors (health, perceptual acuity, motivation) can affect performance. Thus, IQ, the performance measure, may closely approximate the ceiling potential of the individual or may greatly underestimate it.

IQ is a familiar term to most of us. Completion of an IQ test provides a numerical score indicating one's relative position in comparison with others of similar age. An IQ of 100 is considered average, and those who score higher are assumed to have more innate cognitive capacity than those who score below this standard. In general, it is considered an advantage to have a higher IQ, since that should allow one to learn more quickly and effectively in a variety of situations.

The concept of IQ has an age factor built into it. IQ is a measure of a person's relative position, and in order to maintain an IQ score of 100 as the average for each age group, the test score must be adjusted for typical age changes. It is assumed that older people will score lower, and so older persons can maintain the same IQ score they had in earlier years by scoring fewer actual points. For example, a person at age 25 must score approximately 110 to have an IQ score of 100, whereas a person at age 75 can score only 68 and have the same IQ score (Botwinick, 1978).

IQ is an important measure of a person's potential. However, it has become so widely used that it is frequently accorded greater recognition than is appropriate. To place it in proper perspective, it is imperative that we determine what performance characteristics are important for older people before concerning ourselves about the highness or lowness of IQ scores.

For instance, in determining which older workers should be recruited into a retraining program, IQ would be a useful factor to consider, since it provides a general indication of learning ability. Likewise IQ can be used as a measure of social competence; those with very low scores may legally lose the right to manage their own affairs and property. It may also be of use in determining ability to care for oneself, in admission to degree programs leading to new careers, or in determining whether an older employee is competent to continue work or should be retired. In these areas and others, it is generally very low IQ that becomes significant and may cause the person to lose some control over the situation. An average IQ score may be sufficient to meet minimum criteria. Thus, intelligence is a very important consideration in examining a person's potential, but it is not all-important; if a person's intelligence is at least average, then most circumstances require that other characteristics be given greater weight.

Likewise, high IQ scores do not assure a person success, do not indicate social or vocational competence, and may not lead to adaptation to the society or any particular role. IQ historically was developed as a means of predicting success in educational endeavors. Since it deals with cognitive abilities and these are closely related to any learning enterprise, it has proved to be a fairly reliable indicator of performance in an educational setting. It is also very useful in estimating success in employment that has high educational prerequisites. However, there are many areas of life in which learning is not particularly relevant—interpersonal relations, adjustment, physical strength, beauty, commitment, self-esteem, motivation, wisdom. In these areas, other variables may prove to be substantially more powerful determinants of success than intelligence. Thus, intelligence is an important attribute of each person, but high or low scores do not automatically determine the quality of performance that can be expected from that person.

Although *intelligence* is a singular noun, most psychologists would agree that there is no single entity that can be thought of as "the intelligence." Rather, it seems more accurate to conceive of intelligence as being composed of several factors which are more or less distinct and which collectively constitute a summary measure. This is a change from the early conceptualizations of the characteristic: The founders of psychology believed that intelligence was a single factor, which could be measured through an omnibus test. Although contemporary IQ tests may result in a single score, it is acknowledged that this is done for convenience and that there may be significant variation in the scores of the several subtests included in the measure of intelligence. It is probably more accurate to think of "intelligences" which each person has and which can be measured in a variety of ways. These distinct components are likely to be somewhat diverse, so that the person may achieve high scores in some areas and lower ones in others. Some people, of course, may score high in all areas while others score universally low, but some diversity is the norm for people in the average portion of the range.

Intelligence tests are generally composed so that they measure these various factors. The Wechsler Adult Intelligence Scale (WAIS), commonly used with adults, is composed of eleven subtests in two general categories. The Verbal score is calculated from the subtests of Information, Comprehension, Arithmetic, Similarities, Digit Span, and Vocabulary. The subtests entering into the Performance score are Digit Symbol, Picture Completion, Block Design, Picture Arrangement, and Object Assembly. From these eleven tests, it is assumed that the major factors involved in adult intelligence are measured.

These subtests have been used with adults of all ages, although they were developed primarily for younger adults. It is not a surety that the eleven "intelligences" they measure are the most important ones for older people. Schaie and Parr (1981) concluded that it is unlikely that additional factors that will explain more about the intellectual potential of older people will be found, but the importance of the current factors may be different in later life than at the beginning of adulthood. Thus, some of the subtests may be very relevant to the daily functioning of the older person and consequently important; others may be less relevant and less significant.

One conceptualization of intelligence that has received wide acceptance over the past fifteen years is the distinction between fluid and crystallized intelligence (Cattell, 1963). Crystallized intelligence depends on sociocultural influences; it involves the ability to perceive relations, to engage in formal reasoning, and to understand one's intellectual and cultural heritage. It is measured through culture-specific items such as number facility, verbal comprehension, and general information. Thus, the amount a person learns, the diversity and complexity of the environment, the openness to new information, and the extent of formal learning opportunities are likely to be influential in the person's score. In general, crystallized intelligence continues to grow slowly throughout adulthood as the person acquires increased information and develops an understanding of the relations of diverse facts and constructs. Continued acculturation through self-directed learning and education can encourage the growth of crystallized intelligence even after age 60 (Knox, 1977).

Fluid intelligence, in contrast, is not closely associated with acculturation. It is generally considered to be independent of instruction or environment and depends more on genetic endowment. It consists of the ability to perceive complex relations, use short-term memory, create concepts, and undertake abstract reasoning. Items included in tests of fluid intelligence measure memory span, inductive reasoning, and figural relations, all of which are assumed to be unresponsive to training or expertise. Fluid intelligence involves those abilities that are the most neurophysiological in nature and are generally assumed to decline after the person reaches maturity. However, the decline through middle age is quite small; at middle age, scores on fluid intelligence tasks are no lower than in midadolescence (Knox, 1977). The decline, however, continues throughout the remainder of life.

Intellectual Changes over the Life Span

The earliest studies of adult intelligence showed an increase in IQ until the late teens or early twenties and then a slow decline throughout the rest of the adult years. These studies used a cross-sectional design, which tested people of several ages and then compared the scores of current younger people with those of persons who were older. The differences in the scores were assumed to be caused by age. Later studies have used longitudinal designs, in which the same persons were tested at various points over their life span and changes in scores were compared so that trends in intellectual performance could be observed. These studies have reported a somewhat different pattern of change, with less decline occurring and IQ increasing in some cases.

Before examining these trends, however, we must consider once again the great individual differences that exist in intellectual functioning. Any general description of the relation of age to intellectual change will obscure some of the variation observable in a large population. Thus, knowing a person's age is insufficient to estimate whether that person is intelligent or not; likewise, old age should not cause one to assume that a person has suffered such decline that he or she is no longer capable of learning or functioning successfully. Age does have some effect on intelligence, but it does not override many other influencing factors.

Botwinick (1978) has described the "classic aging pattern of intelligence." Over the adult portion of the life span, verbal abilities decline very little, if at all, while psychomotor abilities decline earlier and to a greater extent. Thus, on the WAIS, the Verbal subtests show virtual stability throughout the years from age 20 to 60, while the Performance subtests show decline from the late twenties on (see Figure 1). After age 65 to

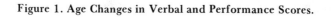

Figure 1. Age Changes in Verbal and Performance Scores.

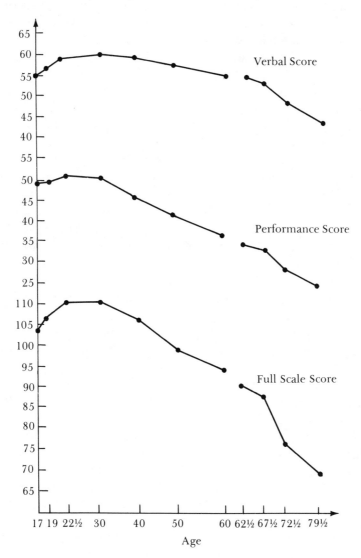

Source: Adapted from J. Botwinick, "Intellectual Abilities." In J. E. Birren and K. W. Schaie (Eds.), *Handbook of the Psychology of Aging.* New York: Van Nostrand Reinhold, 1977.

70, decline in both areas increases but does not reach the point of incompetence. Eisdorfer, Busse, and Cohen (1959) reported that this pattern holds for men and women, black and white adults, persons from various economic strata, and persons both in mental hospitals and in the community. These findings are consistent with the notion that crystallized intelligence is maintained over the adult life span while fluid intelligence declines. Taken together, this decline in fluid intelligence and growth in crystallized intelligence are assumed to approximately balance out, so that the loss of biological potential is offset by the wisdom, experience, and knowledge the older adult has acquired. Stability of intellectual performance of the greatest part of the typical life span would appear to be normal, and persons in their fifties should have maintained learning ability equal to what they had in their twenties, when they can control the pace. Although ability may fall off after age 60, the tasks that become more difficult are those that are fast-paced, unusual, and complex (Knox, 1977).

The effect of age on comparative intellectual performance is not particularly clear; that is, are persons who initially score high on IQ tests more or less likely to suffer declines in performance some years later? Owens (1959) reported that there were no differences among persons achieving high and low scores. Baltes and others (1972) reported that persons with high initial ability declined while those with less ability increased on later testing. Thus, both groups moved toward the mean. Botwinick (1977), however, concluded that people who perform well when they are younger will perform well when older. Bright people will not be outscored by less bright people simply because of the passage of time. However, initial performance of young people is not a good indication of whether performance decline will be great, small, or lacking.

Several researchers have suggested that test results that show older persons scoring more poorly than younger ones may be caused by the disadvantages of timed tests. Since the WAIS subtests on which older people do poorest are timed, and since older people tend to show decline in the speed of central nervous system function, response rate, and perceptual acuity, the lower scores may be more reflective of the slower response than of decreased intellectual potential. Research in which tests were given both in a timed and in an untimed condition, however, have revealed approximately the same decline (Klodin, 1975; Storandt, 1977). Thus, when speed is involved in the testing situation, the difference between older and younger people may be magnified. However, the elimination of the timed condition helps older people only minimally and does not explain the difference in scores between the two cohorts (Botwinick, 1977). Speed alone is not a sufficient explanation for the age differences.

The amount of deficit that occurs after age 70 is also unclear. Although a fairly sharp decline is typically shown, this may be caused by what has been called "terminal drop." This phenomenon, first reported by Riegel and Riegel (1972), is a decline in IQ score a few years prior to death and is thought to be caused by physiological deterioration. For some reason, intellectual functioning appears to be one means of predicting approaching death. If the older sample in any study included a preponderance of persons who were nearing death, their IQ scores would indicate a substantial decline compared with younger persons; however, this may be traced to their nearness to death, not to some other change that occurs around age 70. Thus, intellectual decline that results at this time may be caused mainly by the approach of death and not some cognitive factor. Increased medical treatment, preventive health care, and improved public health may prolong the healthy portion of life and consequently extend the period during which intelligence remains basically stable.

Some of the longitudinal studies have shown a modest increase in intelligence scores from age 20 to 50 (Owens, 1953; Bayley and Oden, 1955; Jarvik, Kallman, and Falek, 1962). Although this may occur, especially in the verbal areas, an alternative explanation for this phenomenon is that the longitudinal design causes the increase because of death and illness of some of the panel members. A longitudinal study tests the performance of the same subjects over a period of several years. In dealing with older people, the number of subjects available for retesting declines with each reapplication. A comparison of those who are retested and those who are not has shown that persons with high intelligence scores are more likely to survive and to continue in the testing (Botwinick, 1977). Consequently, only the initially more able subjects are retested.

Schaie (1975) has suggested an alternative view of life-span IQ change. By designing a study that was both longitudinal and cross-sectional, he has shown that performance is maintained through the adult years, with minimal decline occurring before age 60 to 70. However, each generation scores slightly higher on the IQ measures than the preceding one, and therefore cross-generational comparisons disadvantage older cohorts. His conclusion is that each generation is slightly more intelligent than the preceding one and that comparisons of 20-, 40-, and 60-year-olds do not show declines in IQ scores but generational differences. Each generation maintains its scores, but the following generation scores slightly higher, so that any comparison makes it appear that decline has occurred.

Figure 2 shows these results. Persons who were initially tested at age 25 or 32 have the highest scores. Those first tested at 39 or 46 have the next-highest scores, and those who entered the testing situation at age 53, 60, or 67 have the lowest. However, scores for the youngest group show slight change over the fourteen-year period, scores for the middle group show no change at all, and scores for the oldest group decline substantially only after age 74. Schaie's data suggest clearly that intelligence as measured by the Thurstone Primary Mental Abilities Test is quite stable over the life span and that subsequent cohorts score better than preceding ones.

Generational differences in intelligence may occur because of improvements in diet, in health, in education, in the extent and quality of the mass media, or in other areas that enable people to acquire more information, thus improving performance on IQ tests. It is not clear which of these influences are most responsible for the changes, but age cohorts do seem to differ; each succeeding generation is slightly better than the preceding one. This should not seem surprising when we compare it to the realm of athletics. Each year, some athlete runs a little

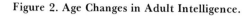

Figure 2. Age Changes in Adult Intelligence.

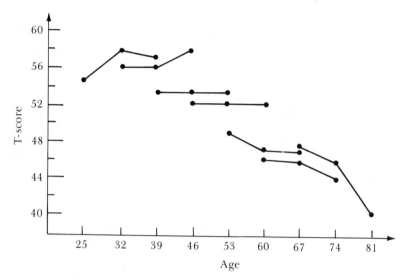

Note: Each curve shows the scores of one group of subjects at three testings over a fourteen-year period.

Source: Adapted from K. W. Schaie, "Age Changes in Adult Intelligence." In D. S. Woodruff and J. E. Birren (Eds.), *Aging: Scientific Perspectives and Social Issues.* New York: Van Nostrand Reinhold, 1975.

faster, jumps farther, or lifts heavier weights than anyone has in the past. Breaking world records is almost commonplace.

Age, of course, is not the only variable that affects IQ. Education, socioeconomic status, and cohort are also major factors in determining the intelligence of any individual. Birren and Morrison (1961) analyzed a large amount of data from the WAIS test and concluded that education is much more important than age in determining IQ. With increased education, IQ scores rise sharply. This does not necessarily mean that education increases IQ. It may mean that people with high IQ are prone to attend school longer or enjoy it more; or it may mean that there is some third factor involved that affects IQ and education. Regardless of the causative relationship, increased education and higher IQs appear to be positively associated.

Likewise, greater socioeconomic status is associated with

higher IQ scores. As noted earlier, crystallized intelligence and some of the WAIS subtests are sensitive to experience and acquired information. These are likely to increase with higher socioeconomic status, since travel, a stimulating environment, availability of books, and encouragement of continued learning are likely to be available. Whichever of these is involved, all are more available for persons at a higher level of income, occupation, and education—the components of socioeconomic status.

Cohort differences are also important. Persons born in 1900 have experienced a world quite distinct from the world of those born in 1950. The "War to Make the World Safe for Democracy," the Great Depression, the Second World War, the changes in political philosophy, the modifications in family structure and permanence, residential mobility, extent of education, and many other variables have created differences in knowledge, attitudes, behavior, and beliefs among the generations. These differences are reflected directly or indirectly in IQ test scores.

Personality is also a major factor in determining intelligence scores. Persons who are self-deprecating, who have little faith in their own ability, who are unwilling to take risks, who are inflexible, or who are suffering from poor mental health are likely to score low on intelligence tests. These factors are often involved when an older group is tested. Societal norms currently provide little support for the value of the older person, and so it is easy to understand why many older people do not value themselves. This negative approach can lead the person to concede defeat before really attempting a task. The amount of encouragement provided by society generally as well as by persons in the immediate environment will have a substantial influence on the extent to which individuals try and, ultimately, succeed.

Considerations in Describing Intellectual Functioning

The measurement of intellectual functioning in later life is very difficult to conceptualize and undertake because there are so many related variables that affect the result. For instance, in designing a study of older people, is the most appropriate sample a randomly selected one, or should the group include only those who are reasonably healthy, with good vision and hearing, and with adequate energy? Since health, perception, and energy are significant intervening variables in determining the IQ scores that will be achieved, including persons with decrements in these areas will severely lower the average score. The score then may not accurately reflect innate intelligence; it will be influenced by noncognitive factors. However, many older people have these difficulties; they are forced to live with them each day, and their functioning depends heavily on the extent of these disabilities. Whether or not persons with these difficulties are to be included in the sample is therefore very important.

In a study by Botwinick and Birren (1963), two groups of very healthy men were given intelligence tests. Although there were no major differences in their scores, the group of men who were judged to be slightly less healthy scored lower than the very healthy men. Significantly, the subtests on which they did most poorly were the ones that are the most sensitive to increased age—the performance section of the WAIS. Thus, even small declines in physical health appear to reduce intellectual functioning, especially in areas in which psychomotor or fluid abilities are involved.

Likewise, in a test comparing older people who had suffered some hearing loss (Granick, Kleben, and Weiss, 1976), persons who had less loss were likely to score higher on the WAIS. In this case, the verbal subtests were most likely to show decline when more hearing loss was present. This result may have occurred because people with more hearing loss were no longer able to maintain vocabulary and knowledge, owing to the limited social interaction currently available to them.

Fatigue is another noncognitive variable that will affect test performance. Furry and Baltes (1973) reported that older people tire substantially during the course of an intelligence test and that if this fatigue factor is not ameliorated, their scores will suffer. Older people in any situation will achieve at a substantially lower level if they are not provided the supportive environment needed to function at the highest level possible.

As Botwinick (1977) emphasizes, fatigue, perception,

health, education, and socioeconomic status are part of the makeup of every older person. When dealing with a group of older persons in an instructional setting, we do not have the option of dealing only with their cognitive potential (innate intelligence). We must try to teach the person who attends the class. These persons may have many disadvantages or disabilities that interfere with their learning unless these decrements are specifically moderated. Since most of us never perform at the level of our potential, older people should not be assumed to be substantially disadvantaged because of noncognitive variables.

We may conclude that the intellectual potential is maintained throughout the major portion of the life span. People even into their eighth decade have the ability to learn and change. However, they often have not cultivated that ability and must expend additional energy to succeed in spite of their growing infirmities and difficulties. The role of the instructor is to understand the areas in which additional help is needed and to design content and process so that learning can be maximized.

Implications of Intellectual Performance

The studies of intellectual functioning across the age span provide a great deal of data on the stability of IQ and the noncognitive factors that significantly affect performance. Teachers of adults and older people should see in these studies some implications that will influence the planning and conduct of instruction. Like all implications, they should be carefully considered in order to assure that they really are drawn from the existing data and that they are relevant to the needs and interests of the involved group (here, instructors of adults). It must be kept in mind that the studies of intelligence have been undertaken for the purpose of understanding a complex and interesting topic and have not been designed primarily to answer the practical questions of the classroom or consultation. Consequently, the studies and the implications that can be drawn from them may not be as useful or as definitive as any of us would like them to be.

Intelligence over the life span follows a classic pattern:

Verbal abilities remain stable until the late sixties or seventies and then decline slowly; performance scores decline slowly throughout the adult years and evidence more rapid decline after age 60. This pattern may be challenged by some researchers, but it is generally supported by most of the reported studies. The implication is that people of any age can continue to learn and to change their behavior. Even beyond age 70, few people are so rigid or so restricted in neurological functioning that they cannot learn when they choose to. The clear message of the literature on intelligence is that there is little reason for hesitation in attempting to teach persons of any age.

The Wechsler Adult Intelligence Scale has been widely used to measure the mental potential of individuals and groups. Scores on this test usually provide some indication of the individual's potential performance in a traditional learning setting. Adults who score high on this test are likely to learn more efficiently and to learn complex tasks more readily if they apply themselves than those who score low (Knox, 1977). One implication in the form of a caution is that a test may prove to be a very inaccurate predictor of other types of performance (for instance, behavioral tasks, likelihood of change in attitude, or social adjustment in a variety of settings). These elements may be objectives in an instructional endeavor, but the IQ test score would be inappropriate for predicting the likelihood of change on the part of the learner. Thus, the IQ score may be of value in a learning situation in which cognitive change is desired, but it is not a measure of all types of learning potential.

Another caution implication is that IQ may be of limited usefulness in assessing the learning capacity of any individual older person. Since there have been no predictive studies that indicate the chance of success in an educational endeavor based on the scores achieved on an IQ test (Schaie and Parr, 1981), reason would suggest caution in placing too much emphasis on test scores. Much remains unknown when attempting to predict an individual's performance. The best we can do is to extrapolate from group data and suggest that when verbal meaning and reasoning are measured, persons at age 60 are at the peak of their educational aptitude, and by age 81 their performance is still 70 percent of what it was at age 25 (Schaie and Parr, 1981). Older people involved in learning situations may be disadvantaged when speed and complex interrelationships are emphasized, but when trying to solve verbal or social problems in light of past experience, they are likely to be substantially advantaged. Thus, age may be a help rather than a drawback when the education is responsive to the learner's current knowledge.

Regardless of their purpose, studies on intelligence in later life show clearly that in the verbal and sociocultural areas decline is least and comes latest. This finding suggests that the cognitive abilities of greatest relevance to the daily lives of older learners are those that evidence the most resistance to decline with age. Instruction that is relevant to the older person's interests, needs, and wants should be learned quickly and efficiently. The usefulness of the instructional content to the learner should be given special emphasis. If the topic is generally familiar to the older learner, if it is of interest, if it can be used in some important manner, the older person will be more likely to be motivated and to learn better.

Individual differences in intellectual performance (as well as virtually every other variable) increase throughout the adult years. Consequently, in teaching any group of older adults the instructor must expect that the intellectual range will be great, experience will be diverse, and individual learning skills will differ extensively. Although recruitment procedures for specific courses may be directed toward a particular segment of the total population, and in fact the participants may appear to be fairly homogeneous, nevertheless great differences will exist. The instructor must be able to provide flexible and occasionally individualized instruction.

A brief pretest may prove valuable in determining the level of knowledge on beginning the instruction, but this is not likely to elicit much information on past experience, preferred instructional style, or intellectual potential. Probably the most useful way of initiating the instruction is to design learning activities that are reasonably simple, can be undertaken sequentially, allow for prompt feedback, and can be increased in complexity and difficulty as the individual or group potential becomes more evident.

Although the data on the ability of older people to learn are quite clear, this information has not yet been assimilated by many administrators and teachers of adults. Too often they accept the stereotype that intellectual potential is lost after young adulthood and are unwilling to commit the effort and resources necessary to assist this older cohort to learn and continue its development. One of the most important challenges arising from these data is the need to convince policy makers, administrators, and teachers of the educational potential that older adults retain and to assist them in designing programs that will take advantage of the learning attributes of older people and minimize their deficits.

This means that any instruction of adults and older persons should be paced slowly enough so that time for acquisition and review is provided, should be related to the experience and knowledge that the older person has, should make provision for the wide range of differences that are likely to be represented in the room, and should provide opportunities for rest and refreshment during the instructional time. These areas will be discussed further in the next chapter.

Likewise, older adults themselves accept the usual stereotypes about decline in learning ability with age and are likely to deprecate their own potential. Until they are convinced they can learn, it will remain unusual for them to place themselves in a situation where they will have to do so. By providing a series of learning opportunities, each with an increasing amount of challenge and each with a high probability of success, older people can be eased into the habit of continued pursuit of educational goals and can be encouraged to modify their beliefs about their own potential.

In the long run, the problem may solve itself. As subsequent cohorts reach old age, they will bring with them high levels of formal education, a greater involvement in adult learning activities, and a stronger self-image. Collectively, these are expected to result in large numbers of older persons continuing their education through formal and informal channels. In the meantime, however, it will be necessary for academicians and practitioners to continue to encourage older persons to learn and to overcome the dispositional barriers to participation in continuing education in the later years.

The research on intelligence in adulthood is filled with discussion of the interference of noncognitive factors in the performance of older persons. It has been suggested that such variables as education, socioeconomic status, health, energy, perception, caution, and motivation are probably more important than age in determining learning performance. Although learning potential may change somewhat over the life span, few people ever learn at a level near their potential, and so noncognitive variables are likely to be major determinants of intellectual performance on IQ tests.

In attempting to teach an older adult, then, assessment of the noncognitive variables may be more relevant than a current measure of IQ. The student's ability to see or hear, to understand and be able to build on past experience, to summon the energy needed to concentrate on learning activities, to overcome the fears and inhibitions that limit involvement, and to decide that learning is a valuable undertaking is paramount. These are areas in which the teacher can undertake an informal, early assessment and use this insight to adapt the instruction to the unique characteristics of the group.

Schaie's work has underscored the stability of IQ over the adult years and the performance differences among various cohorts. One implication is that older persons are disadvantaged by the historical factors of inferior schools attended longer ago, and thus their learning skills have become obsolete. In order to function well and to compete with younger people for jobs, for status, and for power, they need some compensatory education designed to improve their learning skills and overcome the noncognitive interference.

Training studies have shown that learning skills can be improved in later life. For this to occur, older people must have the opportunity and the societal support to continue their education. Community programs are needed that are administered and taught by persons who are familiar with the changes that must be accommodated if optimum learning is to occur.

Some older adults have learned to compensate for many of the intellectual and noncognitive changes. The teacher can assist each older person to continue and improve this accommodation by tailoring the instruction to his or her particular needs. This may require some individualization at times, and it may mean that the usual techniques of lecture and discussion will be inadequate. The current condition of the older person is the primary determinant. By designing the learning situation so that the deleterious effects of noncognitive variables are minimized, the teacher can help the older learner overcome these deficits and approach more closely his or her true learning potential. Specific examples of these actions can be seen in the use of accessible facilities, appropriate lighting, selection of content, creation of a supportive environment, and relating new content to older experience.

The noncognitive factors play a part in the studies of laboratory learning, in the effect on cognitive style, and in the current developmental stage of the individual. Accordingly, they will be discussed in later parts of this book. The emphasis here is not on specific methods of adapting to noncognitive changes but on the fact that they may make it appear that the middle-aged or older learner has a limited capability. In reality, the potential is there for the vast majority of older people, but it is masked by variables that detract from optimum performance. The bulk of noncognitive interference can be compensated for by the creative individual who is committed to continue involvement in learning activities. The teacher of older adults must identify these areas of interference early in the instruction and design a process that reduces rather than emphasizes the deficiencies.

This means that older students are different from younger ones. The instructor not only must know the subject matter and good teaching techniques but must be willing and able to adjust both to the peculiarities of the older group. This adaptation makes teaching an additional challenge—but it is only that, and not an impossibility. The older adult can learn, but the teacher's role in encouraging, facilitating, helping, and persuading will be enlarged. The rewards in appreciation and continued growth are no less exciting than they are at any other age.

5

⊃⊂⊃⊂⊃⊂⊃⊂⊃⊂⊃⊂⊃⊂⊃⊂⊃⊂⊃⊂⊃⊂⊃⊂⊃⊂⊃⊂⊃⊂⊃⊂⊃⊂⊃⊂

Learning
Ability

Learning occurs throughout life. People continually learn through study, through incidental contact with others, through their jobs, and through analysis of their reactions and feelings. This learning process does not change abruptly when a person reaches old age, but differential performance and ability between older and younger people have been reported. The ability to learn has been dealt with in the preceding chapter; this chapter will emphasize the measurement of learning performance and the means by which learning efficiency can be improved.

An immediate caveat must be presented: Learning and performance are not the same. The fact that an item has been learned does not necessarily mean it can be recalled or recognized in every situation. In other words, poor performance on a learning task may mean that insufficient learning has occurred, or it may mean that the performance does not accurately reflect the extent of the learning achieved. However, it is only through the observation or measurement of performance that we can infer learning. Consequently, throughout this chapter, when learning is discussed, it is the observable results of the learning that are measured, not some internal change that has taken place.

Botwinick (1978) has emphasized this distinction, and it should be kept in mind both in reviewing laboratory studies and in evaluating instruction of older people.

Older people, like those of other ages, are very different from one another. Consequently, in measuring the learning performance of this cohort, it must be emphasized once again that any discussion of the average obscures the wide variation in learning performance. Some older people perform as well as younger persons; some score significantly lower. Some older people are extremely rigid in their approach to learning, while others are much more open to new knowledge and experience. Some older persons appear to limit themselves to one methodological approach to learning, while others are able to use many means. These differences require that the teacher of older people remember that the findings and insights described here relate to the average older person and should not be applied in too strict a fashion to any individual or group.

There are three common approaches or predispositions to life-span changes in learning performance (Willis, 1977). These are the expectations that (1) learning performance will suffer irreversible decrement over the course of the life span and that little can be done to compensate for this decline, (2) learning performance is basically stable over the life span, and cohort differences are due to variations in the educational, health, or intellectual levels of the different groups, not individual changes with increasing age, and (3) modest decline in performance occurs in the later stages of life, but this decline is modifiable through some compensatory intervention. This third view is gaining increased support and suggests a major role for education and training in the development of learning skills and the maintenance of learning performance in the later years. By acquiring both skills and content, the person can maintain an acceptable level of functioning, continue as a productive member of society, and facilitate psychological growth.

It is this potential for educational intervention that makes the knowledge of adult learning so relevant and valuable. Over the past three decades, a large number of laboratory studies of learning performance have been undertaken that provide extensive and reliable data on the changes occurring with age that are especially amenable to intervention. The purpose of those studies has been to explore the age-related differences in learning performance (that is, the differences between older and younger learners). Although this has great value and interest, our intent is to identify those findings that may be applied to instruction of older people.

The review of these studies, therefore, will be selective in an attempt to abstract those that are of greatest relevance to the program planner, teacher, and administrator of educational activities for the aged. In doing this, it will be necessary to extrapolate from the findings in an attempt to suggest some instructional applications or principles. Some may find the distance between the studies and the applications too great, but the translation process must be intensified in order to maximize the potential impact on the growing number of instructional programs. Thus, in reviewing these studies, the intent will be to provide a general understanding of the research, to report the more relevant findings, and to identify the implications and insights that are salient to instructors of older people.

Laboratory Study of Learning

Most studies of learning performance have been conducted in a laboratory setting. Several experimental procedures have been used in which subjects either see or hear words, letters, or symbols and then are asked to recall or recognize them. In some studies paired words are presented and the subject is expected to recall which word was matched with which other word. The specific design and method have varied widely depending on the type of hypothesis being tested, but in general, the subject attempts to memorize several words and to recall them after a short time has passed.

This experimental situation provides for experimenter control of many of the possible variables and thus gives a good measure of learning. It is a unique experience for most people, however, and is quite different from the teacher/learner situation in a classroom. Extrapolation of the findings from laboratory studies must therefore be done with care and with the understanding that other intervening variables may substantially modify the results in a classroom setting. Nevertheless, many insights can be drawn from learning studies, and these are of great use to the educator of older adults.

Laboratory researchers generally assume that learning is a cognitive process that can best be understood through examination and experimentation, that it is a complex intellectual process involving multiple elements. Although there are several theoretical models of learning, most researchers would agree that learning involves at least three stages: (1) the intake of the information (through one of the senses); this is often considered to include (a) a very brief storage of the information in its sensory form, (b) "movement" of the information to short-term memory, which occurs when one's attention is focused on the information, and (c) placing the information in long-term memory after some rehearsal, (2) storage of information, generally in the long-term memory in a way that allows the information to be found and recognized at a later time, and (3) searching for, retrieving, and providing the information in an appropriate manner (for example, response to a question). The learning studies have shown that older people may have difficulty with each of these steps and that it is important to identify the circumstances that aid or hinder successful achievement of each step.

Performance on learning tasks is affected by several factors. Intelligence, the learning skills the person has acquired over the years, and the flexibility of learning styles are, of course, key variables. There are, however, several other variables, often called noncognitive factors, that can also have a great effect on learning. These do not involve intellectual ability but nevertheless have a great bearing on performance. Noncognitive factors include visual and auditory acuity, health status, motivation to learn, level of anxiety, speed at which the learning is paced, and meaningfulness of the material to be learned.

Several of these are treated as major variables in research on learning performance. Others, such as perceptual acuity and health status, are not. It should be obvious, however, that persons who are unable to see or hear well are not likely to perform at an acceptable level. They will misunderstand directions, fail to adequately take in the material, and have difficulty responding in written or oral form. These hindrances to learning do not relate to the person's innate ability, but they interfere to such an extent that any learning performance is likely to be severely affected.

Likewise, poor health can be a major detriment in any learning situation. If a person is not able to concentrate on the instruction because of pain, if physical stamina and strength are lacking, or if the senses are dulled through illness or medication, the learner will not be productive. Since the number of days of illness per year increases with age, physical health must be considered in any measurement of learning performance and especially in any attempt to teach individuals or groups. Thus, attention to noncognitive factors as well as cognitive ones is important in laboratory and field learning settings.

Findings from Laboratory Studies

Laboratory studies of learning in adulthood and later life have provided a wealth of data on the changes in learning performance over the life span and the means by which learning performance can be improved in old age. These conclusions are reported in the following sections. In each case, an attempt is made to show the relevance and application of the findings to the instruction of older people. Further elaboration is provided in Chapter Nine, which discusses the instructional process.

Interference. Interference can reduce the efficiency of learning. Although Craik (1977) argued that the data were inconclusive at best, most researchers seem to believe that interference can prevent learning of new material or substantially impede the learning process. There are several ways interference can occur. First, it can result from the conflict of previous, personal knowledge with the new knowledge to be learned. Second, two learning tasks undertaken at the same time can interfere with each other. Third, subsequent learning can interfere with the intended learning. Each of these can prove to be a difficulty in the learning process.

Interference from prior events or knowledge has occurred in studies in which older people were asked to learn nonsense words or symbols. Some of these symbols were contrary to common knowledge—for instance, 6 + 2 = 3. Arenberg and Robertson (n.d.) report studies in which this type of learning proved to be substantially more difficult for older people than learning nonsense symbols that did not conflict with present knowledge—for instance, A + D = F. From a research point of view, these equations are comparable, and so differences in the scores are attributed to conflict with present knowledge.

The teacher of older people could utilize this understanding by emphasizing new knowledge that will be consistent with previous learning, by minimizing any conflicts between new and old knowledge, and by helping the older person unlearn incorrect knowledge. A specific implication of this understanding is that the instructor can benefit from familiarity with the older person and the beliefs, experiences, and knowledge the older learner brings to the instructional setting. If the new information is likely to be in sharp contrast with present knowledge, the teacher should proceed slowly and carefully, since overt or implicit resistance to the new information can be expected.

However, it is possible to use the past knowledge and experience of the older learner in a very positive and beneficial fashion. Studies have shown that older people benefit more than young adults when the material is familiar or is consistent with what they already know (Arenberg and Robertson, n.d.). The past experience and knowledge of the older person can be either positive or negative, depending on its consistency or conflict with the new learning being undertaken, and needs to be given special consideration by the instructor.

A second type of interference occurs when the older learner is expected to attend to two things at once. In laboratory studies this often occurs when subjects are expected to listen to a different word list in each ear simultaneously, remember which light was flashed a few seconds ago, or repeat words while listening to other words. When older people must divide their attention among intake, attention, and retrieval processes, they seem to be especially disadvantaged (Arenberg and Robertson, n.d.; Craik, 1977). When the older person is required to shift attention from one learning task to another, efficiency of learning suffers.

The instructional implication of concurrent interference is that the teacher should concentrate on one task at a time and ensure that one item is satisfactorily learned before the next is undertaken (Botwinick, 1978). If a second task must be learned, it should be postponed as long as possible and should be clearly distinctive so that it is possible to know when one has completed the first task and is moving on to the next (E. B. Bolton, 1978). Apparently, older people need more time to integrate the new learning and to rehearse it before it is well set in the long-term memory. Additional stimulation during this period is likely to result in premature forgetting or inability to adequately retrieve the information.

Another type of concurrent interference results from distractions at the time of learning. These may come from background noise, room conditions, personal anxiety, or numerous other factors. Whatever the cause, if the older person divides attention between the learning task and something else, learning speed and accuracy will decline. Hence, the instructor is well advised to reduce the potential for distraction whenever possible and to help the older person concentrate exclusively on the learning at hand. This may not be easily done, but it is an effective means of increasing learning performance.

A third type of interference, retroactive, occurs when the person completes one learning task and then must concentrate on some other task. This subsequent diversion may impair retrieval, although this is not as well documented as other types of interference (Arenberg and Robertson-Tchabo, 1977).

Instructors of older people are well advised to space the learning experiences sufficiently to allow time for integration, to ensure that the content of the subsequent learning does not conflict with the previous learning, and to follow up later to evaluate the quality of the knowledge retained. The possibility of retroactive interference is sufficient to encourage the instructor to incorporate review, reflection, and application of the learning in order to avoid forgetting.

Pacing. Laboratory studies have shown that older people perform less well when the learning task must be completed under the pressure of time (Canestrari, 1963, 1968). Older people learn more successfully when they are given additional time both to take in the information (presentation rate) and to retrieve the answer (response rate), although a slowed response rate appears to assist them most (Monge and Hultsch, 1971). Paired-associates tasks have proved to be especially difficult for older people, who do less well than younger people when tasks are to be completed quickly (Botwinick, 1978). Canestrari (1963) reported, however, that the learning deficit can be overcome somewhat if the older learner is given additional time, and it will almost disappear when the subject can control the learning pace. Thus, when self-pacing by the older learner is allowed, the learning performance appears to be optimized (Botwinick, 1978; Calhoun and Gounard, 1979).

One result of fast pacing in learning experiments is that older persons make more errors of omission, errors in which they make no response at all rather than risk a wrong answer. Omission errors are much more common for older learners and may result, in part, from inadequate time to determine the preferred response; therefore no response is made. Arenberg and Robertson-Tchabo (1977) suggested that additional time is useful in reducing the amount of nonresponse. Extra time allows a successful search of long-term memory, so that correct answers are forthcoming.

The application of this insight from laboratory research is very direct in a teaching setting. Instruction should be self-paced or, if that is not possible, should be paced rather slowly in order to provide time for both intake and retrieval (Calhoun and Gounard, 1979; Botwinick, 1978). Since the lecture is a form of timed instruction, it should be structured in such a way that material is presented, reviewed, and examined. This may be effectively supplemented by structured discussion and applications that allow the material to be related to previous knowledge, offer time for consideration of the material, and can reduce the psychological pressure of speeded learning.

The importance of controlling the pacing of instruction

cannot be overemphasized. The laboratory learning studies, research on adult intelligence, and practical classroom experience clearly indicate the need for slowly paced or self-paced instruction for older people. In a classroom setting, this will typically require the instructor to reduce the amount of content to be presented and to offer greater clarity, specificity, and depth rather than cover a number of diverse topics. In posing questions to older persons, one should allow increased time for response and take greater care in framing the questions so that they are specific and directed.

Another aspect of pacing involves the length and timing of the instructional sessions. Although data are scarce here, it would seem most appropriate to keep the teaching sessions fairly short and to space them out over several days or weeks rather than continuing a single session for several hours (Shooter and others, 1956). This is consistent with the need for slow pacing, for a time period between learning tasks, and for accommodating the reduced strength and stamina of the older person.

Organization of Material. Learning performance depends in part on whether the person is able to retrieve what has been learned. Within the information-processing model of learning, retrieval depends mainly on how the information is organized, or "filed," in the brain. By organizing information into categories and sequences, or by using some type of visual or mnemonic device, the person is generally able to increase the quality of retrieval.

This has been shown to be especially applicable to older persons. Older adults typically do more poorly than younger adults on learning tasks, and in an attempt to explain this difference in addition to pacing and interference effects, the effect to which people use some kind of organizing strategy has been studied (Hultsch, 1969). Evidence is persuasive that older persons are less likely than others to spontaneously organize as a way to help memory (Botwinick, 1978; Arenberg and Robertson-Tchabo, 1977). When investigators have encouraged older people to categorize words to be learned, scores have improved; and when the organizing strategy was provided by the researcher, then scores improved significantly. This appears to be especially true for older people who have poor verbal skills; the weaknesses in the organizing strategies of highly verbal older people are less pronounced, so that this type of assistance produces minimal improvement (Gonda, 1977).

Learning performance of older people can be improved by helping them organize the material in better ways and by encouraging alternatives to rote memorization. This can be done through the provision of "advance organizers," aids to help the learner appropriately direct his or her attention (E. B. Bolton, 1978). Many older learners have difficulty following the content because they cannot anticipate what will be taught and do not see the whole that is being presented. It is often helpful to provide an introductory overview in which the entire lesson is given in outline form. This provides an early opportunity to see the "map" that is being followed, an insight that is especially useful for older people (Botwinick, 1978).

Advance organizers can also provide the bridge between what the older person already knows and what is to be learned in the present session. They can indicate the size, shape, extent, and orientation of the content to be covered so that dimensions can be appreciated in advance. Examples of advance organizers include the provision of an outline of the class session, the course, or the program; sets of notes to follow; initial summaries of the content; and lists of facts, concepts, or issues to be examined. These, of course, need not be provided in written form, but when that is the procedure, it does provide a guide that the learner can review at any time.

In discussion-type settings where the content is to be determined by the group, it may be impossible to provide an outline ahead of time. However, once the planning process is completed, it should be possible to write on the blackboard a listing of the topics, schedule, or persons who will be involved as well as a statement of the purpose or goal being pursued. These should be helpful in guiding the discussion and maintaining a clear direction in the learning session.

A related aspect of this topic can be seen in studies in which older people are asked to reorganize the knowledge before responding. For instance, they are read a list of words or numbers and then asked to repeat them in reverse order. Studies have shown that older people do significantly more poorly on this type of activity than younger persons (Craik, 1977), since they must not only remember the material but reorganize it. Thus, the older person faces not only the learning problem but the interference effects of two different processes.

This finding has clear implications for instruction of older people. If the content is presented in one way and the older person is expected to apply it some other way, the transition may cause difficulty. Accordingly, if the overview is provided in five points, it would seem appropriate to construct the lecture in the same five points. If the outline deals with examples or case studies, then the testing (if there is any) should deal with the same type of application. Generally, older people should not be expected to acquire abstract information and to make the transition to practical application themselves. Whenever possible, the instruction should be provided in the format that is to be used. Most instructors of older people are probably familiar with the situation in which the older person takes what is said too literally and is unable to generalize the material or apply it to comparable settings. The reorganization process is not an easy one, and it should be minimized whenever possible.

Another means of improving learning performance is through the use of mediators—that is, the association of the word or information to be learned with some other word, image, or story that can be remembered easily. As with other organizing strategies, older people are less likely than younger ones to consciously and regularly use some type of mediators. Rather, they are likely to use rote memorization to remember new information. Studies have shown that when older persons are assisted in using mediators, their scores improve. Some researchers have hypothesized that visual mediators (such as forming a picture of the word or information) are more effective in improving learning performance than verbal mediators; however, Canestrari (1968) found little difference. Both were helpful in improving the organization and remembering of the new information.

In group instruction, mediators are useful in showing the

relationships between facts that are known and those that are being learned. They can tie the new information to the old and help to show where the new knowledge fits in the person's scheme of organizing information. Since older people are not likely to use these mediational devices automatically, their learning efficiency can be improved by helping them form pictures, stories, analogies, or examples in order to make the tie and find the organizing variable. This can be done through encouragement of notetaking so that the person will indicate how the new information can be used and where it fits with the old. It can also occur by helping the person develop little stories or pictures that help him or her recall specific information.

Although not particularly useful in many situations, the chaining of words or ideas is helpful in recalling lists. Each item of a list is related by a story or picture to the next. Thus, when the first word is recalled, it should be possible to recall the whole list by remembering the tie (picture) to the next word. Another method is to relate the words in a list to a numbered series of learned words. For instance, if you remember that one is *fun* and relate the first word to *fun,* it can be remembered more easily. If two stands for *shoe* and the second word is related to *shoe* by a small story, it too may be more easily recalled.

The implication from these data on the use of organization and mediative devices in learning is that the instructor needs to provide the time and opportunity for the learners to apply the new information, in either a mnemonic or a nonsense way, or to relate it to previous knowledge. This not only provides the additional time that has been identified earlier as necessary but may reduce interference with previous knowledge. These strategies and devices can improve the quality of learning, although the amount of content covered may need to be reduced because of the time involved in the application process.

Motivation. It is generally accepted that older people are less motivated when approaching a learning task than younger people. Obviously, a desire to succeed and a commitment to conscientiously address the task are important elements in successful learning performance. Since older people are known to have less general interest in learning, and since many laboratory tasks have little meaning or relevance to the older person, it has been assumed that older learners do less well because they are less motivated. Hulicka (1967) reported that older persons refused to continue to attempt learning tasks that involved "such nonsense." This type of reaction has been reported by other researchers and has been interpreted as indicating low motivation.

One means of increasing motivation is to make the learning undertaken more meaningful to the individual learner. Calhoun and Gounard (1979) reported that older people learned significantly more of highly meaningful material than of material that was medium or low in meaningfulness. They concluded, as did Woodruff and Walsh (1975), that understanding the needs and wants of the older learner and directing the content toward those meaningful areas will result in greater motivation as well as greater learning.

Another approach to meaningfulness may be through the level of concreteness of the material. Several studies have pointed out the decline in abstract behavior with increased age (Botwinick, 1978); older people may be unable or unwilling to deal with problems, even in the laboratory, that are distant from present reality. Arenberg (1968) reported that older people had an extremely difficult time completing learning tasks involving abstract elements (forms, colors, numbers). However, when the elements were changed to more concrete items—particular beverages, meats, and vegetables—the older learners accomplished the task much more easily. Thus, it would appear advisable to present instructional components in ways that are as concrete and as personally meaningful to the older student as possible.

Other researchers have found contradictory results when measuring the motivation of older people in a learning task. Powell, Eisdorfer, and Bogdonoff (1964) took blood samples and measured galvanic skin response and heart rate of older subjects involved in a learning study and reported that older persons had higher levels of arousal, indicating greater involvement, than younger subjects. Older people experienced greater stress in the learning situation and performed the learning task more poorly than younger persons.

Subsequent studies (Eisdorfer, Nowlin, and Wilkie, 1970)

have shown that if the degree of arousal is reduced by medication, older learners improve their performance. This suggests that the older learner may be so motivated or involved in the study that his or her emotional state interferes with cognitive processes. By overreacting to the stress of the situation, the subject may withhold responses, score poorly on the learning task, and further increase anxiety in a vicious cycle (Elias and Elias, 1977).

One means of overcoming this overarousal is by providing a supportive learning environment. If older people are placed in a situation in which they are expected to compete with others or to be evaluated on their performance, they are likely to be overaroused and to do less well. Ross (1968) reported a study in which three sets of instructions were given to older subjects. One was considered to be supportive, one neutral, and one challenging. Older persons did substantially better when given the supportive instructions, less well with neutral instructions, and least well with challenging instructions. The conclusion was drawn that a positive expectation and supportive learning situation are likely to reduce the threat of the learning experience and to result in greater learning.

It has long been assumed that if correct responses are rewarded and incorrect ones are not, subjects will learn most quickly. A study by Leech and Witte (1971) indicated that if all responses were rewarded, although correct ones more strongly than incorrect ones, older persons could be persuaded to make some response and thus reduce the errors of omission. Learning tends to be poorer when the learner does not respond in some way, and the method of rewarding every response assists older persons to take a chance and perhaps learn something in that process.

The implications of these motivation studies are important for teaching older adults. First, it should be obvious that older people will be more highly motivated if they are learning meaningful material. Their interest will be heightened, and their commitment is likely to be better. It is therefore imperative that the instructor know what their needs, wants, and interests are so that the appropriate materials and methods can be used.

Second, if anxiety causes a decrease in learning efficiency, then the instructional setting should be designed to reduce the fear of failure, the chance of being made to look foolish, and the need to compete for rewards. By designing instruction at an appropriate level of complexity, by setting a relaxed pace, and by reducing the threat of failure, the instructional experience can become more successful and enjoyable. This can occur mainly through the attitude and approach that the instructor brings to the learning setting. However, a supportive environment also depends on the supportiveness of the learners toward one another. Only through real interaction can group cohesion and support develop so people can begin to feel free to express their ignorance, needs, and wants and thereby learn more deeply and effectively.

Third, the reward for participation in the instructional setting should be clear and regular. To assume that the older student is able to stand defeat and has the necessary self-confidence to persevere regardless of the results may be inaccurate. Constant monitoring of the supportiveness of the climate, of the extent to which people are being made to feel they are a part of the situation, and of the extent to which they are appreciated and valued regardless of their academic background or achievement is necessary for continued involvement and progress.

Sensory Modality. Several studies have attempted to determine whether visual or auditory input is more effective in learning. Although all of us learn both by reading and by hearing the spoken word, questions have been raised about the extent to which one is superior to the other. McGhie, Chapman, and Lawson (1965) reported that auditory means are generally slightly superior than visual when the information is to be retrieved within a very short period. Visual means may be superior, however, if the information is to be held in long-term memory for some time (Taub, 1975).

Several studies have attempted to determine whether learning is improved when one type of presentation (visual or auditory) is supplemented with the other. If the learner is provided visual images and hears the same material simultaneously, learning should be improved. In general, this has proved to be the case. Arenberg (1968) provided an additional insight in that the supplementation was done in both an active and a passive manner. Subjects learned a word list under one of three experimental conditions: looking at the words, looking at the words while the experimenter read them (passive), or looking at the words and reading them aloud (active). The results supported the hypothesis that supplementation in either the active or the passive form was valuable and that active supplementation was more helpful.

These studies suggest that teachers of older adults may facilitate learning by using both of the major senses, especially when this can be done simultaneously. Increased learning is likely to result if the instructor provides written material for the learner to follow during a lecture or uses the blackboard to list important points. However, a caution must be added. If the oral and the visual presentations are not similar, older students may experience the interference that occurs when they divide their attention. Thus, if the written materials are quite different from the oral presentation, less rather than more learning may result. The teacher must carefully choose the material to be presented in written form so that it closely conforms to the lecture presentation. Simply finding a pamphlet or other handout may not be helpful unless it is closely adhered to.

Another inference to be drawn from the studies of modality relates to the active/passive aspect of the learning. Persons who were active in the learning process, even in such a minimal way as saying aloud the words to be learned, succeeded to a much greater extent. Most teachers have assumed that activity is a valued part of the learning enterprise, but this assumption underscores the need to continue involvement of the older student, to seek forms of activity related to the new learning, and to encourage the learner not to passively soak up the knowledge but to see personal and perhaps silent ways to be active.

Feedback. Studies have shown that older persons are assisted in their learning when they are provided feedback on their performance (Hornblum and Overton, 1976; Schultz and Hoyer, 1976). Since the older person often continues to use improper or ineffective means to address problem-solving or learning situations even after these have proved to be unproductive, the feedback is especially useful when it includes suggestions for alternative approaches.

The implications for instruction include the obvious value of allowing the older learner an opportunity to rehearse the behavior or learning under the teacher's guidance so that corrective feedback can be provided. Since the older person typically requires a longer time and a greater number of trials in order to achieve the desired learning, feedback on the amount of progress being made and the current level of functioning is generally of value.

As with most suggestions, negative results can occur. Older people are typically less able to accept negative feedback and continue to do well (Bolton, 1978). Since they often have less interest, greater anxiety, and a lower self-concept, they are likely to experience greater detrimental results from negative feedback. Consequently, every attempt should be made to avoid a judgmental, critical position; and a more supportive, helpful posture should be taken whenever possible.

Similarly, older people should be helped to avoid errors to the extent possible. Since they tend to remember errors and repeat them, it is most advisable to design the situation so that successful completion of the task is likely (Arenberg and Robertson, n.d.). With mistakes, the older person's self-concept is likely to fall, and continuing commitment to the learning experience is reduced (Crawford, 1978).

Superior Learning Capabilities

Little research has been directed toward discovering areas in which older people have superior learning abilities compared with younger adults. Most of the research has involved paired-associate studies, which showed very early that older people were likely to exhibit deficits. One approach that offers some promise has been reported by Woodruff and Walsh (1975). In their study of EEG alpha rhythm, older people proved to be superior. The task involved the operant conditioning of brain waves. Electrodes were attached to the subject's scalp and connected to an amplifier to form a feedback system. The subject was instructed to maintain the same tone, which indicated alpha brain-wave activity. Old people reached the performance criterion in fewer trials than younger people.

Although this is only one study, it suggests that there may be areas in which increased age is an advantage in learning rather than a detriment. In this case, Woodruff and Walsh speculate that the reason for older persons' superior performance may be the result of self-awareness that has been developed over a longer period of time "in their bodies." Similar results might be found if additional creative approaches to learning and training were undertaken. If these were found, they might guide instructors to the strengths of older learners, which could be very helpful in overcoming a feeling of inability and a low desire to learn.

Summary

Laboratory studies of learning performance have consistently shown that older people score lower than younger adults. These cross-sectional findings may be due mainly to the lower educational levels of the current cohort of older persons, the less challenging and supportive learning environments in which most of them live, or the history through which this cohort has lived. The results may have little to do with any decline in the individual's cognitive ability. Although researchers and educators had concluded that age-related decline generally occurred, some are now suggesting that cognitive stability can continue throughout the adult years and that growth is possible with continued education and a supportive environment.

The studies reported have shown that older people are disadvantaged, compared with younger persons, if a time limit is imposed. The older person typically requires more time, especially for retrieving the information and overcoming the tendency toward response omission. Older persons rarely use learning strategies; they do not spontaneously use classification strategies and are unlikely to employ mnemonic devices as learning cues. They are therefore limited to rote memorization and other habitual approaches, which are likely to be used even after their ineffectiveness has been shown.

Interference with learning can occur in several forms. Previous knowledge that conflicts with that being taught can interfere, as can distractions at the time of learning and subsequent events or knowledge. Reducing this interference will achieve the most efficient learning and facilitate recall.

Motivation has been shown to greatly affect learning, as does a supportive environment that reduces anxiety and encourages risk taking. Either oral or written input is useful in learning, and using both at the same time may offer advantages in some situations, as can feedback on the progress the learners are making. Although there are some ways in which increased age can be a benefit in learning, these remain generally underexplored and minor compared with the detrimental aspects that have been identified.

However, it is evident that well-planned instruction is useful in assisting the older person to learn more efficiently and develop new learning strategies that will be transferable to other settings. This knowledge is helpful to teachers and other helping professionals working with older people and provides the basis on which to build a quality instructional program.

6

ΟΙΟΙΟΙΟΙΟΙΟΙΟΙΟΙΟΙΟΙΟΙΟΙΟΙΟΙΟΙΟΙΟΙΟΙΟΙΟΙΟΙΟΙΟΙΟ

Physical and Perceptual Changes

In planning and conducting instruction for older people, some program planners suggest that this population is so unusual that a set of distinct principles, different from those used in teaching adults or children, is required. Those supporting this idea of a "gerogogy" generally base their arguments on the physical changes that occur with age and suggest that alternative instructional procedures are required. Although physical and perceptual changes are significant in later life, the instructional adjustment is typically one of emphasis rather than of kind (Marcus and Havighurst, 1980). These aging-related changes do require consideration in the development of educational programming, and this chapter will deal with several of them, including vision, hearing, general energy level and other physical changes which have implications for instruction.

The physical and perceptual changes of aging are likely to be slow, and accommodation is typically made throughout the life span. Consequently, many people may not realize the extent of the sensory declines and may adjust with little awareness of the process. Reductions in the acuity of vision and hearing result from injury, disease, and age-related changes. The inter-

92

relationship of these is complex, and so it is typically impossible to determine which are exclusively age-related and which include some environmental causes. Over time, the changes affect not only perception but personality and behavior as well. As shown later in this chapter, some unusual behaviors can be understood through an awareness of perceptual decline. Thus, persons who become lost, who are antisocial, or who even evidence paranoid tendencies may have suffered physical impairment of their senses rather than experiencing some mental disorder.

Although the physical and perceptual changes are prevalent in cohorts over age 60, a great deal of individual variation occurs among members of any cohort. Caution therefore needs to be exercised in concluding that all older persons have lost their ability to see or hear well. Consequently, the discussion in this chapter assumes that normal persons will have experienced some reduction in sensory acuity but that the use of artificial aids and behavioral modifications will enable most persons to adjust to these losses and function relatively normally into their seventies and eighties. The instructor of older people, however, should be aware of the potential losses in any group so that additional compensation can be facilitated. Frequently, the older learner is functioning with little margin, and the environment needs to be as well designed as possible in order for the perceptual senses to function well.

Vision

Visual acuity is of extreme importance to anyone attempting to function independently. It is the major sense used in mobility, it provides continual stimulation to the mind, and it is essential for reading. Although many people manage to function without the visual sense, it is necessary to make major accommodations in order to function in a learning environment without the use of one's eyes. Typically, older people are less willing to make this extensive commitment and consequently are not found in educational settings when visual capacities have been substantially reduced.

Legal blindness increases substantially over the life span. Between ages 40 and 64, approximately 250 persons per 100,000 are legally blind. Between ages 65 and 69, 500 per 100,000 are legally blind; over age 70, nearly 1,450 per 100,000 are (Fozard and others, 1977). These figures indicate the substantial increase in eye problems with age. Another way of measuring these visual problems is to use the criterion of corrected vision at or before 20/50. At this point restrictions are usually imposed on a person's right to drive. At age 65, approximately 8 percent of the population has 20/50 vision or worse. At age 75, the number increases to 15 percent, and at age 85, it reaches 40 percent (Fozard and others, 1977). These statistics indicate the substantial increase in visual problems that occurs during the later stages of life. The decline in visual acuity does not begin at age 65 or 75 but commences in early adulthood. The accumulated decline, however, does not generally interfere with most people's functioning until reasonably late in life.

The aging process includes several typical changes that occur in later life. Two that are most relevant to educational endeavors involve the size of the pupil and changes in the lens of the eye. Many other changes typically occur, but most of these have little implication for the design and conduct of instruction for older people.

Pupil Size. The pupil of the eye is the opening through which light is admitted. From adolescence on, the size of the pupil declines, and the flexibility (ability to increase or decrease in size) is reduced. As a result, as people age, the pupil lets in less light; consequently, older persons need greater amounts of lighting in order to function adequately. At age 60, approximately one-third as much light is admitted as at age 20. At age 80, a person needs about three times as much light to read as a teenager does (*User's Guide,* 1976). Consequently, substantially greater lighting is needed in a classroom setting where older people are participating.

Lens. The lens is the optical instrument of the eye that focuses incoming light waves on the retina. Throughout life, the lens of the eye continues to grow, although it does not increase in size. The cells become more closely compacted until there is a loss of elasticity, resulting in farsightedness, or the inability to see close objects clearly. This typically occurs after age 40 and forces most people to resort to bifocal glasses or reading glasses in order to adjust. The continued growth of the lens causes the difficulties most middle-aged persons experience and reduces the ability to focus on close objects.

A second change in the lens is the increase in its opacity over the life span. In the extreme, this opacity results in cataracts, which can be treated only by surgical removal. In their sixties, about 9 percent of the population have cataract difficulties. During the seventies, the percentage increases to nearly 18 percent, and in the eighties, about 36 percent have major cataract problems (Fozard and others, 1977). Cataracts, however, are only the final manifestation of the increasing opacity of the lens. Before it becomes necessary to surgically remove the lens, the increased opacity begins to scatter light rays as they enter the eye and causes a glare, making it difficult to function in an environment where there is one bright light source. This is especially critical if the older learner is expected to sit looking toward a bright light, such as an exterior window in a classroom. This light will diffuse in the older person's eye and make it nearly impossible for him or her to see anything in that direction.

A third change in the lens of the eye is yellowing. Although it is not clear just what causes this, the result is that this coloration screens out some of the dark green, blue, and violet light rays, making these colors harder for older people to see. Consequently, red, yellow, and orange are more vivid to the older person and are preferred colors to use on blackboards, signs, or printed materials.

The aging of the lens also reduces ability to adjust when moving from a brightly lit room to a dark one. Older persons have difficulty in this adjustment because their eyes are not able to handle the extremes of brightness or darkness as well as younger persons'. They do not seem to be slower in making this adjustment, but their final accommodation is less complete than that of the younger person. Consequently, older people are more hesitant to drive at night where the bright lights of oncoming cars are likely to blind them momentarily before they must quickly adjust to the darkness of the empty road.

Implications for Education. Several implications can be drawn from the available knowledge on changes in vision with age. Perhaps the most general conclusion is that older people should be encouraged to control their own lighting whenever possible. Just as self-pacing is desirable to accommodate individual differences in learning rates, in any situation where lighting is adjustable, the older learner should have as much control as possible over how the lights are set. This might be done by lowering or closing blinds, by turning on some of the lights while leaving others off, or by having desk lamps in some of the learning areas. Although this may be difficult to implement in many settings, it is most helpful if the person can control his or her own illumination.

A second implication is that older people will generally need more light than younger people. Rooms in school buildings that have adequate illumination for children or young adults may have insufficient lighting for older learners. The increased illumination should be diffused as much as possible to ensure reduced glare and should come from behind and above the older learner in order to optimize vision.

A third implication is that larger print should be used in all the materials provided to older people. This is relatively easy to do, since many books can be purchased with larger type, handouts can be designed this way, and large writing can be used on blackboards or bulletin boards. Print also becomes more legible when there is high contrast between the paper and the ink. The use of red, yellow, or orange colors is often valuable, and whenever possible the cooler colors of blues, greens, and violets should be avoided.

Light-dark adaptation can be facilitated by waiting a short period after turning off the lights before beginning to show a film or slides. Likewise, the lights should be turned on slowly after completing the audiovisual presentation. A similar period of accommodation should be facilitated when the older learner is moving from a brightly lit classroom to a dark parking lot or from a room with subdued light to a bright outdoor location. A transition room or space will help, especially if the older person can be encouraged to tarry there a few moments in order to aid the adjustment.

Overall, the accommodations for visual change in later life are not so great as to require a whole different learning setting for older people. However, the decreased visual acuity of the older person requires some instructional adjustment and is one area in which planning can substantially increase learning efficiency.

Hearing

Decreasing hearing acuity is widely recognized as one of the typical attributes of later life. Although it does affect many older people, one need not assume that everyone over the age of 65 or 75 or 85 has deficient hearing. When hearing loss does occur, however, it is likely to have a major impact on social interaction and to reduce participation in educational activities. Since hearing is such an integral part of daily life, those who have lost substantial portions of their hearing are likely to experience social difficulties.

Reduction of auditory acuity is likely to increase the risk of accidents in the physical environment because people are less likely to benefit from the warning that hearing often provides. In addition, reduced hearing acuity is likely to limit interpersonal communication, often resulting in paranoid tendencies as hard-of-hearing persons become convinced that others are excluding them from communication or talking about them. Other emotional problems can result from reduced hearing, including depression caused by lack of social interaction and feelings of inferiority, which occur when one can no longer effectively participate in verbal interchange.

Strangely enough, a hearing loss is accorded less sympathy than are other physical decrements. While a blind person may engender concern, a deaf person is more likely to be shunned and ignored. Persons with only modest hearing loss are likely to be avoided, since it is often difficult or embarrassing to interact with them; older persons with a hearing loss are likely to conclude that people do not like them because they are excluded from or are unable to hear the conversations going on around them.

Rehabilitation of the older person with a hearing loss is difficult. Many older persons believe relief is impossible and so fail to seriously pursue the steps to increase their communication ability. Hearing aids are available but are frequently unused by persons with hearing problems, and helping professionals may control the older person's activities to such an extent that the person loses the ability to conduct his or her own life. Hearing rehabilitation takes constant effort by the older person. Frequently, this causes too great a strain for the older person to handle.

The major hearing loss that occurs in later life is called *presbycusis*. It is characterized by progressive bilateral loss of hearing for tones of high frequency due to the degenerative physiological changes in the auditory system as a function of age (Corso, 1977). It involves both peripheral- and central-nervous-system aspects of hearing. In all likelihood, presbycusis results both from the aging process and from environmental factors such as a noisy environment, disease, and accidents. Along with older persons' reduced capacity for hearing sounds loudly enough, it is one of the two major hearing difficulties of the elderly.

Hearing loss begins early in most people, probably about age 20, and continues throughout life. Its prevalence is lowest in the early years, with approximately 42 persons per 1,000 experiencing a hearing loss between ages 17 and 44, increasing to 114 per 1,000 from ages 45 to 64, to 231 per 1,000 in the age range of 65 to 74, and finally reaching 398 per 1,000 among people 75 and over (Schow and others, 1978). After age 55, men tend to show more hearing loss than women, although this may be caused by environmental conditions (noisy work settings) rather than some physical inclination (Corso, 1977).

Older people with a hearing loss must concentrate more consistently and carefully in order to understand conversation. In laboratory studies, older subjects are likely to be more cautious and to not indicate the presence of a tone until it is clearly audible. Rather than risking being wrong, they prefer to make no response. This behavior frequently carries over to normal listening situations. Older people may prefer to ask that a statement be repeated or may ignore it unless they are sure of what has been said. In order to optimally use the hearing they have, they typically must listen carefully and concentrate on the verbal message. This is a tiring and frustrating undertaking, as anyone can experience by trying to carry on a conversation in a noisy room or by listening to a poorly amplified play.

Because reduced hearing acuity does not engender social sympathy, many people, both older and younger, try to conceal this loss. They are likely to use such accommodations as lip reading or staying away from difficult situations rather than wearing a hearing aid. Even when an aid is available, it typically is difficult to adjust, and many people never use it extensively. With denial of the existence of a hearing problem, the person must continually be on guard, concentrate more, and try harder to hear what is occurring in the environment.

Volume. One of the typical auditory losses that occur in later life is the reduced ability to hear sounds as loudly as before. This change is widely recognized and leads some people to assume they must speak more loudly when conversing with an older person. This will be sufficient accommodation for many older listeners if the environment is free of extraneous background noise, but it may prove inadequate in a setting with competing sounds.

Pitch. A second typical change in the older adult's ability to hear is reduction in the ability to hear high-pitched sounds. In younger people, ability to hear sounds within the range of 1,000 to 10,000 cycles per second (cps) is common. After age 65, however, it is unlikely that most people can hear any sound above 8,000 cps. This deficit may reduce the enjoyment of music, but it does not interfere greatly with understanding speech. However, some older people lose the ability to hear sounds above 4,000 cps or 2,000 cps. In this situation, speech becomes very difficult to understand even though it is loud enough to be heard. Conversational speech generally falls in the range of 1,000 to 8,000 cps, and it is the unvoiced consonants (*s, c, t, p, g,* for example) that are high-pitched and therefore difficult to hear. In this case, increasing the loudness of the speech (which for most of us also means increasing the pitch) will not help older persons understand what is being said.

Educational Implications. The loss of hearing acuity in later life has a number of implications for the design and conduct of instruction. The most obvious is that teachers should make their presentations in a loud voice with as much precision in diction as possible. In general, it is preferable to speak more slowly so that the older listener has the opportunity to consider the words and meanings slightly longer. In addition, it is appropriate for the speaker to face the audience and to have sufficient light on his or her face so that the participants can see clearly any visual cues that are provided. Since many older people supplement their hearing with lip reading and other clues derived from gestures and motions, it is imperative that these be clearly visible.

Likewise, in a learning setting where there is considerable discussion, each participant should sit in a position where he or she can see others who are speaking. This may require a circular seating arrangement or asking persons to stand and face the group when they speak. Many participants need encouragement to speak loudly and to keep their hands away from their mouths when speaking. Demonstration of appropriate techniques by the teacher will usually not be sufficient for the class; regular encouragement of clear and loud speech will often be required.

A second implication results from the reduced ability to hear higher frequencies of pitch. Whenever possible, the speaker should lower the pitch of his or her voice. This may be difficult for women to do, and those with high-pitched (squeaky) voices may prove to be impossible for the older students to understand. However, most people are able to reduce the pitch and consequently to increase their understandability.

A third implication is that interfering noise should be eliminated or reduced to the extent possible. Background conversation, traffic noise, and mechanical sounds interfere with the understanding of speech (Bergman, 1971). This means that the instructional classroom should be quiet and able to be screened from interfering noise. Frequently the outside noise can be eliminated or reduced, but the participants converse among themselves, creating an undercurrent of whispered discussion. Although this may indicate interest and sharing of the content, it is likely to interfere greatly with hearing of lectures or discussion and needs to be eliminated. The older learner will quickly agree that it is a bother and generally will support its reduction.

A fourth implication that can be drawn from the literature and practice is the importance of ensuring that the older student's attention is secured before the speaking begins. As pointed out earlier, comprehension requires more attention and commitment by the hearing-impaired learner. The older student who misses an introductory statement because of inattention may have difficulty understanding the rest of the presentation. Consequently, it is necessary to gain the students' attention before starting as well as to give them a clear idea of what is going to be presented.

Finally, it is important to continue receiving feedback on whether the older persons in the classroom are understanding what is being said. It is relatively easy to ask people whether they can hear and understand, but it is probably more effective to allow for discussion of issues the instructor has raised. This can show relatively quickly whether the group has been hearing and whether the material presented was understood.

In general, then, the suggestions for the alteration of instruction in order to ensure hearing by older persons are similar to those drawn from the laboratory studies of learning (Chapter Five). Older people will do better when the pace is slowed, the presentations are clear, interference is reduced, attention is maintained, and feedback is consistently used. Although older people vary considerably in their auditory acuity, most classrooms of older people will include some persons with hearing loss who need the indicated accommodations in order to function optimally.

Energy Level

Numerous physical and psychological conditions affect the level of energy that older people have to invest in learning. In general, it is assumed that people over 65 are likely to have lower levels of strength, vigor, and endurance. This tends to be true, and the program planner and instructor must consider this situation in order to ameliorate the negative impact that reduced energy may have on the effectiveness of learning. There are many interrelated factors, the major ones being physical health, mental health, and physical conditioning.

Nearly 80 percent of people over 65 suffer some chronic physical condition that has little likelihood of being cured. These limit the mobility of about 20 percent of the older population and force the others to accommodate with appliances (glasses, hearing aids, crutches, and so on), behaviors (such as withdrawal or caution), or medication (Tager, 1981). Some of these conditions are simply an inconvenience and with modest accommodation do not really affect the functioning of the older person. However, many reduce the vital margin of energy and enthusiasm that the older person has and limit his or her desire and ability to undertake challenging and enlivening educational activities.

Many health conditions reduce the energy level of the older learner. Chronic diseases, recent surgery, and mild infections are prevalent among the older population and tend to have a debilitating influence. Each of these conditions may be under treatment by various medicines, and the overuse of drugs can prove to be a major hindrance to the vital functioning of the older learner. Older people make up 10 percent of the population but take one quarter of all prescribed medications (Tager, 1981). Many older people regularly take several prescription and over-the-counter medications that may reduce their intellectual acuity and physical functioning. In the classroom, this reduced energy may be manifested as listless behavior, lack of interest, or unwillingness to participate actively. Reduced energy makes the older student less likely to enter into the learning experience and to benefit from it.

Common mental health problems such as depression may also reduce learning. Depression is characterized by fatigue, sleeplessness, low self-esteem, and anxiety. Although it may be chronic, recurrent, or acute, while it exists it is likely to keep the older person from functioning well, especially in a demanding classroom setting. About 20 to 25 percent of the older population suffer from occasional depression (Plopper, 1981), and so it is a major concern when teaching a group of older people.

Depression may deter older persons from enrolling in any educational endeavor because the negative feelings discourage accepting any challenge or involvement. In such cases, it may be a recruiting consideration rather than an instructional one. However, in a group of any size, there is a reasonable chance that some of the participants are suffering some form of depression and that it will reduce learning efficiency.

Physical conditioning may also affect the older person's ability to successfully complete a learning experience. Since many older people do not consciously strive to maintain good muscle tone, they lose the strength and stamina needed to be mobile and undertake new activities. They report that they are too old and tired to participate in instruction requiring several hours of attention and involvement. For some, the physical difficulties may be great, but in many cases the physical ability has been lost through disuse rather than any particular accident, disease, or medical intervention.

Educational Implications. Although not all older people suffer reduced energy level, it is common enough so that the instructor of older adults will want to consider several accommodations. First, class sessions should not be as long as for younger people. Probably two hours is the maximum for many older people, and that may be too long if the learning is intense or physically demanding. Although there are certainly persons who will desire and be able to handle longer sessions, this seems to be a good limit for many older people.

Second, even two-hour sessions are too long to conduct without some kind of a break or chance for the learners to walk about and redirect their attention. The need for change comes from both the physical need to move about and the need to relax a little and to take some refreshment. Serving coffee or tea and a cookie is useful as a stimulant to the older learners and a way to increase their energy level.

A third implication can be seen in the need for the instructor to be sensitive to gradually building physical capacity. Instead of beginning with the hardest work, as may happen in undergraduate education, the instructor might prefer to phase in the work so that the older person is enabled to slowly build a capacity through the course. That is, if it takes a good deal of energy to handle the learning, the older person should be helped to gain that energy by working into the "intellectual exercise" gradually rather than having to plunge in too fully.

Finally, instructors should be aware of any changes in the energy or enthusiasm level of the older student. If a person becomes quiet, withdrawn, or sad, it may be that some physical or emotional problem is interfering that needs to be settled before good learning can continue. When this occurs, it is important for the instructor to keep priorities in perspective and not expect the older person to ignore problems in order to keep learning. The physical or emotional needs must be met before the learning can be pursued effectively, and so the instructor may want to help or find other assistance rather than assuming that the depressing or other enervating condition can be ignored.

Other Physical Changes

The aging process is not limited to the senses of hearing and vision and the general level of energy. All body systems are affected by the progressive process of aging. These changes occur across the life span but begin to affect behavior between the ages of 65 and 75 for most people. The human being has a great margin of strength and capacity beyond what is needed for normal daily living, but this margin begins to become very thin as people reach retirement age. This is evidenced in many ways, only a few of which will be mentioned here, since they are the ones with direct relevance for the design and conduct of instruction.

With increased age, people are less able to adjust easily to major fluctuations in temperature. More older people die from heat prostration and hypothermia than younger people. This occurs because the older body is not able to compensate for the extremes of temperature and tends to follow the outside temperature, resulting in physical difficulties for the older person. Although most classrooms are neither so cold as to threaten freezing nor so hot as to cause heat strokes, it is important to realize that very cool or hot temperatures will have greater effects on older learners than younger ones. Most older people prefer the room somewhat warmer than younger people (in the mid to upper 70s) and become quickly uncomfortable when the temperature moves outside this range.

A second change involves reduced mobility. Older people typically do not walk as quickly or as agilely as younger ones. The flat-footed gait of an old person is a common stage affectation but reflects the adopted style of many older men and women. A somewhat bent posture may also become common, resulting in less ability to notice objects ahead and above the person. Classrooms located in areas that are hard to reach, require climbing steps, have slippery floors or thick rugs, or require long walks are likely to prove difficult for older people. They will probably avoid them but, if they do participate, will complain about the difficulty of access.

Likewise, instructors who include physical movement in the classroom or field visits to other agencies or settings will need to keep the mobility conditions of the older person in mind. A "walkthrough" in which the possible obstacles are identified and the extent of travel is considered will be helpful to assure the older participants that the reduced mobility will not prove to be a problem.

A third change involves bowel and bladder control and has implications for the classroom. Since older people find it necessary to relieve themselves frequently, adequate and accessible restroom facilities must be available, and sufficient time should be provided for a "bathroom break." Since some type of urinary difficulty is not unusual, older persons leaving the classroom with some regularity should not be assumed to be evidencing a lack of interest in the course; their physical needs are merely taking priority over their intellectual ones.

Summary and Conclusions

The physical changes occurring throughout adulthood result in cumulative effects by later life that have implications for the design and conduct of instruction for older people. They result in slowed reactions, need for greater visual and auditory stimulation, and reduced levels of energy and physical stamina. The instructor will need to remember these characteristics and to time the instruction in such a way that these decrements do not reduce learning efficiency. This should not prove to be extremely difficult, but without some awareness of the physical changes, it is possible that the best of instructional intentions will be wasted.

7

OIOIOIOIOIOIOIOIOIOIOIOIOIOIOIOIOIOIOIOIOIOIOIOIO

Stages of the Adult Life Span

The preceding chapters have presented the evidence that older persons typically retain the intellectual capacity to learn and that the skills needed for learning can be refined and developed well into the retirement years. In assisting middle-aged and older persons to increase the number of learning attempts and their learning efficiency, educational program planners must consider the desires and needs of adults—what they want to learn. Since change occurs over the adult years, it is not surprising that the interests and reasons for learning are different during various parts of the life span. As persons experience changes in their physical condition, as technological advances impinge on them, as family adjustments are required, and as employment and avocational interests are modified, learning needs change.

The adult life span is not a single, unitary period. It involves a variety of tasks, adjustments, and challenges that come from both within and outside the individual. These adjustments have been described in at least three ways. First, they can be viewed as resulting from the physical senescence that occurs over the life span—the physical stability of the early years and the subsequent decline which occurs after the early twenties and which progressively affects the person's ability to function. Physical changes accelerate in the later stages of life and increasingly interfere with normal functioning, causing the person to accommodate more extensively. The lowered capacity is significant because it reduces the physical margin maintained by the person, resulting in more catastrophic implications when illness or accidents occur.

Second, the changes of adulthood can be described as occurring primarily within the consciousness of the individual. Motives, drives, interests, and expectations change as one passes through the adult years. Various periods of life may be characterized differently in terms of their psychological emphasis. Young adulthood may be a time for acquisition, middle age a time to exercise power, and old age a time to reflect and contribute to others. The motivations change, primarily because of internal psychological states that are generalizable to most individuals and are predictable across the life span.

Third, the changes of adulthood can result from the sociocultural factors that impinge on the individual from the family, community, or culture. We have been conditioned by our society to expect to complete certain events within prescribed periods of time. For instance, completing one's formal education, obtaining a job, being married, receiving a promotion, and retiring are all events that most people expect to experience. They may occur at any time in life, but most of us could identify ages at which they most "appropriately" occur. Technological and cultural development affects the perception of these time periods. Today the increased pace of knowledge acquisition has made learning a lifelong process, marriages are occurring at all ages, and people are moving into and out of the job market in their sixties as well as their twenties.

The adult life span, then, is not a totally predictable path that people walk in unison. It can be interrupted by tragedies, by sudden good fortune, or by twists of fate that move the person rapidly toward cherished goals or greatly retard progress. Although there are stages through which most people progress, some never experience the typical attributes of physical decline, motivational change, or social expectations. However, they are unusual and should be viewed as the exceptions to the typical life course.

Another way in which adults differ in life-course experience occurs because of cohort differences. The historical experience of persons now old is substantially different from the experience of those who were old in 1900 and from that of those who will be old in 2050. The Great Depression, the world wars, the rapid technological advances have all played a part in molding the current cohort's attitudes, behaviors, and expectations. Thus, we need to be cautious in assuming that contemporary middle-aged and older people are typical of persons at this age in the past or in the future. One example will illustrate this point. Older people today are generally described as being more politically conservative than younger people. One might conclude that people grow conservative as they age. This conclusion is probably incorrect. A more probable explanation is that contemporary older persons were socialized in a time when political attitudes were more conservative. Today's older persons have maintained their political attitudes over the years and so, by comparison with younger persons, are conservative. They have not changed; society has.

In this chapter, life-span development will be viewed from several perspectives. A great deal of scholarly work has been undertaken in a variety of disciplines, especially the fields of psychology and sociology, where research has taken a life-span orientation over the past twenty years. This orientation is important to the field of education, for it begins the clarification process that will help the program planner understand the social, psychological, and physical condition of middle-aged and older persons in order to determine the most effective learning processes and content for this clientele.

This concept of life-span development is useful because it provides the educator of middle-aged and older persons a framework on which to build educational programming. Since needs of individual adults are diverse and desires are fluid, the life-span perspective can assist in determining typical situations and challenges that face these persons so that appropriate educational interventions can be encouraged. The educational program planner can construct a life-accompanying curriculum, a series of educational experiences that will help the person anticipate and meet the challenges that are likely to be presented during the life course. The life-span perspective will also provide a way of targeting specific types of participants and identifying subsequent client groups who may be encouraged to undertake educational experiences.

Life-Span Development

Life-span development is a widely used term in social and behavioral science at this time. There is a general realization among scientists that change does occur throughout adulthood, and a great many researchers have tried to conceptualize the process so that general explanations of adult behavior could be achieved. The result has been a variety of descriptions of life-span behavior, with no one approach receiving general acceptance as a complete explanation for adult development.

Most students of life-span development would agree that adulthood encompasses the peak of the growth stages that were begun at conception. It continues with a longer period of relative stability covering young adulthood and early middle age and includes some intellectual and physical decline in the later years of life. Thus, life-span development is not limited to physical or psychological growth. It includes growth, stability, decline, and horizontal change. It is not a value position limited to positive change but relates, rather, to changes of decline as well as growth (Knox, 1977). Thus, the term refers to generalizable change that occurs during the adult life span, and the study of life-span development is an attempt to describe and understand that change in light of the developments that occurred previously and to anticipate those that will follow.

The adult life span, however, is not one constant period of change. Probably none of us could adjust to eternal change. Rather, the understanding of the adult life span suggests that people go through periods of change alternating with periods of stability. Frequently, the stability will last for several years and then be broken by a decision, an event, or a need that results in change. These are typically called "marker events"—predictable turning points in the life cycle (Cross, 1981). For example, a mother decides to go back to work after her children leave home, widowhood forces a man to seek new living arrangements for social and nutritional reasons, or retirement provides increased leisure time that can be used in a variety of ways.

Once accommodation to events of this type has occurred, a period of stability is likely to set in, allowing the individual or the family to enjoy the new status. This stability may last for many years in the case of the mother who successfully returns to work, or it may be relatively brief in the case of the retiree who fails to settle on a meaningful avocation. During the life course, there is a variety of typical periods of stability and of change that have been identified. Although not every person will experience them all, they will affect most of us. For some, the periods of change may come suddenly, causing great dislocation and confusion. Others may find that the changes occur almost imperceptibly and one period of stability seems to flow into the next with little notice. For instance, an unexpected death, accident, job loss, or divorce may cause a change which was not anticipated and which can be accommodated only with the greatest effort. At the other extreme, some persons phase out of the work role gradually and replace their vocational commitments with voluntary and hobby activities without seeming to notice the change. They send their children off to college while taking on greater community responsibilities and later relinquish those responsibilities for recreational activities. Consequently, the change may be rapid or slow, distracting or unnoticed, expected or unplanned.

When discussing the adult life span, it is most convenient to describe different life periods in terms of the age of persons. For instance, middle age can be described as the period from age 40 to 55; later maturity could be from age 56 to 75; and old age, over age 75. Although this is convenient and easily understandable, it is open to a great deal of criticism. Since there is substantial variance in the chronological age at which typical transitions occur, use of age as the primary description of the period is likely to cause as much confusion as clarity. A 55-year-old may be experiencing life more like a 75-year-old if he has had unusual illnesses, accidents, or other traumas. Or he may see himself as, and act like, a 35-year-old if health and society support that behavior. Thus, when ages of the various stages of life are used, they should be considered illustrative rather than as a precise attempt to anticipate the timing of events or stages.

The remainder of this chapter will deal with three basic aspects of life-span development—physical changes, psychological stages, and sociocultural phases. By approaching the area from these three perspectives, it is possible to describe the current state of knowledge, to show the alternative concepts, and to suggest some insights that educational programmers might find useful. Each of the three approaches will be examined in terms of three time periods—middle age, later maturity, and old age. These terms are used in rather traditional fashion and refer typically to individual behaviors and outlooks rather than a particular chronological age. These three divisions of the adult life span are relatively well accepted at this time, although it is certainly possible to suggest additional substages, as some researchers have done (Levinson, 1978).

Taken together, these three life periods and three approaches offer an overview of the research and theory developed over the past sixty years. This conceptualization is useful in helping us understand the process of adult development so that instruction can be effectively designed. By building on this knowledge base, it is possible to identify educational interests and needs of middle-aged and older persons that are conceptually sound, resistant to fads, and applicable to current conditions of contemporary education. The conceptualization is especially valuable in identifying potential clients for various content areas, since it has been shown that education is one of the primary resources adults use to assist them in dealing with transitions.

In a study of adults and their involvement in educational programs, Aslanian and Brickell (1980) discovered that 83 percent of the educational participants identified a change in their lives as the reason for engaging in learning. Many of them expected to face a life-change point (job, marriage, empty nest, financial opportunity) and realized that in order to successfully complete that life change, they would need additional information, skill, or insight. The life change, then, was the trigger that moved them to pursue education. By understanding who these persons are who will be needing help with their change points, educational planners can become more efficient in designing and conducting instructional programs. They can identify audiences, more accurately predict enrollment, and more successfully determine the level and orientation of instruction that is offered.

Physical Changes

Life-span development can be viewed as primarily a physical phenomenon. When this approach is taken, adulthood is typically seen as a time of physical stability that increasingly becomes decline. As the person nears the end of life, the decline becomes more pervasive and has a greater impact. Most physical characteristics do show stability through the early stages of adulthood and then begin the irreversible pattern of diminution that continues throughout the remainder of the life span. However, before assuming that only negative results occur, it should be noted that most of us are not forced to use the full extent of our physical capacities throughout most of our lives. We are capable of greater physical feats than we are typically required to undertake, and so the decline may not be noticed until well into middle age, when it may begin to interfere with normal functioning.

Likewise, the rapidity of decline is not determined solely by some biological clock that runs within each of us. It is also affected by the ways we live—amount of exercise, diet, number and type of accidents, and smoking and drinking. People who live healthful lives typically discover that the physical declines come more slowly and less pervasively than they do to people who treat their bodies in less sustaining ways. Thus, physical decline varies radically from person to person. Our genetic directions and our lifetime accumulation of insults or supports combine to make us decline more or less rapidly than the average person.

Middle Age. Decline does occur, and it is difficult to reverse the process. In middle age the potential of retarding the process exists, but it is more difficult to reverse the declines once they occur. Those readers who are beyond age 35 or 40 will recognize the discipline it takes to return to jogging, bicycling, tennis, or even square dancing after months or years of abstention. Actions that previously were considered routine now take great effort, and breath and stamina are often in short supply. Likewise, eye-hand coordination deteriorates as visual acuity declines and fine-muscle skills are lost. In some cases the decline results from disuse—our inactive life-style, lack of physical challenges, the pressures of everyday life. In these cases, practice and perseverance can restore much of the skill or strength. However, in other areas the physical aging of the body cannot be easily overcome. The professional basketball player will not become youthful with additional conditioning, nor will the competitive swimmer regain championship form.

The physical changes of middle age do not occur through an event (as do social or psychological transitions); rather, the multiple changes occur slowly and are recognized only when one attempts to engage in an activity, previously easy, that is difficult now. The changes can be seen in the wrinkling of the skin, the thinning of the hair, and the thickening of the waist, but these are only the symptoms rather than the basic changes that affect the middle-aged person. Recognizable declines in energy, stamina, strength, and coordination are the more important characteristics of middle-age development. They typically do not interfere with normal life activities, but they bring the disturbing realization of the imminent decline of the body.

The educational implications of physical development in middle age are not as impelling as they will be later in the life cycle. However, there are several areas in which instruction may prove to be of value if the motivation to participate can be secured. These include an understanding of the normal aging process and an awareness of how this process can be slowed or can be speeded up through excessive smoking or alcohol consumption. As people reach middle age, they realize that the changes are occurring; however, they typically do not interpret the changes as serious (and typically they are not). Consequently, the motivation to learn more and to retard the decline is not great. Today, the widespread interest in nutrition and exercise provides a great deal of cultural support for instruction in this area, and it may be expected to continue in the future as the younger persons who have initiated the interest move into middle age.

Likewise, physical development provides a backdrop for the interest of the middle-aged in the physical changes that are affecting their parents. The middle-aged person typically accepts some responsibility for the parent who is over 70 and who is experiencing some health condition that may affect mobility or activity. A desire to know how serious a condition is, whether it can be controlled or cured, and how life-styles can influence its future course may encourage middle-aged persons to become involved in health-related courses that explore the later stages of life. Similarly, interest in rehabilitation from premature strokes, heart attacks, or accidents may offer opportunities for course instruction. In a variety of ways, the initial impact of physical decline can be used as content in continuing educational programs for middle-aged persons.

Later Maturity. Later maturity is a stage at which the physical changes appear to accelerate. The accumulating declines become more noticeable and begin to affect adults' behaviors and expectations. Illness is more common, lowered energy levels may reduce the will to undertake new responsibilities, and ability to engage in strenuous activity is reduced. At this stage people are much more likely to feel daily their reduced physical prowess and to adjust their work, recreation, and family activities accordingly. This is not to suggest that people in this stage of life are incapable of continuing normal activities; rather, they typically accommodate with intellect, experience, and caution rather than relying on physical strength, speed, or agility. Examples include active people who decide to walk rather than jog, sedentary people who find it tiring to be on their feet more than a few minutes, and employees who find themselves exhausted after a week's work when they previously retained sufficient energy to look forward to an exciting weekend.

Designers of educational programs will find that persons in later maturity are aware of and interested in the physical developments of this stage of life. As physical changes become more apparent, many questions arise regarding the normal aging process as contrasted to the illnesses of the period. Since decline and illness are very distinct items, it is helpful for people to realize the difference and to understand when a physician is necessary and when the condition is something that is best ignored or tolerated. Courses in such areas as nutrition, exercise, cancer, heart disease, arthritis, and other chronic diseases are likely to draw concerned audiences and to provide helpful and valued service to this client group.

Old Age. In old age physical development takes on a constraining and debilitating aspect. Old age, by definition, is a time when the physical changes have forced the person to constrain activities and to reduce mobility, activity, and participation. Although people may reach old age at different chronological ages, typically they have lived 75 to 85 years and are nearing the end of life when the most severe of the physical declines are experienced. Although a person may live in old age many years, the primary purpose of medicine (and to some extent of education) is to postpone as long as possible the onset of "old age" and to maintain the attributes of middle age and later maturity as long as possible.

The term *old age* is used here to mean a period of life denoted by extensive physical decline; it is not simply a particular age. Persons 80 years old can still be in later maturity if their health and energy allow it and if their psychological state supports it. Persons who are the "old-old," or in "old age," have experienced so much physical decline that health conditions become the center of their social and physical world. The encouraging aspect is that people can frequently move back to later maturity from what would appear to be "old age." Heart disease, cancer, stroke, or broken bones can so severely affect older persons that they appear to have completely lost their vigor and strength. However, today it is possible to find increasing numbers of persons who, though experiencing this trauma, regain their physical abilities and return to normal functioning. Medical science provides these modern miracles, but education plays the role of helping the individual and the family recognize that a second chance exists and identifying the means by which its use is optimized. By assisting with rehabilitation, by continuing encouragement, by making persons aware of the likelihood of recovery, and by offering educational opportunities phased to the developing characteristics of the older person, real service can be provided.

Too often, educational providers go into nursing homes, hospitals, or rehabilitation facilities with the assumption that little will result from the educational offerings. They believe that persons in old age can only be entertained as a prelude to death rather than that they can be reclaimed to useful functioning. By seeking the rehabilitative possibilities for the older person, educators too can be assisted in helping to reclaim the person's skills and talents. Thus, it should be clear that the physical changes occurring from middle age through old age provide a variety of educational needs that can be used by program planners to serve these clients. Although the exact age at which these concerns become important for adults will vary, most people will find that there is a time when the physical changes do reach their consciousness, and they therefore become concerned about learning more so that they can preserve their health and vitality.

Developmental Stages

Psychological study of life-span development has emphasized theories linking personality formation to chronological age. The assumption in most of these approaches is that life is a continuum in which the person progressively moves upward through a series of stages of personality development, finally reaching the highest state in old age. "Old age" in the psychologist's sense is not akin to "old age" in the physiologist's sense. It is not a period of dependency and limited mobility; rather, it is the time when the person is seeking to overcome the limitations of the physical body and achieve the highest level of psychological development. People can, of course, truncate their psychological development at any time, and hence lifelong progress is not assured. However, through internal change and social supports, the person can meet the challenges of each period of the life span and continue psychological growth.

Since G. Stanley Hall's *Senescence* in 1922, psychologists have attempted to describe the stages of personality development. Some, like Hall, saw these stages as few—in his view, simply "before the peak" and "after the peak." Others, such as Buehler (1962), identified several stages—need satisfaction, adaptive self-limitation, creative expansion, establishment of inner order, and self-fulfillment. Perhaps the best-known and most widely accepted conceptualization is that of Erik Erikson (1963), who described eight stages of development across the life span. His theory befits the conception of life-span continuity, with successful resolution of issues within the early life stages aiding and strengthening the ability to meet and resolve future challenges.

Erikson identified eight distinct but interconnected stages stretching from birth to death. The first six stages of development occur in childhood, adolescence, and entrance to adulthood and will not be addressed here, since they do not deal with the adult life span. However, stages seven and eight are of interest. Stage seven is called generativity versus stagnation, and involves the conflict between self-absorption and devoting some energies to guiding the next generation, which can include one's own offspring and the community in general. For many people it is a struggle between settling for what they are, for continuing interest only in their own career, family, or friends, and moving outside themselves to devote time and energy as contributions to the welfare of the larger society. Although the naive idealism of youth may have faded, the task is to move one's attention to others after the basic conditions of adulthood have been met.

We can see this occurring as persons in their forties and fifties become involved in local politics, serve on boards of organizations, contribute to charities and local agencies, provide volunteer services, and increase their interest in contemporary world events. Education can be of assistance in this task by raising awareness of social issues, by making options known, and by developing the skills needed to serve successfully in policy-making and leadership positions. Frequently, adults do not prepare for these roles but move into them serendipitously as their availability is recognized and opportunities present themselves. More encouragement is needed to make preparation valued; the future may see more development in this area as the need for volunteer service expands and available persons recognize multiple opportunities. Education can also be useful in expanding the individual's horizons through study of world history, politics, literature, drama, or philosophy. As people expand their interests in others, instruction in local, state, national, and international events offers many opportunities for the program planner.

It would appear that people who do not successfully respond to the challenge of middle age that Erikson identifies, those who stagnate rather than gain generativity, are unlikely subjects for educational programming which offers challenges to growth and which expands the knowledge and interests of the individual. They are likely to be more interested in themselves and their families. Accordingly, their choices of educational offerings may resemble those identified in the section dealing with physical development in middle age and later maturity. Thus, persons who do choose to continue their education in this area are likely to be growth-oriented and may respond very positively to a variety of methods and approaches, while those interested in physical development may be thought more likely to favor a conservative approach that incorporates a supportive environment rather than a challenge to growth.

Erikson's eighth stage of development occurs in *later maturity* and carries over into *old age*. It reflects the nearing completion of life and involves reflection and consideration of its meaning and importance. The task of this stage as Erikson describes it is to achieve a sense of integrity, acknowledging satisfaction with the course of one's life in contrast to dissatisfaction and despair over the choices one has made and the results of past decisions. This time for reflection and consideration is a necessary conclusion to the "examined life" and allows the person the luxury of undertaking review and synthesis with no other purpose than to assess the implications and determine the meaning that life has had. If the review is successful, it will likely lead the person to a sense of transcendence, an understanding that life is more than the body and that the meaning of life is not measured in physical attributes, material possessions, or social accomplishments. However, if the life has not been lived well, if the review is not successfully undertaken, or if the greater meanings are not sensed, the person will reach a sense of despair over the ending of the physical life and the opportunities that have been squandered.

The educational implications of Erikson's eighth stage are easy to identify. They include the provision of an opportunity for people to examine, with supportive help, their lives and the meaning they have had. This can occur through a variety of content. For instance, the currently popular courses in autobiography provide a way for people to look at key life events and to search for their meaning. By undertaking this in a group setting, the individual can be assisted to extract insights from other persons' life events and to apply them to his or her concerns. By seeking especially important times and persons, the individual is aided in reaching some conclusions about the parts of his or her life that were important and the impact they had on the rest of the life course. Another way of approaching this life review is through the study of the humanities—literature, religion, philosophy, drama, or music. This approach is less personal than the autobiography, but it allows the older person to explore the insights that other cultures and other times provide. Frequently, the study of a topic will last only a short time and will quickly give way to the meaning that the topic has for the individual. When this occurs, it should not be seen as a lack of interest in the course material but rather as what it is—an attempt to apply it to the major question facing the older person, the struggle to achieve integrity.

We can see, then, that the psychological developments that occur in middle age, later maturity, and old age offer some insights into the educational needs and desires of potential participants. Middle age is a time when the individual has reached the peak of his or her power and influence. The person is typically no longer driven to achieve but considers himself or herself to be the driver of others. It is a time when mentor relationships are developed and assistance to the next generation may take precedence over greater acquisition. Relationships with people begin to have greater value than material gain, and enjoyment of oneself and one's role replaces the desire for pleasure. Relationships with parents are likely to improve as the older person's needs increase and the middle-aged child begins to feel more at ease about a mature relationship.

By later maturity these changes are even more pronounced. The desire for greater comfort, the willingness to let others face the new challenges, the concern for security rather than opportunity all seem to be much stronger. Although health and energy may remain high, there is a withdrawal from the pressures of the world and a desire to let social interaction provide the stimulation needed. Physical changes may reduce the ability to undertake demanding activities, but typically the person restricts the challenge more than is required by the physical limitations. As interest in the past increases, a lack of understanding of the present is evidenced. It is a time of loss of friends and relatives; and as this occurs, people turn to an examination of themselves.

Finally, old age is a time of disengagement, caused mostly by physical infirmities. People typically are constrained by the limitations; some overcome these with their attitudes toward life and others, while some become so absorbed with their difficulties that they hardly realize others exist. Interest in the rest of the world, when it exists, is of a rather abstract nature. It is not so much that the world is not there as that it has little impact on the lives of the very old. They are preparing for another experience, and it takes much of their attention. During this period of life, persons have learned to do less and are in the process of learning to be more.

Sociocultural Phases

The third approach to life-span development emphasizes the role played by the society in moving the individual through

the life span. Just as some change comes from physical development and internal expectation, some occurs because the social
environment has been organized in such a way that it encourages certain behaviors and not others. This means that there are
appropriate times for people to get a job, raise children, retire,
and withdraw from community activities. These social expectations are not consistently enforced—for example, some people
choose to marry late in life or never leave the work force—but
they form a backdrop against which the individual measures his
or her own progress, as well as a series of quasi-legal sanctions
when they are not adhered to.

These phases are not hierarchical, as were the psychological developmental stages. They are linear in that one follows another, but there is nothing that requires one to marry before retiring, for example. Thus, successfully completing one phase
does not mean that the next will be easier or harder because of
the previous experience. Sociocultural phases are typically initiated by a marker event—a circumstance that indicates the end
of one period and the commencement of another. Examples of
such events include a wedding, the birth of the first child, a divorce, finding a job, changing jobs, the last child leaving home,
the death of a spouse, retirement, a serious illness, appointment
to an important civic position, and loss of a record or title. In
each case, a new phase of life is heralded by a public event,
often a ceremony, which typically results in new expectations,
roles, and rewards.

Havighurst (1952) has described these sociocultural
changes in terms of developmental tasks that occur midway between an individual's need and a societal demand. He suggests
that the tasks are a way of identifying a "teachable moment" in
the life of the individual, a time when the person is ready to
learn in order to facilitate the needed change. Havighurst's
teachable moment provides a conceptual support for the finding
of Aslanian and Brickell (1980) that people tend to see learning
as a way to facilitate the required adjustments when life changes
are needed. Aslanian and Brickell stress that education is a preventive mechanism; it is often undertaken in advance of the
marker event as a preparation for the anticipated change.

Havighurst identified six age periods. Only two of these deal with middle age and later maturity; they will be discussed here. Middle age is described as a time when the person has great influence over society. The developmental tasks of this period arise from environmental pressures related to family, employment, and community. Havighurst identified the tasks as these:

1. Assisting teenaged children to become responsible and happy adults. This entails providing worthy role models, offering guidance as well as freedom, and understanding.
2. Achieving adult social and civic responsibility. Peak levels of social influence create social responsibilities to future generations and society at large.
3. Reaching and maintaining satisfactory performance in one's occupational career. Changing career patterns make it necessary to expect career change throughout the life span. Middle age, however, is typically a time when people change careers, move up rapidly, or realize that they may have reached their occupational peak.
4. Developing adult leisure-time activities. With time freed from family responsibilities, the person needs to identify meaningful activities that balance the work role and provide opportunities for future development and expansion.
5. Relating to one's spouse as a person. This task emphasizes the need for mutual understanding, affection, and support during a time when the family typically is changing from a several-person to a two-person unit.
6. Adjusting to aging parents. This implies meeting mutual needs in an attempt to satisfy both generations. The extent to which needs are defined and responsibilities are assumed varies among and within cultures, among social classes, and among individuals.

These developmental tasks provide a variety of learning opportunities. Middle-aged persons can reasonably predict that the marker events will occur and can decide well in advance which will require new knowledge or additional skill in order to be successfully completed. Assistance in understanding the human development that their children are experiencing will be useful, since some middle-aged persons suffered great difficulty in breaking away from their own family unit when they were young. Achieving social and civic responsibility can be aided by greater understanding of the community, awareness of the needs of various ethnic and disadvantaged groups, and understanding of how community organizations function.

Occupational change in middle age offers many learning opportunities. Since most people must change job roles or be upgraded in their current position, learning related to professional specialties, legislative changes, or new technologies will be needed. One obvious example is in the area of computers. Most middle-aged persons had little exposure to the use and potential of computers in their formal education. Those working in offices are likely to have the opportunity to use a computer for word processing, accounting, or planning within the very near future. In order to make the most efficient use of these new tools, the middle-aged person could benefit from some exposure to them and the ways they can be useful in the person's particular field.

Leisure-time activities may be learned through informal means, such as conversations with friends, coworkers, or family. However, this frequently results in an applied approach that may exclude some vital aspects of the area. To gain a more comprehensive overview, middle-aged persons may choose to undertake a formal learning period in which they seek the greater insight, complexity, and interrelationships of various elements, movements, facts, and so on, that can be acquired. This seems also to be true of relating more closely to one's spouse. It can occur with little formal education, but "marriage encounter" programs and interpersonal groups appear to be popular with middle-class persons and may well spread to other socioeconomic groups. The opportunities of learning in order to deal more adequately with one's older parents have been described earlier and so will not be dealt with here except to emphasize once again their value and interest to many older people.

Havighurst identified the final stage of development as later maturity. He indicated that it was fundamentally different from other stages in that it involved more of a defensive strategy, a holding onto the life that one has rather than seizing more of it. In identifying the learning tasks of later maturity, he combined the sociocultural with the physical. Of the sociocultural tasks, he mentioned the following:

1. Adjustment to retirement and to a reduced income. This significant change in later life provides the opportunity for increased leisure time, while economic resources are frequently reduced—by as much as 50 percent for a large part of the population.
2. Adjustment to the death of a spouse. This is a task that more women than men face. It involves social and personal adjustments as well as economic ones.
3. Establishing an explicit affiliation with one's age group. This is very difficult for some older persons. They try to reject the idea that they are growing old, and so they reject affiliation with others whom they perceive to be old.
4. Meeting social and civic obligations. These are similar to those of middle age except that there is now more time and less competition in developing appropriate activities.
5. Establishing satisfactory physical living arrangements. Economic and family considerations typically encourage change of housing in later maturity. This may be to a congregate living setting, to one with health care provided, or simply to a warmer climate.

Education can help the older person successfully complete each of these tasks. It can provide the preliminary information needed to help the person gain a realistic understanding of retirement, make appropriate plans for retirement, and adjust more completely to the challenges presented during this period. Likewise, it can be used to prepare couples for the eventual loss of one partner by helping each to understand the contributions of the other and to rely on himself or herself more than on the partner. It can also be useful in adjusting to the loss of the spouse through discussions with others who have sustained simi-

lar traumas and have learned to find other means of companion-
ship and support.

Establishing explicit affiliations with one's age group is
especially difficult for some older persons. They reject the idea
that they are old, and they seek to maintain contact with those
who are perceived to be middle-aged rather than their cohort.
Education can be useful to them because different cohorts are
likely to have different experiences and interests. Through autobiography, history, contemporary events, and other topics, people can come to realize the value of affiliation with their own
group, whether it is the old or the young. This can also happen
when older persons become interested in improving their social
or economic state. Typically they band together with others to
challenge the policy makers who are perceived as offering insufficient support. In this process, the older advocate finds that his
or her greatest allies are those who are of the same generation.
They have comparable needs and interests and so are most likely to share motivations and plans. Education can assist the development of participative skills and can bring persons into
closer communication with those of their own age.

Social and civic obligations can be met best by knowledgeable and skilled persons. Education can provide this background and can help people choose the places where they can
make the greatest impact. It can also help older persons find
alternative activities when the responsibilities become too great
and the physical limitations reduce the energy and stamina. Finally, education can be a means of exploring the variety of
housing opportunities available to older persons. Since appropriate living accommodations are so important to the future adjustment and life satisfaction of older persons, choosing appropriate housing is a crucial undertaking. Exploring the variety of
options, identifying the values of each of the possibilities, and
learning from the experiences of others can facilitate an informed choice and encourage a better living situation.

Educational Adaptations Related to the Life Span

Viewing the life span from the three viewpoints of physiological, psychological, and sociocultural development provides

insight into the multiple aspects of the life course. Some development is generated from within the individual, while some results from external forces. These viewpoints offer differing insights that educators can use in selecting content areas and designing instructional programs. Adults experience all three types of development but may be more cognizant of one rather than another at any particular time. Some persons are extremely aware of physical declines and health difficulties; others are struggling with personality growth; and others are most conscious of the external job or family changes that are affecting them.

Cross (1981) has attempted to integrate these three viewpoints by posing a life-span conceptualization that she termed "Characteristics of Adults as Learners" (CAL). She suggested that these life-span developmental processes can be described graphically in order to clarify their meaning and to show their distinctiveness, as in Figure 3. The physiological dimension can be shown as a smooth curve rising in the early stages of life,

Figure 3. Life-Span Developmental Changes.

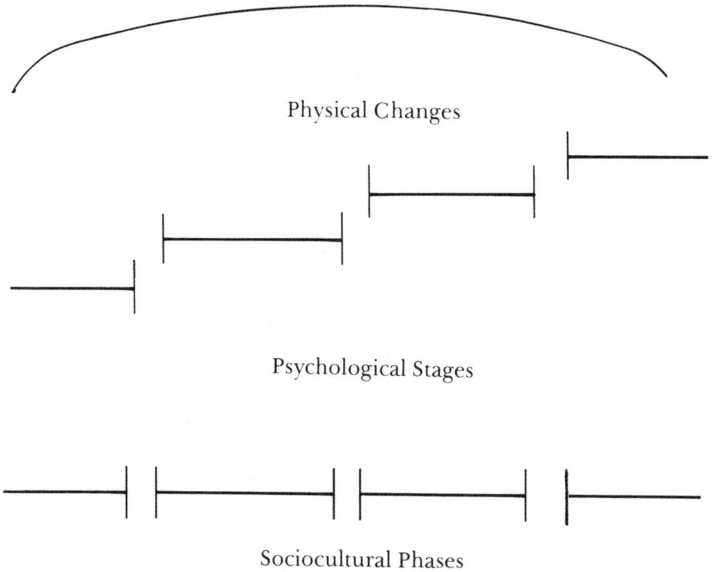

Physical Changes

Psychological Stages

Sociocultural Phases

Source: Adapted from K. P. Cross, *Adults as Learners: Increasing Participation and Facilitating Learning.* San Francisco: Jossey-Bass, 1981.

maintaining some stability through the middle years, and declining in old age. This curve would vary depending on the characteristic shown, but the general curve holds for many physical attributes. Cross suggested that the role education can most appropriately play in addressing physical development is largely adaptive; that is, educators must adapt the instructional process to reduce the impact of the physical decrements, and content should be oriented toward helping people understand and adjust to these changes. Thus, the role of education is to increase the person's ability to compensate, a common reaction of most people. The accommodation, however, can be improved by more accurate anticipation of the changes, skill in alternative behaviors, and awareness of the natural and institutional support system.

This accommodation can be facilitated by designing the instructional methodology to reduce the speed of instruction, increase the illumination, help students organize material better, and use the knowledge that the older learners already have. (See Chapter Five for specifics.) In terms of content, interests are likely to be in the areas of exercise, nutrition, health promotion, rehabilitation, specific diseases, and services available in the community. People want to know what physical changes to expect, how to deal with difficulties, ways to distinguish aging from illness, and places where helping services can be obtained.

The second dimension, psychological development, can be graphically illustrated as a series of stages, each higher than the preceding, separated by transition points. There may be several stages across the adult life span or a very few. In terms of Erikson's conceptualization, the final two stages would be generativity and transcendence, but these could be broken into smaller steps and shown as in Figure 3. The role of education, in terms of psychological development, can be viewed as challenging the person to recognize the existence of the next stage and motivating the person to try to reach it. Through sensitization, knowledge giving, and skill development, the educator challenges people to reach their maximum potential. This process may cause learners to examine their current assumptions, redefine their goals, and explore the insights that others have acquired.

This dimension can be implemented by teachers who demand more than the students believe they can give, by dealing with content which is not only interesting but applicable to the circumstance of the older person, and by offering courses that allow for personal exploration and examination. Psychological growth does not come by simply absorbing additional content knowledge; rather, it is acquired through the examined life, and this occurs both in a group setting and in individual contemplation. The person who accepts the challenge in later life is likely to be somewhat hesitant but aware of the need and desirous of achieving the new goal.

Sociocultural development is shown as life phases, again separated by a marker event, but no phase is superior to the preceding. This is shown in Figure 3 as a series of phases continuing throughout the life span in a generally predictable order but without the requirement that one precede others. In this area, education has the role of helping the person anticipate the marker events and prepare for adjustment to each new phase. This does not mean that older persons are expected to simply accept whatever the new phase offers, but through greater knowledge and skill, they can understand more completely, respond more adequately, and adjust more quickly.

Educational experiences in this area are very common. They include preparation for retirement, second-career development, hobby initiation, advocacy training, and financial planning. Frequently, the educational offering appeals to persons anticipating the event, but not always. It has surprised many community educators offering retirement preparation how many participants are already retired. They often wish to know what they should have done or to confirm the wisdom of the decisions made without formal preparation. Thus, educational offerings can be useful in this area both as preparation and as general knowledge for those who have experienced or are experiencing the sociocultural change.

Summary

A life-span developmental perspective has become much more common in the social and behavioral sciences. It offers insight into the changing motivations, interests, and needs of adults as they pass through a series of changes, phases, and stages. It has also become of interest to institutions of higher education as they begin the process of adapting to the changing age demography of the nation. The work of Chickering and Associates, *The Modern American College* (1981), has taken life-span development as its theme as it describes the purpose of American colleges and universities to be the facilitation of intentional developmental change throughout the life span. Awareness of the importance of middle age and later life to higher education and to other social institutions will continue to expand in the future. By utilizing the current knowledge of life-span development, the educational program planner will be able to better understand the needs and wants of the clientele and to design programs that more directly address these aspects of the adult years.

8

OIOIOIOIOIOIOIOIOIOIOIOIOIOIOIOIOIOIOIOIOIOIO

Educational Needs
and Wants

Irving Rosow (1967) in his classic book on housing for
the aged drew a distinction between the problems that older
people have and those that experts think they have. In trying to
identify the most needed instructional programming for older
people, we can draw a similar distinction, for their educational
needs (what experts think they should have) and their wants
(their preferences or desires) are often substantially different.
Londoner (1978) cited studies that indicated no significant relation between what a panel of experts perceived to be the educational needs of a group and what the same group perceived
about its own needs. Hunter (1977) reported similar findings in
comparing educational interests of older people with those suggested by a group of agencies offering educational programs to
them. The determination of both needs and wants is important,
and the distinction between them is crucial in program planning, in selecting instructors, and in setting program goals.

Educational needs are perceived lacks or weaknesses in
the knowledge, attitudes, skills, or values that older people
have. In general, they are determined by authorities through
conjecture and the application of theory; they are typically ad-

131

dressable through some educational intervention. Educational needs may result from the inadequate formal education received by older people, the passage of time since formal schooling was completed, social change, individual development, or a lifelong desire for personal or psychological growth.

These needs, determined by theorists and educators, typically are important at a high philosophical level and are consistent with the idealized values of education and social service organizations. They are attractive to society at large and thus are readily defensible when their consumption of resources is questioned. Educational needs are consistent with the high purposes of instruction and offer good rationales for continuation and expansion of instructional programs for older people. They may not be recognized by older people as real needs, however, and may be inaccurate determiners of program content.

Educational wants, in contrast, are the salient desires or preferences of older people. They are those content or skill areas that are generated or selected by older people in community groups or institutional settings when asked about their preferences for learning activity. Educational wants may occasionally appear frivolous to educational planners. They may include topics which are primarily social or recreational and which can only peripherally be called education. The preferred topics may also be so tentatively held that they may appear to change with each whimsical suggestion, thus providing little indication of the "true" wants of the older person.

This seemingly insecure commitment to a particular want may result from little real interest in education. If older persons are asked to choose the five most interesting educational topics from a list of course titles, most people will comply. But we should not conclude that this indicates the person's major preferences. Those chosen are the highest interest of the choices provided, but since many older people evidence little or no interest in any form of education, the choice may have little meaning. It may be similar to a child's irrelevant question "Would you rather be able to fly like a bird or an airplane?" The answer is of little consequence, since neither is a likely possibility.

Program planners occasionally have difficulty in defending their programs if they cater totally to the educational wants of older people. Recreation has its place and value, but most educational institutions are expected to offer instruction, not leisure-time enjoyment. Consequently, a program of bridge, trips, bingo, and dancing is not likely to be viewed as very important by school boards or college deans. To defend the consumption of resources, program planners need to show that some real education is being offered, and too frequently educational wants do not readily correspond with this imperative.

Educational planners have not always drawn the distinction between the educational wants and needs of older persons. They have often assumed that wants and needs are identical and have programmed on that basis. In reality, this often means that needs are considered but wants are not. Some programs, however, have been oriented so completely to the participants' desires that the offerings have little relation to an educational curriculum. Conscious determination of the appropriate mix of courses directed toward wants and needs is important to successful programming. The extent of the sponsoring organization's influence, the staff, the funding plan, and the policy of the agency will determine the outcome.

It should be kept in mind that great variation exists in the older population, and few needs or wants are found in all older people, except in a very abstract form. Needs and wants depend on the educational level, income, employment history, experience, health, and geographical location of the clientele to be served. These factors determine the expressed interests or wants of different groups.

In addition, cohort changes modify educational wants and needs. The current cohort of older people has less schooling, poorer health, and a different set of experiences than will older people in ten, twenty, or thirty years. Hence, the educational planner must consider the unique characteristics of this cohort of older people when designing an educational experience. Their location, mobility, health status, and life experience may result in interests and needs unique to them, not readily generalizable to other groups or individuals.

This chapter will not deal with the multitude of local,

ethnic, and experiential variations of the older population. These are too individual for a work of this type. It will, however, deal with the educational needs as identified by several authorities in the field and with the educational wants as these are reported in the literature by several individuals and organizations who have queried older people about their preferences, designed programs based on this information, and reported these findings.

Educational Needs of Older People

Educational needs generally emerge from the analysis of the condition of contemporary older people through some frame of reference. Needs are typically determined by observation of older people and conjecture about the elements that could be improved. Many educationists have written about these needs, but Howard McClusky's background paper on education (1971) for the 1971 White House Conference on Aging is the best-known example. In subsequent writings, McClusky (n.d.) identified five categories of educational needs. He correctly emphasized that these were not the only needs of older people, but he argued that these were the needs that could be most effectively addressed by instructional interventions. Thus, he defused the criticism that educators attempt to solve problems which are not appropriate or which are unresponsive to instruction. His categories of need are as follows:

Coping Needs. Some needs result from the decrements that occur in the process of aging and from the obsolescence that results from unused skill or capacity. These include the survival needs as well as those that allow adequate functioning in a complex and interrelated society. They encompass such items as ability to control food, housing, and clothing needs; sufficient health care; stimulating social interactions; consumer competence; and skills needed for daily functioning. Unless these needs are met at a minimal level, it is generally not possible for the person to survive or to have any surplus energy to devote to growth or altruistic activities. These coping needs are similar to the instrumental needs described by Londoner (1978), Hiemstra (1973), and Marcus (1978) and the adjustment needs that Donahue (1952), Frank (1955), and the Academy for Educational Development (1974) have identified.

An educational program designed to address coping needs would be based on a response to changes in the condition of the individual and to overcoming obsolescence in dealing with societal change. This approach would emphasize remedial education designed to overcome weaknesses or omissions in the formal education of childhood and youth. This would include literacy education, the development of reading and writing skills, or consumer instruction designed to help the person deal with the daily decisions necessary for survival in a complex and challenging environment. Specific elements of this type of education could include such areas as (1) instruction about normal physical changes of later life and identification of adaptive strategies to facilitate adjustment, (2) instruction on social changes such as those brought on by death or illness of a spouse, the reduction in employment or voluntary roles, or the need to make new friends that results from changing one's residence, (3) instruction on economic changes resulting from retirement, double-digit inflation, or government income-supplement programs, (4) instruction on emotional or affective changes, including attitudes toward one's own aging, the stereotypes and biases held by others, and adjustments to the realization that "I am old," and (5) instruction on psychological changes, including the adjustment to changes in memory and intelligence, reduced visual and auditory acuity, and personality development.

In each of these areas, some older people face substantial adjustments that, if more completely understood, could be successfully accommodated. This education is an appropriate undertaking for many types of organizations and institutions, and response from older people should prove to be positive.

Expressive Needs. The second category of needs identified by McClusky is termed "expressive." These are needs for activity or participation that is engaged in for its own sake. The reward for involvement is intrinsic to the activity itself, and interest alone is sufficient motivation for participation. Enjoyment results from the physical or social activity, from the spontaneity involved, and from the exhilaration of new experience.

For many older people, time has not allowed exploration or cultivation of all their interests; there has been insufficient opportunity to sample many of the possible arts, sports, and academic areas. Retirement provides somewhat more available time; and so revival of old interests, development of long-postponed relationships, and learning of new skills are now possible. These activities are not expected to lead to a degree, a job, or higher status. They are undertaken because they are fun or challenging or interesting. They allow the person to express himself or herself in a way that has not been possible during the preceding years.

Londoner (1978) suggested that educational needs and outcomes fall into two categories: instrumental and expressive. Expressive educational activity is an end in itself, not designed to achieve some postponed outcome but resulting in immediate gratification. He concluded that this result is positively viewed by many older people and that most educational programming for older people falls under this rubric.

Expressive needs can be met through several types of educational programming. The most evident are leisure-time pursuits that result in a renewing of the person. The preferred diversion varies from person to person, depending on interests and background. Educational experiences emphasizing creativity, such as art, music, and drama, provide obvious examples of this area of educational programming. A considerable number of older people evidence interest in these areas through their participation in, and continued support of, the arts. Their involvement can be expected to lead to increased creativity and improved self-image (Frank, 1955; Linton and Spence, 1964). On another level, arts and crafts are included in this category, since they are typically undertaken for their own enjoyment and allow the person to seek out and develop unrecognized talents (Donahue, 1952).

Social relations are another important and enjoyable component of this category. Development of personal friendships and contacts and maintenance of these relationships through shared activities and collegial undertakings provide great satisfaction and comfort to older persons (Thorson, 1978).

By reducing the tendency toward disengagement and facilitating activity and social integration, it may be possible to provide much worthwhile sharing of experience and insight and to continue the integration and growth of the person.

Contributive Needs. The third category of need is titled "contributive." It indicates the altruistic desire of most people to assist others in coping with current problems and in achieving their developmental tasks. People have a need to give something that is of value to others (Moberg, 1962) in order to fulfill themselves. Through this endeavor older people are likely to increase the opportunity for social involvement, personal status, and increased self-worth. The service provided may take the form of volunteerism with local health and welfare agencies, with churches, or with government programs for older people. Whatever the avenue of their service, the resource of time, understanding, and skills can be of extensive value to older people and to the community generally.

Education has a key developmental role to play in meeting contributive needs. It can be the means by which older persons identify their potential contributions, mobilize their resources, and direct their time and service in the most meaningful manner. Education also has a role in developing and directing the contributive impulse. Without knowledge of the available opportunities for service, people often waste precious energy and become discouraged about the value of their contribution. The development of specific skills through an instructional program can help the person more realistically assess his or her expectations about what can and should be achieved.

Influence Needs. People of all ages have the desire to make some difference in the general functioning of society, to effect some meaningful social change. Influence needs indicate the expectation that older people too will be involved with the larger issues of citizenship and social concerns; they will want to direct a portion of their energy toward these more general areas. This may be done through the typical political processes, through participation in voluntary and community groups, through service organizations, or through participation in quasi-governmental structures.

Education can help fulfill these needs by identifying the most appropriate roles, developing personal or group skills, providing social supports, and assisting in evaluating the results of the activities. Since older people typically have more discretionary time than do many persons in their middle years, the opportunity for participation in this area is great. However, older persons' current level of knowledge and skills may prevent optimum participation. The complexity of government programs, community politics, and bureaucratic turf protection may require fairly sophisticated knowledge approaches that are available only to the well educated.

This area, however, offers the opportunity for educational institutions to begin the process of instruction that will result in a growing activism and participation of older people and may serve to improve the quality of life for us all. Thus, the investment here may be repaid in direct benefits through modification of laws and statutes, regulations, and community priorities.

Transcendence Needs. The final category of needs that McClusky identified is transcendence needs. These are needs for gaining some deeper understanding of the meaning of life, the review of what a life has been, and the movement beyond the physical declines occurring in the body. Although transcendence needs are evidenced at all ages, they are perhaps most imperative in the later stages of life, since death is clearly in view and the mortality of the physical self is increasingly evident.

The development of an understanding of a deeper meaning in life is suggested as a major educational need by several writers (for example, Moody, 1976; Erikson, 1980). They conclude that older people want and need to examine the purposes of life as they can identify them, that they will want to explore their relationship to religious beliefs and precepts, and that their declining circle of friends and peers will cause them to become more introspective. The search for meaning occasionally takes the form of life review (Butler, 1975; Butler and Lewis, 1977). This is a penchant of older people to reexamine their lives and identify the critical points around which changes occurred. Outwardly, older people may evidence a desire to live more in the past than in the present, but this behavior indicates the importance of life review if the person is to find the meaning he or she seeks.

Growth of the person beyond the limits of the body is the third part of transcendence needs. People in the later years realize the inevitability of death and typically begin a process of becoming reconciled to it. They begin the process of transcending the limitations of the physical self and seeking the meaning of existence. This may occur in a religious context, or it may take the form of solace through one's children or other productions.

Education can play a role in each of these aspects of transcendence. It can provide understanding of the meanings that insightful people of other ages and cultures have attached to life; it can offer a supportive and stimulating setting for reminiscence; and it can facilitate thoughtful contemplation and learning to replace the restraints of the body. By individual or group process, older persons can be helped to examine and weigh the insights of others and to seek for themselves that understanding which will settle their restless search. Through guided exploration, they can be helped to understand the criteria by which successful lives are measured and to consider their own level of satisfaction.

Educational Wants of Older People

Educational wants of older people are those preferences, interests, or desires that are indicated by older persons themselves. These, of course, vary greatly from one group to the next and from one person to another. Mailed or group questionnaires often ask the respondent to select the most interesting and motivating educational topics. Other methods include the use of advisory committees, observation of existing classes for indications of additional interest, informal discussions with potential participants, and analysis of enrollment behavior as a means of predicting future interests and wants. Although most educational program planners will try to use some systematic approach to collecting these data, difficulties frequently occur.

None of these approaches, however, is very reliable. The

questionnaire is probably the most widely used of the planned approaches. Persons who have enrolled in educational programs or are perceived to be potential enrollees are asked to complete a form that lists many possible educational opportunities, generally in the form of a list of course titles. The data from this approach should be handled with care, however, for there are several potential drawbacks. First, the questionnaire's existence indicates to most respondents the bias of the investigator. We would not ask people about their educational interests if we did not expect and want them to have those interests. Consequently, respondents are subtly encouraged to choose areas that may not be salient or of real interest to them.

Second, Hiemstra and Long (1974) have shown that in at least one study the respondents' perceived educational needs were not related to the needs that the same persons demonstrated through a paper-and-pencil test. When items are discussed at some length, the results frequently differ from those of a bare listing of interests chosen with little reflection.

Third, there is also a distinction between indicating on a questionnaire that one is interested in a particular topic or course and taking the action step of enrolling in that course. March, Hooper, and Baum (1977) reported that respondents in their survey were likely to choose many educational interests but were not at all likely to enroll in any of the courses that were subsequently offered. Thus, the data generated by a mailed questionnaire may result in a collective response that has relatively little value for program planners in a specific area or for a more general discussion of educational wants. However, the reported data are all that is available, and so they are reported here with the caution that they should not be taken too seriously when one begins to consider program planning.

In general, it is clear from several studies that reported interest in learning declines with increasing age (Cross, 1979). This seems to be true across the life span, but a more precipitous decline is observed after age 55. Johnstone and Rivera (1965) report that, of persons in the 50–59 age group, 65 percent expressed interest in learning new things, while only 53 percent of the 60–69 age group indicated such interest, and 35 percent of the 70–79 age group did so. Since these general findings appear to be supported in every study, it is reasonable to believe that some cross-sectional decline does occur.

This does not necessarily mean that as people age, their interest in education lessens. That may be the correct interpretation, but other explanations are also possible. For instance, since interest is more closely related to level of formal education than to any other factor (Johnstone and Rivera, 1965), it may be that the lower educational level of the older cohorts is the explanation. Then, too, it may be historical effect—that is, for some reason, people born in the early twentieth century are less likely to have learning interests than people born in other times. This may be the result of the Great Depression, of previous experience with schooling, or of some other factor. Whatever the reason, decline due to age is only one explanation.

Cross (1979) reviewed thirty studies of educational interests of adults, including the aged. She reported that adult learners were generally pragmatic; they wanted some visible payoff from the instruction. The more disadvantaged persons were more likely to want vocational help from the classes. Men were more interested in job training, while women appeared to have more general or expressive interests. Advantaged adults indicated that the intrinsic rewards of education were their main concern, social interaction being a major reason for participation. One can conclude from these studies that the content is not the only or even the primary motivation for attendance for many people.

There has been one major attempt to develop a dichotomy of educational wants of older people in order to create some generalized understanding of this area. As briefly discussed earlier, this is the division of educational wants into expressive (or intrinsic) gratification and instrumental (or deferred) gratification. Londoner (1978) has developed this conceptualization from Talcott Parsons's work on structural-functional analysis. Educational experiences that provide immediate gratification are called "expressive." An expressive course is not designed to be of value in some distant future but is enjoyable and fulfilling to the person immediately. Courses that are useful in achieving some future goal are classified as "instrumental"; that is, they are useful as a tool to obtain a future job, promotion, credential, or status. For instance, a course such as music, art, drama, crafts, or humanities may be taken for the enjoyment (expressive), while another such as high school completion, retirement preparation, skill upgrading, or political advocacy may be selected because of instrumental wants.

The conceptualization fits with our discussion of expert-perceived needs, and empirical testing of the concepts provides considerable data on the preferences of older adults. Several studies have shown that older people have primarily instrumental wants (Hiemstra, 1972, 1975; Goodrow, 1975a; Burkey, 1975). These studies typically involved small numbers of respondents, and their conclusions are challenged by other studies that have shown older people to prefer expressive instruction or have found no preference for either expressive or instrumental (Whatley, 1974; Bauer, 1975). These conflicting data suggest that it is overly simplistic to assume that older people generally want exclusively instrumental or expressive instruction.

To make the best use of the expressive/instrumental dichotomy, it is necessary to deal with discrete elements of the older population rather than to consider the undifferentiated whole. Studies indicate that there is less preference for instrumental instruction by white-collar older persons (Hiemstra, 1973) and by those with greater amounts of formal education (Hiemstra, 1973; Burkey, 1975), although other studies do not report support for this distinction. Marcus (1978) addressed this situation with more sophisticated statistical analysis and concluded that persons who were younger, with less education and lower desire for enjoyment in the learning situation, were more likely to indicate instrumental education wants and preferences. Higher socioeconomic status (income, occupation, and education) and being female were likely to be positively associated with expressive utility being perceived and desired. Older people were likely to see the education they engaged in as being expressive regardless of the instructional intent. Older people do not perceive education as a means of solving practical problems (instrumental) but, rather, as a means of immediate gratification through enjoyment of intellectual stimulation, social interaction, and interesting leisure-time use (Marcus, 1978).

We may conclude, then, that it is unclear whether older people want instrumental or expressive education. Probably both can be well received, but in order to achieve success, they should be aimed at different subgroups of the population. Expressive education is generally more desired by persons with greater education, higher occupational level, and less pressing coping needs. These tend to be the persons who typically participate in education. Instrumental instruction may appeal to persons with problems or needs that can be addressed. However, they are typically nonparticipants, those who tend not to enroll and who expect little of direct value if they do participate.

Several studies have reported the instructional wants of older people. Hendrickson and Barnes (1964) interviewed a sample of 2,307 persons over age 65 and reported that the greatest educational interest was in religion, problems of growing old, gardening, travel, physical fitness, and grooming. Other topics receiving high interest included psychology, managing financial affairs, history, public affairs, and foreign relations. These researchers found women to be more interested in the domestic area and the arts, while men were more likely to name public affairs, travel, and household mechanics as areas of interest.

Galvin and others (1975) have reported on a survey of older persons' educational wants undertaken by several community colleges in the Los Angeles area. They reported that coping with problems of life, health, and finance was the greatest interest, retirement preparation was second, and social development and training for voluntary service third. Categorized in another way, about 60 percent of this sample indicated interest in hobby and recreational subjects, health and nutrition, consumer education, and supplemental income.

A survey reported by the Central Bureau for the Jewish Aged (1971) indicated the educational interest of older persons who participated in senior centers. It concluded that the greatest number were interested in instruction about current issues and health, consumer, and nutrition education. Little interest was expressed in employment-oriented instruction, formal classes, or cross-generational groupings.

Hunter (1977) interviewed 100 older persons in a small community. She reported that the top-ranked interests were travel, crafts, sewing, health information, bridge and chess, Social Security, sports, physical fitness and exercise, music appreciation, and Medicare/Medicaid. She cautioned against the generalizability of these data, however, since three times as many older people refused the interview as agreed to participate.

Hoffman (1978) reported on a survey of interests in the area of arts programming. Although he received only a 5 percent response, he summarized the 1,015 returns in terms of their priorities within the humanities. The topics of most interest were the relationship of older people to society, state history, religion, problems of aging, travel, and antiques.

We may conclude from these studies that the interests of older people are, like those of the population as a whole, extremely diverse and complex. Some topics emerge persistently, such as religion, health, financial affairs, history and contemporary events, and travel. Skill-related instruction, such as arts and crafts, bridge, or gardening, is also commonly mentioned; other topics, such as science and technology, are generally absent.

Summary and Conclusions

Educational needs and wants of older people are not necessarily the same. The needs emerge from the social and developmental context of the individual but may not be perceived to be salient to the individual's current interest. Wants, in contrast, are an indication of the individual's preferences and desires at the moment. They may, however, be temporary, transient, and lightly held. Most educational programs are likely to attempt to meet both needs and wants, a result that does not easily occur when dealing with a complex group of people.

In designing educational programming for older adults, it is usually necessary to include some experiences that will be well received by the participants. These will be useful in encouraging initial participation, in developing an attitude of cooperation, and in ensuring the acceptability of educational participation. In the long run, however, it is generally necessary for educational planners to offer courses that are viewed as more substantive and more directly related to the community and individual needs. This occurs because funding sources and supervising administrators require an indication of greater payoff from their organization's investment. Thus, a range of educational offerings stretching from the entertaining and enjoyable to experiences designed to help solve problems would appear to be appropriate for most educational programs.

9

Selecting Methods
of Instruction

Facilitation of learning by older people is the theme of this entire book. This chapter, however, is perhaps closest to this specific topic and as such is an attempt to integrate many ideas and apply them to the conduct of educational activities for older people. Some of the points have been made in previous chapters; they are reemphasized here to provide a single statement that can be used by program planners and instructors. Because the chapter is oriented toward providing instruction in a classroom setting, references are typically made to courses, workshops, or instructional groups. This has been done for convenience, and the same or similar considerations will be useful in a variety of other settings (planning group, informal discussion group, individualized instruction, or other learning environment where an instructor and at least one student are present).

The older learner is the primary consideration in the planning and design of any instruction. Most education of older adults is oriented toward the perceived wants and needs of the learner, and accordingly the current level of knowledge, attitudes toward self and learning, life experience, preferred methodology, and content orientation are typically determined after examining the real or anticipated audience of the instruction. This is not to say that every educational experience for older adults must be unique in planning and design, but it does suggest that knowledge of older people in general and of the intended participant in particular should be a major influence on the design process. The instructor needs a general understanding of the unique characteristics of this particular audience and must provide regular opportunities for feedback from the group in order for their perceptions, reactions, and evaluations to modify the instructional process when it strays from their preferences. The educational design is planned and monitored to keep the older learner in mind and to provide opportunities for dialogue and agreement on objectives, setting, content, and methods.

Any discussion of older learners must emphasize the wide individual differences within that group. The 45 million people in the United States over age 55 include a vast variety of intellect, experience, motivation, interest, and skill. They vary more from one another than do people at younger ages, and on many variables they have more inner-cohort differences than exist between them and other age groups. One of the self-evident phrases in gerontology is that as people age, they become more like themselves. In so doing they become different from others; thus, an educational setting is not likely to include a homogeneous group of persons, regardless of the course, sponsor, or instructor.

As Chapter Three indicated, older people who participate in educational programs are likely to have higher-than-average levels of education, income, occupation, and social activity; in addition, they have had more diverse experiences and enjoyed a complex environment that has encouraged individual change and growth. Thus, on the average, a self-selected group of older learners will be different from the older population in general and will have greater intellectual skills. In the recent past, it has been mainly the more highly educated older people who chose to enroll in educational activities. This appears to be changing as many older people participate in groups that include education along with recreation, social services, health programs, financial planning, and advocacy. Instruction for individuals or groups who are not self-selected but who engage in education through some other initiative—for example, nutrition program participants, retraining of older workers, family counseling groups, or compulsory attendees of driving schools—is likely to include people with even more diverse backgrounds and with great differences in their experience, learning skills, interests, and motivation.

Furthermore, members of the current older cohort have a particular history that greatly affects their ideas about education and its value to them and to society. The contemporary older cohort was born before 1920, and most of its members can remember both world wars and had their social values shaped by the Great Depression. Intercontinental travel, television, and residential mobility have all developed during their lifetimes, but these elements may not have influenced their values and philosophy as did the Great Depression. This event and the accompanying dislocations led many of the current older cohort to accept a somewhat conservative philosophy, to retain traditional values, to rely on their own resources, to conform to social pressure, to be frugal, and to accept their fate with limited complaint.

Educated in the 1920s, most members of this older cohort did not complete high school, and they remember education as involving rote memorization, strict discipline, academic rigor, classical content, and limited relevance. The concept of life-span education was not common at that time, and so most of these people view formal education as preparation for life, valuable to the young but somewhat unusual for persons such as themselves. Because education was not expected to be pleasurable, stimulating, or useful, it was not considered a voluntary pastime. Hence, the current older cohort may be less well prepared for educational participation and less likely to seek it out than future cohorts of older people will be. Their expectations may be of a traditional, formal process that is neither enjoyable nor relevant. Consequently, the educational planner and the instructor may face a variety of difficulties before the course ever starts.

Just as older people differ from children, so the instruction designed for them needs to differ from that developed for children. Although some would argue that older people are so distinctive that a special methodology should be created for them (*gerogogy* has been suggested as its name), it is neither practical nor necessary to separate older adults too completely from middle-aged learners. Consequently, with the reminder that health, perceptual, and energy changes must be considered, it is the contention here that the instructional conceptualization called "andragogy" offers a great deal of insight and usefulness when considering education of older people.

Andragogy

Andragogy is a term used to describe the instructional process for adults, differentiated from pedagogy, which is for children. The distinctions between the two may be summarized by suggesting that the traditional (pedagogical) view is that education is the transmission of knowledge from teacher to student. This philosophical position is no longer appropriate, since knowledge changes so rapidly; andragogy emphasizes an alternative position, that the purpose of education is the development of learning skills and the continuing practice of those skills throughout the liftime. Developed and refined by Malcolm Knowles (1980), andragogy emphasizes the relationship between the teacher and the learner and encourages facilitation of a cooperative planning, instructional, and evaluation climate that is most supportive, most conducive to learning, and best received by adults. Andragogy assumes that adults are volunteers for learning; that is, they are not required by law or custom to participate in formal learning situations but do so because they find it of interest or value. Thus, they are able to choose to leave the learning setting at any time, especially when they find that they are not learning the type or level of content they desire.

The instructor is the key to the effective development of andragogical instruction. He or she must be able to share with the adult students the responsibility for the learning and must be conscious of the learners' feelings about both the content and the process (Meyer, 1977).

Andragogy makes five assumptions about the adult learner. Each of these has relevance for instructors of older people, although some need modification. These assumptions are as follows:

(1)   *Adults are increasingly self-directed.* After adolescence, people become independent and are able to take responsibility for their own acts as well as their own education. Past experience with the educational system may not have prepared the person for this role, but there is a desire to accept it, and the andragogical teacher will help encourage it. Thus, the learner is a partner in the planning, conduct, and evaluation of the learning process and not the recipient of some preplanned set of learning experiences over which he or she has no control.

Although some of the older cohort are institutionalized or dependent on others for care and support, over 90 percent are caring and providing for themselves physically, socially, economically, and personally; thus, they fit the model of the independent adult. It is reasonable to assume, therefore, that in educational settings many older persons will be hesitant to revert to the subservient role expected of children. They are more likely to set their own learning goals, to specify outcomes they desire, and to use methods and skills they have found to be effective. Accordingly, the program planner and teacher are well advised to include these older learners in planning the objectives, content, and methodology of instruction. Since older persons are volunteers in the learning enterprise, they are likely to continue their participation in those experiences that they find valuable, enjoyable, and relevant and to depart from those that do not meet these criteria.

Some older people, however, do not fit this model of an independent learner. Some persons have internalized negative stereotypes about the intellectual capabilities of older people to the extent that they bring a very low self-concept to the learning situation. Because many of them have had little recent exposure to a classroom setting, and because they may have had limited successes as students in their younger years, they have little real evidence of their ability to function in a classroom setting during later life; hence, they rely on the social stereotypes and their own fears. These are typically negative and cause people to enter the instructional setting with the expectation that they are too old to learn, too ignorant to contribute anything, or too unskilled to keep up with the group. This reduced belief in their ability often causes them to assume that they will fail and creates a self-fulfilling prophecy. They expect little of themselves and confirm this level of achievement by having a high anxiety level, being reluctant to participate completely, and dropping out when failure appears possible.

As a defensive mechanism, some older learners do not attribute success or failure in a learning situation to their own actions or efforts. In general, they believe that the outcomes of their attempts to learn are determined by factors other than their own persistence and skills. They choose a somewhat passive role in which they participate but do not commit themselves completely; they do not perceive that by increasing their efforts they are more likely to succeed. Consequently, if they fail, there is nothing else that can be done in subsequent attempts that will increase the likelihood of success. The results are determined by factors outside themselves (Okun and Siegler, 1977). This belief protects them from taking the responsibility for failing, since it was not in their power to do otherwise, but it means that they do not successfully complete the learning experience and that there are no remedial steps they can take to increase the likelihood of success in the future. Thus, once a downward spiral of failure is begun, there is no way of reversing it by the student's initiative. These people, then, do not move toward increased self-direction in their learning but move away from it, relying on others to help them or withdrawing from the instructional situation.

Bolton (1976) suggested that this negative process can be addressed through a humanistic approach to education. This has many similarities to andragogy, since it emphasizes the involvement of the older learner in the planning and implementation of the instructional process. If many means of involvement are provided and a supportive group develops, Bolton found, older people do perceive themselves as investing a considerable portion of themselves in the learning experience and, consequently, perceive themselves successfully completing it.

Belbin and Belbin (1972, p. 166) add to this understanding by emphasizing the role of the instructor in helping the student overcome his or her feelings of insecurity. They suggest that "the adult trainee seems to look at his instructor as an ally, rather than as a model, and he seeks in him the qualities that are sought in friendship. He seems to be looking for an acceptable person and a sensitive communicator rather than a master craftsman." Thus, the most effective role for the instructor is one of supporting the efforts of the students rather than attempting to set an example that they feel they cannot achieve.

The extent of educational self-direction by older learners may vary greatly. For those with high self-concepts who have successfully completed other learning activities, the self-directed learner may become the usual posture, but for the many who have had little or no formal education in the past decades, substantial instructor support may be needed to maintain their participation and to guide their initial learning activities.

Adults have a rich background of experience that can play a vital role in the type and extent of learning that is achieved. They have both a greater volume of experience than a child and experience that is of a different type. "To an adult, his experience is him. He defines who he is, establishes his self-identity, in terms of his accumulation of a unique set of experiences. . . . An adult is what he has done" (Knowles, 1980, p. 44). Since the experience has a great deal of time and energy invested in it, it takes on substantial worth to the individual. When this experience is not used or is minimized, the individual is likely to feel rejected both intellectually and as a person. Thus, in a classroom setting, validating the experience by allowing it to be shared, to be used for comparative purposes, and to illustrate various concepts or facts will enhance the value of the experience, will underscore the worth of the individual, and will provide a link between the previous and the new knowledge.

Knowles (1980) suggested that this experience background has at least three andragogical implications. First, adults are more experience-based in their learning style. They are likely to learn more efficiently with, and to prefer, instructional methods that allow for their involvement, encourage active participation, and simulate life situations. Second, adults seek practical application of the new knowledge and continue to look for ways to apply what is learned. While children may be satisfied with vague promises that the knowledge will be useful at some future time, adults are more likely to attempt to relate what is being learned with what they need to know. Third, adults who have had much experience may have become somewhat rigid, adopting the position that only their experience is valuable and that conflicting knowledge that is outside their experience is unacceptable. When this happens, experience becomes a major hindrance to learning, and extensive unlearning may be necessary before new learning can result.

Experience is an especially significant asset for older people. Since their formal education is typically less extensive than younger people's, they use experience as their basic reference and knowledge base. It is not surprising that they will attempt to relate it to the learning enterprise. This can be seen in their preference for discussion, informality, problem-oriented instruction, and personal involvement in the instructional process. Such involvement is consistent with andragogical practice and proves to be usually applicable to older learners.

Most older persons learn by relating the new knowledge or insight to that which they have acquired previously. This striving for consistency of understanding means that the new material may be readily integrated into the cognitive structure of the older person, but it also means that material that conflicts with previous knowledge is likely to be rejected or quickly forgotten. The instructor is likely to find it both useful and effective to relate the new content to the learner's old knowledge and to find ways to show relationships. This can often be done by encouraging discussion around the examples that older people can suggest, by relating an insight to experiences that older people may have had, by encouraging older learners to speculate on how well some new behavior will work, or by providing opportunities to question both the new knowledge and the old experience.

The value of experience and past learning is especially important in instruction that develops psychomotor skills. In pottery, lapidary, painting, piano, dancing, and other courses in which body movement or eye-hand coordination is important, the past of the older learner will prove to be a major influence on the starting point and the rapidity of development. An assessment of previous experience in the area will be helpful, as will continued support for those who are making their first attempts in areas such as these.

As pointed out in Chapter Five, older learners are likely to prefer learning settings with greater involvement and emphasis on practical applications of the content. Likewise, they are prone to experience the problems caused by experience-based knowledge. As Moody (1978) has pointed out, the experience of older people can be both their greatest resource and their greatest stumbling block, the strength of their wisdom and the tragic flaw of dogmatism. All of us are familiar with adults who have restricted the breadth and diversity of their experience, who have sheltered themselves from broadening and complex experience by refusing to accept anything other than what they believe to be true. The years of experience are used to support biases rather than provide insight and understanding. When this occurs, experience becomes the opponent of new learning and makes teaching extremely difficult if not impossible.

The content and skill that an adult chooses to learn depend largely on the stage of development of the individual. There is a "teachable moment" when a person recognizes the need for and value of learning some particular information. These moments occur throughout the person's lifetime. As people pass through life stages, they are required to make a series of adjustments, many of which can be aided and facilitated by learning. Havighurst (1952) identified three periods of adulthood that have typical developmental tasks, adjustments that are required of most people. A successful curriculum for adults will need to be designed so that the needs of these stages are addressed and so that education can help the individual successfully meet these challenges.

This is especially relevant to instruction of older people who face serious adjustments. Havighurst (1976) refers to such adjustments as learning tasks and identifies the following: adjusting to decreasing physical strength and health, adjusting to retirement and reduced income, adjusting to the death of a spouse, establishing an explicit affiliation with one's age group, adapting to new social roles, and establishing satisfactory physical living arrangements. Each of these provides the opportunity for education to assist in its successful completion.

One implication of this andragogical assumption is that adults of different ages are likely to be facing varying developmental tasks. Since the interest in particular content may be related to the current developmental tasks, people are likely to select themselves into age-segregated classes. Thus, courses that deal with retirement, adjustment to old age, chronic diseases, and nursing homes are likely to appeal primarily to older people or middle-aged persons concerned for the welfare of their older parents. Likewise, programs aimed at understanding the meaning of life, second careers, or the use of leisure time may be of special interest to persons in later maturity.

As has been pointed out previously, older people are not all alike. However, it is appropriate to note that many older people will face similar tasks in later life and that education may be the method chosen to address these tasks. When this happens, the classroom can best facilitate learning by seeking some degree of agreement on what the problems are that are being addressed and by adapting the instruction to the developmental needs of the majority of the group.

Adults are problem-centered in their learning. They participate in educational programs in order to find solutions to the problems that confront them. They are motivated to learn what is useful, relevant, and helpful rather than to seek out courses or curricula that are based on the abstract categorization of knowledge, the basis for disciplines, and the traditional content organization. Motivation to enroll in an educational experience is caused by some interest or need; learning is an active process in which the individual searches for answers and the teacher is present to facilitate that process.

The material presented to older learners, then, is best designed to be meaningful to them. This occurs when they have had a part in determining topics and methods and when the instructor is familiar with their backgrounds and expectations for the educational experience. Meaningful material must meet another criterion, however. It must also be at the appropriate level of complexity. Since some older learners will bring an extensive background of experience and insight in particular areas, the instructor should not assume that older learners are novices in the content area. They may not have a well-rounded or theoretical knowledge, but they are likely to choose to enroll in courses that have some relation to past interests and experiences. Thus, they may bring a great deal of intuitive knowledge or experience and will demand that the presentations and discussions be at a level that provides new insights and content.

Likewise, older learners are likely to find concrete content to be more relevant than abstract or theoretical content. Since they often seek to use the new material in some way, they are typically more interested in application than in generalized understandings. Instruction, then, is likely to be well received if it includes both specific content and instructional methods that allow the content to be presented in applied ways (observation guides, using raw materials, role plays and simulations, specimens, manuals, or worksheets). The transition from abstract instruction to application is difficult for many adult learners; it is helpful when the instructor can present material in a manner that needs less translation to the form in which it will be used.

One way to accomplish this is through an example or model of behavior that can be observed and replicated in one's own life (Knox, 1977). If the learning has some specific outcome, such as a particular behavior, skill, or activity, it is often helpful to expose the students to a person who has recently learned the attribute. This provides some encouragement for the struggling learner as well as clear expectations of what the outcome will be at the end of the instructional endeavor. A recently completed painting, a sculpture, a poem, a retirement financial plan, a nutritional plan, a physical exercise, or a recent relocation to a different living arrangement can provide an example of successful task completion and a clear model for the current learner.

As children and young people, most of us implicitly assumed that life was unlimited, that there was no end to the future before us. By middle age, we came to the realization that the years remaining were limited, and this awareness often caused us to focus our vision on what seemed a reasonable life span. Older people generally have a more limited interest in the distant future and are likely to be concerned with the present and the immediate future. As a result, their educational interests are related to current problems, interests, and uses. The idea that instruction will provide knowledge that may be of some use in the dim future has little appeal to older learners. They are most interested in dealing with current situations or building on lifelong interests that may be deepened through further study.

Educational content, then, is best oriented toward the relevant. This does not mean that only instruction in consumer affairs, health adjustments, or family changes is desired. On the contrary, much of the instruction for older people includes content on the historical, philosophical, and religious aspects of life. These offerings, however, are not esoteric excursions into academe but may be viewed as attempts to better understand the meaning of life and the results of the learners' lives. Old age is a time of bringing together, of understanding the disparate, of making sense of those elements that have occasionally seemed senseless. Education can do this through a variety of content, but most of it involves content and process that have meaning, use, and value in the present and near future.

It must be emphasized once again that not all older people will fit this pattern. Some persons have a lifelong history of educational participation and may well continue it into retirement regardless of its utility. Harris and Associates (1975) reported that the primary reason given for educational participation by a national sample of older people was the expansion of general knowledge. Covey (1980) supported this conclusion by reporting that learning for the sake of learning was the primary reason given for educational participation by a sample of senior auditors at a western university. Each person in this sample had participated in education throughout his or her lifetime and continued to do so into the later years without changing purpose or objectives. Like Houle's (1961) lifelong learners, these persons participated because it was enjoyable and habitual rather than to solve some problem. It may be assumed that persons of this type are in the minority in educational programs offered outside regular credit courses, but it is not unlikely that some of them will appear in most instructional programs, especially if the program offers high-quality and innovative instruction.

Adults are more motivated by internal incentives than extrinsic rewards. A degree or certificate, a promotion or reward, a new job or a higher status is often not as important as the discovery of knowledge that will solve some problem. The motivation is to improve, to problem-solve, to understand, rather than to meet someone else's expectations. Thus, older learners need to be participants in objective and goal setting as well as in carrying out the educational plan. They need to help determine and measure the progress that is being made as well as take some responsibility for their own learning.

Since society has relatively little concern about the development and roles of older persons, there have been few social rewards or sanctions for older persons who participate in education. In a sense, we collectively have not cared whether they succeed or fail, since it does not directly affect productivity, citizenship, or family development. Motivation for participation, then, has had to come from within the older learner rather than from some external encouragement by society. This means that the reasons for participation will differ and will be related to the older person's perceived needs and current interests.

This makes the desired outcomes from the learning situation the primary motivating force for the older person. Often these are considerably different from those of the instructor. On some occasions, it may be that the motivation for the older person is the social interaction that occurs during the coffee break and not the content of the course at all. If this is so, then the emphasis on solid content, good lectures, helpful audiovisuals, and clear textbooks will not be as important in the success of the course as will be group projects, open discussions, and a supportive group atmosphere. For the instructor to succeed in the instructional endeavor, there must be a reasonably clear understanding of the factors that have motivated the older learner to participate and the expectations that the student has for the learning experience.

Application of Andragogy to Older Learners

The assumptions about learning in adulthood made by the conceptualizers of andragogy have some direct implications for the design and conduct of instruction for older people. These can be grouped into two general categories: the role and expectations of the student and the faculty member and the psychological climate that is desired for the classroom. In each of these areas, andragogy offers some insights that can be supported by empirical research and/or alternative conceptualizations.

Role of the Student. In any adult education, the student takes a more central and significant role than in the education of children. Rather than being directed by the teacher, the adult learner must be permitted to be an active participant in the determination of both the content and the methods to be used in instruction. It is necessary, therefore, that both the teacher and the student accept this increased influence and seek to operationalize it in a manner agreeable to both. It may prove difficult for some instructors to share the authority of their position, but in the long run it will result in greater relevance of learning and student commitment.

One means of implementing the expanded role of the student is for the instructor and the older learners to devote substantial time to the diagnosis of the learners' needs and wants. Although younger people may be asked to suggest topics or strategies for their learning, they generally do not have the option of leaving an instructional experience that they perceive as irrelevant. As voluntary learners, older persons may seek other activities if the instructional program is not adjusted to their wants and needs. This means that substantial time must be spent before or at the beginning of a class or workshop to determine the participants' level of functioning as well as their wishes for the educational experience. In short classes or workshops the instructor may want to begin instruction as soon as possible in order to use all the available time. Although appearing efficient, in the long run this may prove counterproductive.

The older student must be allowed the opportunity to consider and affect the goals of the instructional experience. Although the teacher or leader may have greater knowledge of both the content and the methodology, this superior insight is not the only determining criterion. The purposes of the older learners must also be incorporated into the goal setting. This can best be achieved through a period of structured discussion early in the class in which learners' expectations, questions, problems, and interests are explored in a supportive and open atmosphere. By providing the opportunity for group members to identify and clarify their own expectations, the instructor can gain additional insight into their level of knowledge, assess what outcomes will best meet their expectations, gain some insight into their individual levels of functioning, and determine some of the resources the individuals bring to the group. An additional and perhaps more important outcome is that the instructor immediately indicates his or her interest in the wishes of the older students and the commitment to accept them as partners in the planning and execution of the course or workshop.

The assumption being made by the instructor is that the older learner is a self-directing individual who comes to the instructional setting with some particular problem, interest, or need. By developing the relationship with the teacher in a way that facilitates the older learner's ability to pursue his or her own goals and address his or her own problems, the instructor is building on the assumptions of andragogy and encouraging the continued growth and independence of the older person. Since many older people have had limited formal education experience, they may need assistance in developing this self-directing role. They are likely to be hesitant to express their wants, or they may conceal their preferences within oblique verbiage. The instructor will need some patience to sort through this discussion and find the interest or need. It can be done, however, if a supportive and open atmosphere is established early in the course and if it is maintained by both the instructor and the group.

The assumption is often made that older students prefer older instructors. It is not unusual for older students to comment that a younger instructor is not likely to have much to say about any meaningful subject. Both personal experience and research, however, suggest that this need not be a major concern for most instructors. Rindskopf and Charles (1974) point out that in having older and younger students evaluate younger and older instructors, there were no differences in perceived effectiveness. Although older people rated all instructors more highly, both young and old instructors were well received. This finding suggests that younger people should not be hesitant to undertake instructional assignments with older students if they are knowledgeable about content and methodology.

Finally, the roles of the student and the teacher in the evaluation process need to be clear. Since older learners are likely to exhibit greater anxiety around the whole learning experience, evaluation, especially if it involves testing, can be a very threatening undertaking. Most evaluation during the period of formal education involves determination of how much the student has learned. Most older students desire to avoid this (Goodrow, 1975b). In the education of adults and older people, the evaluation focuses more completely on the quality of the instructional experience rather than on the older learner. Thus, evaluation is likely to be an assessment of how well the students liked the experience, how relevant it was, how well the level of content fitted their needs, or how well the instructor presented and clarified concepts.

It is one of the clearest insults to self-sufficiency of the older learner to have the teacher evaluate the student. The evaluation can be cooperatively done with a comparison of the level of functioning before and after and a determination of whether the intended learning was achieved. In a sense, it is a rediagnosis of the person's learning needs (formative evaluation) rather than a judgment on his or her progress.

Older learners, however, may still be expecting evaluation to be a measure of their knowledge or skill and consequently fear or avoid it. They need to discuss with the instructor the purpose, value, and use of evaluation and agree how it will be done. If they can accept that it is an attempt to measure the value of the course rather than their performance, they are likely to accept it more readily and to reduce some of their anxiety.

It should be kept in mind, in seeking older persons' assessments of a learning experience, that they are likely to be very thankful for the opportunity, to appreciate anything that is done for them, and to offer few critical comments (Rindskopf and Charles, 1974). Since they often expect little assistance from outside the family, a college, hospital, community center, or public school that offers a program for them is viewed as being especially generous and is graciously received. They often do not consider the ways that the experience could be made better but simply use any evaluation instrument or discussion to indicate that it was fine. Hence, totally complimentary comments should not automatically be assumed to be a reflection of the program but should be seen as due partly to the accepting nature of many contemporary older people. The major exception to this statement may be groups of senior citizen advocates who are seeking to establish greater visibility and services for older people and thus may have become more discriminating and verbal about services and opportunities for older persons.

Classroom Climate. The psychological climate of the instructional setting is also an important consideration in designing and carrying out instruction for older people. Since the older learner is more likely to be hesitant about involvement and more apprehensive about new situations, the climate will be a major force in determining whether the older learner will participate fully or will withdraw from the learning session. The climate of the instructional setting needs to be a warm, caring one with mutual respect between student and teacher. This generally means that dialogue is encouraged at any time, that both see their roles as participants in the teaching/learning process, and that each respects the knowledge and experience of the other.

Participation in a learning setting is an indication that the current level of knowledge, understanding, or skill is less than the learner would like it to be. This indicates a lack on the part of the potential learner that is publicly acknowledged and indicates the desire to improve. Since many older people have heard and accepted the negative stereotypes about old age, they are likely to have a lower self-concept and not to set high expectations for themselves in a learning situation.

A positive self-concept supports learning. The person has more confidence in himself or herself and is able to approach the learning experience with the expectation of success. Such self-confidence allows older persons to open themselves to new ideas and experience, to take some risks, and to try out new behaviors in the protective environment of the classroom. However, self-confidence, risk-taking, and positive assumptions about success are opposites of the expectations of many older people. They may have historically had little success in school, and so they expect the same outcome today.

It is especially important, then, not only that the teacher be supportive and hold positive expectations but that the family, friends, and colearners accept positive assumptions. By having the support necessary to initiate the learning and the positive reinforcement for continuing, the older person can develop the confidence to take risks, to seek to do well, and to participate without the constraints of anxiety and fear.

History is very important here. Because current older people have been outside the learning setting for many years and because they experienced autocratic education in their youth, they are likely to be somewhat unsure and perhaps even anxious in an andragogical classroom. On the one hand, they expect education to be structured, teacher-centered, and content-oriented; on the other hand, they wish to participate, to draw on their experience, and to take some leadership in determining content and method. This ambivalence is likely to be demonstrated in a reluctance to participate at first and a tendency to observe and listen and to measure the instructor's approach before becoming actively involved.

The instructor must not only discuss his or her approach to teaching but explore the students' expectations of themselves and the instructor. This can be undertaken early in the learning experience so that both student and teacher have a clear understanding of each other's expectations. The instructor, however, must be sure that his or her statements are in fact those that are believed and will be acted on. Too often, we are likely to describe ourselves as progressive, democratic, and student-oriented, only to be criticized later for not being willing to allow the others in the learning setting to have some of the responsibility for goal setting and process determination.

The instructor sets the initial climate by the way he or she deals with the learners individually and collectively. By allowing the group a voice in goal setting and instructional planning, the instructor begins to show that the learners are also important. The manner in which they are addressed, the attention paid to their comments, the way their experience is used in the instruction, and the patience with those who speak or learn slowly will affect the willingness of others to become completely involved.

The group climate will also affect participation. The instructor will do well to encourage the development of group cohesiveness, knowledge of other students, and student-to-student interactions. If this occurs, the students will find the learning environment comfortable and enjoyable and will be likely to maintain their participation. Without such a climate, however, they are likely to terminate their attendance as soon as the content has met their needs.

Since social interaction is a major motivator for participation of many older people, it is necessary that a supportive and interactive group be developed. This can be done through sharing names, backgrounds, interests, and wishes for the class. It can also occur through small-group projects and extensive discussion. More likely, however, it will occur during the breaks or before or after the class session when persons of similar interests will seek one another out for continued discussion of the content. Throughout the process, the instructor should keep in mind that the older persons in the group are teachers as well as learners. They can learn much from one another, and this learning will be encouraged when they talk together, seek to help one another clarify needs or thoughts, or support the struggles of the others. The instructor can normally deal with only one person at a time, but the class as a whole can involve everyone in some interaction. Thus, greater involvement will normally mean greater learning.

For this to occur, however, the older students will have to become convinced that it is appropriate for them to express both their hopes and their fears regarding the learning process. Thus, the communication must be open, honest, and meaningful. For some older persons this will come naturally and no encouragement will be required. For many, however, the idea of opening themselves to new ideas is frightening. For most of our lives, we try to pretend that we are informed about every subject. In the learning experience, however, it is necessary that people admit what they yet need to learn and that they find ways to obtain it. This requires not only encouraging people to listen and comment but creating a feeling that the group will support everyone and that the sharing of meaningful concerns is acceptable and expected.

Thus, the instructor's role may be considered to be one of setting the tone of instruction, modeling an open and supportive posture, and strongly supporting the worth of each individual's input; the instructor is not a lecturer or information giver in a traditional sense. Both the group atmosphere and the content need to be nonthreatening so that learners will continue to seek to be involved and to understand.

Summary and Conclusions

Instruction of older people is an art and will require additional time and effort before it can become precise and predictable. The instructor must consider many elements of the learning transaction and base a variety of actions on personal judgment. However, some suggestions seem to hold promise for those who would improve their instruction and attempt to help others do so. Perhaps the most important of these is that both teachers and learners differ, and both must be understanding in order to be most effective. This means that the instructor must gain some insight into the students' historical experiences, their be-

liefs and values, and their contemporary situation. Likewise, the
instructor must know something about himself or herself. It is
extremely important that instructors understand their own
biases, preferences, and skills and use them in the most effective
manner.

Older students typically participate in educational activities because they expect to find satisfaction or enjoyment. Consequently, they must see progress and understand the plan being
followed. This means that the older students need to understand the instructor's goals and values as well as their own. This
can often be facilitated by open discussion of what the students
hope to accomplish and the role they expect the instructor will
play. If there are differences in perception, they can be explored early in the instructional process, and appropriate resolution can be achieved.

Instruction of older adults, then, is a cooperative undertaking in which the participants are both learners and teachers,
both helpers of others and seekers for themselves. The instructor sets the initial tone for the experience, provides the rules for
participation, and helps the students accept the shared responsibility. The instructor is an equal, but only in terms of worth
and contribution. He or she is somewhat more than an equal in
influencing the entire learning process. Thus, the instructor's
role is of crucial importance and should be entered into with
good content preparation and a conscious plan for the way stu-
dent/instructor relationships will be developed.

10

CIOIOIOIOIOIOIOIOIOIOIOIOIOIOIOIOIOIOIOIOIO

Teaching and
Learning Styles

The insights derived from research on intelligence and learning in later life provide a base of knowledge on which to build instruction for older people. They do not, however, help in categorizing types of older learners so that instruction can be designed on a more individualized basis. Although everyone would agree that there is great variation in the older population, relatively little has been done to determine the most effective methods, content, and instructors for older persons having various characteristics.

Likewise, the studies on classroom learning of older people do not provide much assistance. They have concentrated on instructional results—whether the students learned and how well they liked the type of instruction they received. Thus far there has been little conceptualization of various types of older learners and limited development of measurement instruments that can show instructional outcomes with particular groups of older learners. Until this is undertaken, we can expect that all instruction will be less effective than desired and less well received than possible.

This chapter suggests a conceptual approach that divides

older learners into two general categories and offers promise for improving the results of instruction when it is designed for either of these groups. It deals with the cognitive style of older people and, through both theory and empirical research, provides a way of predicting the most appropriate content, process, and instructor for a group of older learners. The chapter includes a discussion of cognitive style, its relation to behavior, its use in instruction, and its application in the design and implementation of instruction for older persons.

Cognitive Style

The conceptual approach presented here, titled "cognitive style," is an attempt to understand, measure, and predict behavior based on the characteristic modes of perceptual and intellectual functioning that each of us has as well as to understand and categorize individual variation in the modes of perceiving, remembering, and thinking. Cognitive style describes the manner and form that perception and cognition take in individuals. This varies greatly, and the distribution can be displayed along a continuum between two poles.

Field Dependence/Independence. Nine or ten conceptualizations of cognitive style are currently being examined in research studies. The particular approach chosen for review here is called field dependence/field independence and has been clarified through twenty-five years of research by Herman Witkin and his associates. Witkin (1976) suggested that the simplest way to gain an understanding of the concepts "field dependence" and "field independence" is to describe the situations originally used to ascertain these differences in individuals.

One kind of test is conducted in a completely darkened room. The apparatus consists of a square frame coated with luminous paint and a rod pivoted at the same center as the frame, also coated with luminous paint. This is all the subject is able to see. Rod and frame can be tilted clockwise, together or separately. In a typical trial the subject, on opening his eyes, finds rod and frame in tilted positions. If he reports that the rod is tilted, he is asked to adjust it to a position where it appears upright, while the frame remains in its initial position of tilt.

People . . . differ markedly . . . in how they perform this task. At one extreme of the performance range are people who, in order to perceive the rod as upright, require it to be aligned with the surrounding frame. If the frame is tilted 30 degrees to the left, they will tilt the rod 30 degrees to the left; and when the rod is in that position, they will say it is perfectly upright. If the frame is tilted 30 degrees to the right, they will then tilt the rod 30 degrees to the right and say the rod is perfectly upright in that position. At the other extreme of the performance range are people who are able to bring the rod close to the upright more or less independently of the position of the surrounding frame (Witkin, 1976, pp. 39-40).

People who adjust the rod to parallel the frame are considered to be more field-dependent, while those who ignore the position of the frame are more field-independent. The degree of congruence of rod and frame determines the placement of the person along the dependent/independent continuum. There are other methods of determining cognitive style, such as the identification of a simple drawing within a complex one, but the results are highly correlated. Some persons are heavily influenced by the entire perceptual field, and some attend to an aspect of the field apart from the whole. When the whole field dominates a person's perception, that person is said to fall at the field-dependent end of the continuum; when a person's perception is not influenced by the surrounding field, the person is considered to fall at the field-independent end. This distinction in cognitive style appears to be relatively stable and to be closely associated with thinking and problem-solving behavior.

It should not be assumed that people are completely field-dependent or field-independent. Most persons will fall toward one end of the continuum or the other, but some will score in the middle range. Likewise, there are people who have behavioral tendencies that include both field independence and field dependence. In general, people who are field-independent can behave as though they were field-dependent, while people who are field-dependent find it nearly impossible to "act as though" they were field-independent.

Cognitive styles differ from abilities in several ways. Witkin (1976) indicated that these differences include the fact that cognitive style describes typical behavior while abilities generally deal with maximum levels of performance. A second distinction is that abilities generally have a value connotation (either good or bad) while various cognitive styles are only different from each other; one is not better than the other. Thus, it is never better to have low ability than high ability, but there are many cases in which field independence is better than field dependence or vice versa. A third difference is that abilities are unipolar; that is, they run from zero to a lot. Cognitive style is bipolar; there is a continuum along which the individual's style may fall, so that any person may have strong or weak tendencies toward a particular style and its accompanying behavioral pattern.

Cognitive style is not related to intelligence. Persons with either field dependence or independence may have high or low IQs. Likewise, creativity is not related to one's cognitive style. Thus, the way the person perceives the world is not likely to affect creativity or intelligence. An architect, who is likely to be field-independent, may be very creative in his or her field, but a writer, who is likely to be field-dependent, may also be creative.

Cognitive Style and Behavior. Through a long series of research projects, it has been shown that persons who are field-dependent behave differently than those who are field-independent. For instance, field-independent persons are likely to be analytical in their approach to a situation. They are likely to be able to examine the various elements involved apart from the whole, to ignore social pressure, and to work from an inner frame of reference. Often field-independent persons will choose college majors and subsequent professions in areas such as mathematics, biology, science, engineering, or technology. They tend to prefer working alone, to be internally directed, to be less constrained by tradition and convention, and to make more references to themselves than field-dependent persons.

Field-dependent persons, in contrast, are likely to perceive more globally. They are likely to be conscious of interpersonal relationships, to be more social, more people-oriented, more concerned about social interaction, and more conventional in dress and behavior. They are likely to choose college majors and professions in the humanities, social sciences, teaching, rehabilitation, or selling—those areas in which there is greater involvement with other people and with the concerns of human beings rather than abstract or inanimate objects. In both communication and behavior, field-dependent persons are likely to modify their typical patterns to coincide with others with whom they are dealing. When interacting with a field-independent person, the global individual is likely to become more like the independent person in speed, style, and patterns of speech. (For a summary of the correlates of field dependence/independence, see Witkin, 1976.)

The distinction between field dependence and independence can even be seen within professional areas. It has been shown (Nagle, 1967) that clinical psychologists (those whose work is the most applied and most concerned with human problems) are likely to be more field-dependent than experimental psychologists (those at the more abstract end of the continuum). This is doubtless a result of both the self-selection of the students and counseling given by departmental faculty.

Since field-dependent persons are more perceptive of the social environment, it is not surprising that they are more attentive to people and communication. They spend more time looking at the faces of those with whom they are interacting; they remember verbal messages better; they prefer closer physical positioning of persons communicating; they make fewer references to themselves and more to others; they are prone to be guided by persons in positions of authority; and they are likely to adapt their interpersonal style to agree with the style of others. In general, then, the field-dependent person is more attuned to the social and communication environment, is more likely to perceive it completely and to adapt to it, and is more aware of and concerned for the other person(s) in a social setting.

Field dependence/independence is also associated with several demographic and developmental characteristics. Women are more likely to be field-dependent than men, especially during the late teens and early years of adulthood, the time when there is the greatest sex differentiation (Rehermann and Brun, 1978). Amount of schooling also affects cognitive style; persons with more formal education are likely to be field-independent (Reherman and Brun, 1978; Tramer and Schludermann, 1974). The public school system and our institutions of higher education have placed a premium on analytical abilities, have emphasized the natural sciences and mathematics, and have used a system that encourages rigorous instruction, competition, and discipline. These traits all relate closely to the model of field independence and doubtless have had an impact on recent generations of students.

Field dependence appears to change over the life span. Children are generally field-dependent but increase in independence until about age 17. After that time, field dependence gradually increases throughout the remainder of life (Lee and Pollack, 1978; Panek and associates, 1978; Tramer and Schludermann, 1974; Schwartz and Karp, 1967; Comalli, 1965; Comalli, Krus, and Wapner, 1965; Axelrod and Cohen, 1961). Thus, the older population appears to have more field-dependent people than younger cohorts do. This may result from a disproportionate number of women, the lower level of formal education of the current older cohort, or ontogenetic change that is part of the aging process.

It is not completely clear what causes some people to be field-dependent and others to be field-independent, but it would appear that early socialization is very important. Persons who become field-independent are more likely to have experienced early encouragement of autonomous functioning. A child who is encouraged to make his or her own decisions and to be responsible for his or her own actions will likely become analytical and field-independent. This pattern has been shown to occur in other cultures and appears to be consistent whether it is in America, Western Europe, or Sierra Leone (Witkin, 1976).

Teaching, Learning, and Cognitive Style

The behavioral differences and preferences between field-independent and field-dependent persons have major implications in the classroom. Since teachers spend most of their time with other people, it is not surprising that they are likely to be more field-dependent as a group (Witkin, 1976). However, as in other professions, there is substantial variance, math and science teachers being more field-independent and social science and humanities teachers being more field-dependent.

Cognitive style influences behavior in the classroom. Field-dependent teachers are likely to prefer the use of discussion methods, since they involve more social interaction and interpersonal communication. They are also more likely to use democratic procedures in the classroom and to attempt less direct ways to affect student behavior. Field-independent teachers, in contrast, are likely to prefer lecture formats, which involve greater instructor dominance, emphasis on information giving, and a more structured procedure. It is possible to be more orderly, more precise, and more controlled in presenting material through this method and to ensure that the students have had access to all the important information. The emphasis is on the information, however, and its transmission, rather than on the student and his or her reaction to it.

Students likewise are influenced by cognitive style. The amount of knowledge they acquire in a learning setting is related to the congruence of their cognitive style with the instructional process used (Witkin, 1976). If the cognitive style and the teaching method are in agreement, the amount of learning will be increased. Field-dependent students will learn more under, and are likely to prefer, discussion or discovery methods, ones which involve them in greater social interaction and in which they can gain the support of the teacher and other students.

Field-independent students are likely to learn more under

conditions of intrinsic motivation, since they are most frequently directed by inner drives rather than social pressure for acceptance. Little difference between field-dependent and field-independent groups has been found when external rewards are used, but criticism tends to have a greater influence on field-dependent students than on those who are more analytical in their approach.

It can be seen that the match of student and teacher is very important if the best learning is to be achieved. However, this match (or mismatch) is also important for the satisfaction of each with the learning situation. Students who have teachers with the same cognitive style are likely to describe them in highly positive terms, to view them as better teachers, to relate better to them, and to seek them out more often for advice (DiStafano, 1969). Likewise, teachers who are matched with students are likely to perceive the students as being more intelligent, learning more, and having more positive personality characteristics. The positive interaction when cognitive styles are consistent probably results from shared interests, shared personal characteristics, and common communication modes. Surprisingly, both students and teachers are able to determine agreement of cognitive style (even if they do not identify it by name) within as little as one-half hour of experience with each other (Witkin, 1976). Cognitive style appears to be obvious after only a short time and to begin to affect performance almost at once.

Just as teacher and student interact, the content also interacts with the learner and the teacher. When the student's cognitive style coincides with the content, the student is likely to do well. When they conflict, the result is generally not so positive. It has been shown (Witkin, 1976) that students who were field-dependent were more likely to change curricula than field-independent students were. Frequently, the move was from the sciences and mathematics to the humanities and social studies. One reason was a mismatch of content and cognitive style, and another was that field-dependent students were not as inner-directed and so had more difficulty settling on one content area or career line. However, the key to successful education from the cognitive-style conceptualization was to achieve agreement of student, teacher, and content so that both learning and satisfaction were optimized. In order to do that, the teacher must know something about his or her cognitive style and must be able to assess that of the student.

This can be done relatively informally through exploring the student's interests, preferences, and successes, or it can be done through the use of a short written test (Oltman, Raskin, and Witkin, 1971), which can be given with little skill. This assessment should prove helpful in designing instruction and determining agreement of content, instructor, and student.

One caution should be made here, however. Most of the research on cognitive style has been conducted with children and adolescents. Although a few studies have shown that the concept has use for older people, the statements on behavior and instruction are generally drawn from research on younger cohorts and so should be taken with a bit of caution when applied to older learners. However, it would appear that there are several ways in which knowledge of cognitive style can benefit instruction of older people.

Application to Education of Older People. Most instruction of older people has apparently assumed that older students are basically unitary in interests, capacities, skills, and preferences. With the exception of the discussion on instrumental and expressive education, the literature has made scant reference to variation among older learners, and conceptual categories of older learners have not been suggested. Consequently, formal instruction for older people has shown limited variations; in reviewing these offerings, it becomes evident that program planners have implicitly assumed that the older students are universally field-dependent. The course content is primarily in the humanities, social sciences, or leisure-time area; little of it is analytical in nature or involves the natural sciences.

Instructional methodology has consistently emphasized group-process approaches in which discussion, social interaction, and informal settings are common. Whenever possible, instructors are encouraged to make learners feel at ease, to reduce their anxiety, to deal with their needs and wants, and to involve them in the planning and conduct of the instruction. Teachers are generally selected not only because of their knowledge of the subject matter but on their ability to interact well with students, to be sensitive and perceptive, and to relate the content to the experience of the older learners. Thus, the typical instructor is expected to be field-dependent.

Older persons who enroll in these instructional programs are also likely to be field-dependent. Often they are attracted by content that emphasizes human and social knowledge rather than that of the physical world. They also expect to find the programs conventional in nature and taught by an instructor who brings a background of formal educational preparation in the field of specialization. They appreciate the emphasis on social interaction with much group discussion, a time for refreshments, and a supportive atmosphere encouraged by both the instructor and the sponsoring organization. No tests or rigorous activities mar the enjoyment of the course where persons share their experiences and learn together through mutual interest, trust, and encouragement.

In many ways, then, current instruction designed specifically for older people appears to be based on the premise that these learners are field-dependent and prefer this approach to content and methodology. Instruction for younger students, however, is usually designed around field-independent preferences—lectures, teacher authority, technical content, a challenging environment, and competition among students. This kind of instruction is likely to appeal to those students who are field-independent in their approach and thus far has not been very successful in involving older learners.

In many cases, colleges and universities have attempted to recruit older persons into regular college courses either on a space-available basis or as regular students. This has typically been unsuccessful, since most older students prefer the more comfortable and supportive style of instruction that is offered to them in age-segregated courses or in the noncredit, community service portion of the college curriculum. However, it is necessary that we continue to examine the distinction between field-dependent and field-independent instruction in order to determine how it will be most useful to administrators and instructors dealing with older learners.

Research on Cognitive Style in Later Life. Initial research in this area has been undertaken at the Gerontology Program of the University of Nebraska at Omaha. It originated with a 1977 study on the effect of classroom variables on older learners' preferences and performance. The original hypothesis was that older learners would prefer, and do better in, the most informal, least threatening learning situations. The results of this study, which was carried out with a group of 180 persons aged 55 and older, gave no support to this hypothesis. The older persons learned significantly more in discussion than in lecture situations, but there was no significant effect of class size or instructional setting.

Perhaps more important, the behaviors observed in the classes were not consistent with theory that describes older persons as fearful of formal learning settings. The students who enrolled in the consumer education classes were very comfortable in a traditional classroom situation, wanted to participate in the class discussion, and had the same fear of exams as any group of undergraduates. What was noticeable, in fact, was their high level of social interaction, their mutual support and lack of criticism, their marked preference for discussion, and their need to relate the course content to experiences in their own lives and the lives of their friends.

In analyzing the observed behaviors and outcomes, it became clear that the results could be explained if the participants were predominantly field-dependent in cognitive style. This could have occurred through the self-selection process of enrolling in the class. Since no test of cognitive style had been administered as part of the original research, there was no way to examine this hypothesis.

Another set of classes for older persons was offered during the fall of 1978 with approximately 180 enrollees in eleven course sections. During the third class session, participants took the Oltman, Raskin, and Witkin Group Embedded Figures Test, one of the standard instruments for determining field dependence/independence. The test consists of a series of complex figures in which a simple figure is embedded. The subjects were instructed to find one of the simple figures in each complex form and to trace its outline on the test booklet.

Because the task was new to so many of the participants, and because an unknown number may have had visual or motor disabilities that could have resulted in inaccurate scores, only those tests in which the participants completed the practice section satisfactorily were used. With this restriction there were 124 usable test scores.

The test score range is from 0 to 18, with lower scores indicating field dependence and higher scores indicating field independence. For this group of participants, the mean score was 4.0, with a range of 0 to 16. The scores clearly suggested that the persons who chose to enroll in class were predominantly field-dependent. If the midpoint score of 9 is used to dichotomize the respondents (and a natural division of scores did occur at this point), only 4 percent of the women and 16 percent of the men could be described as field-independent. These figures compare with roughly 40 percent of women and 60 percent of men who were field-independent in studies of younger persons (Witkin, 1976). Comparisons of men and women in this sample indicated that men had a slightly higher tendency toward field independence (means were 5.35 for men and 3.65 for women).

For participants in this noncredit education program, the hypothesis that they would be field-dependent rather than field-independent in cognitive style was supported. This conclusion was confirmed by the behavior of the participants; they evidenced a preference for discussion, referred to personal experiences to understand conceptual points, and interacted and socialized extensively.

Since people who are field-dependent tend to learn better in group-centered or discussion settings, it is logical to assume that these are the persons who would self-select themselves into group learning (that is, class) situations. Conversely, persons who are predominantly field-independent tend to prefer either lectures or self-paced, independent learning and may prefer to enroll in educational TV courses or to learn on their own through reading.

Implications for Instruction of Older People. These preliminary research data confirm that cognitive style may play some part in the selection process by which older people choose to participate in group instructional programs. It would appear reasonable, then, to suggest some implications from this approach to cognitive style for educational programming involving older people.

Age-segregated, noncredit courses in which older people voluntarily enroll (such as those offered by public schools, colleges and universities, senior citizen centers, and nutrition sites) are typically selected by field-dependent people and should be more successful in fostering learning by using discussion presentations and group-centered teaching techniques, by maximizing positive feedback and minimizing criticism, and by selecting instructors who are themselves field-dependent. For the minority of persons who are field-independent, the instructor should provide reading or self-paced audiovisual materials for supplementary use.

Age-segregated, noncredit courses that emphasize content dealing with human interactions, social concerns, contemporary events, and quests for meaning are likely to be of the most interest to older students. Courses on religion, history, current events, and mental health will be preferred over scientific courses, mathematics, technologically oriented course content, and logic. If an educational institution wishes to enroll greater numbers of older students, the people-oriented courses will most likely produce the desired result.

Age-integrated classes (such as those in the regular course offerings of a college or university) are more likely to attract older students who are field-independent, since these courses are generally assumed to be more formal, analytical, and content-oriented. This perception may account for the low level of enrollment by older people in these courses.

Learning situations in which persons are not self-selected (such as instruction in self-care techniques for heart attack or stroke victims, safe driving courses, courses explaining dietary plans for persons suffering from chronic or acute conditions, or classes in the preparation of income tax returns) could obtain the best results by providing a choice of learning options, allowing people to learn either through discussion classes or through self-paced instruction.

Conferences and large meetings that by necessity must

use a lecture format are likely to prove ineffective for educating many older people. Although field-independent persons are likely to prefer this form of presentation, those who are active in community groups, representatives of boards and advisory committees, and volunteer leaders are likely to be field-dependent and consequently less appropriate participants.

The Group Embedded Figures Test can be used at the beginning of a course or workshop to quickly determine the cognitive style of individuals. This information can be used to verify the appropriateness of instructional plans, to determine participation in subgroup activities, or to assign students to instructors.

Learning situations involving heterogeneous participants could be improved by providing several alternative learning activities that reflect various learning styles and allowing the participants to choose the ones that fit best with their preferences and inclinations.

Conclusions

Much remains unknown about teaching and learning; the cognitive style conceptualization would appear to offer one fertile area for exploration. Data clarifying the preferred learning style of a group of older students would make it possible to plan instruction that would be well received, would facilitate efficient learning, and would develop a positive relationship between the student and instructor. To date administrators have sought to identify the good classes and to continue to offer them to older people. Perhaps the next step should be to identify the style, content, and instructor that would suit a particular group of older students and then use this knowledge to design instructional settings having high expectations for successful learning.

11

○I○I○I○I○I○I○I○I○I○I○I○I○I○I○I○I○I○I○I○I○I○I○I○

Retraining for
Extended Employment

Education of older people is often assumed to deal primarily with their coping, expressive, contributive, and self-
actualization needs. These are of major significance and do meet
the current concerns of many older people. However, the area
of job-related retraining is also of importance and tends to be
overlooked in reviews of instructional offerings for people past
middle age. Because current demographic and labor force trends
are changing the composition of the work force, it is likely that
retraining will become a crucial area in the future.

Retraining of older workers is typically included in what
is called "industrial gerontology." Sprague (1970) defined this
as the study of employment and retirement of middle-aged and
older workers. It involves such subareas as aptitude testing, job
counseling, vocational training and placement, job assignment
and reassignment, retention of workers, job design and redesign,
preparation for retirement and transition to retirement, and
public and private pension systems. The area of industrial gerontology will not be covered here in its entirety; rather, the issues
and practices of training and retraining middle-aged and older
workers will be emphasized. This chapter addresses this area by

181

dealing with the current involvement of older people in the work force, the productivity of older workers, employer reluctance to retrain older workers, the values of retraining, the methods that have been shown to be most effective, the results of retraining, and some current programs designed to help update the skills and knowledge of the older worker.

Training and retraining by business and industry are a major undertaking costing, for example, approximately $2 billion in 1975 (Lusterman, 1977). Nearly 4.3 million workers are involved annually in all types of training programs, the most common of which are conducted during working hours for current employees. The extent of training varies by occupation and level, with management and technical personnel the most likely to be involved on a regular basis. Little of this training, however, is directed to older employees.

In an interesting comparison of persons who participated in retraining and those who did not, Smith (1973) reported several differences between these two groups. In general, those who volunteered for retraining had a less stable occupational history, a clearer view of what the future had in store, higher ambitions for their children, greater economic commitments, and higher intelligence. In addition, they were more likely to be young. Smith concluded that participants in training programs were superior intellectually and had a higher drive for success. These characteristics are more typically found in younger rather than older workers.

When retraining for older workers is conducted, it typically involves persons who have not been of interest to educational gerontologists, for older workers are often defined as those over the age of 40 or 45. For instance, federal discrimination legislation makes anyone over age 40 an older worker; the U.S. Department of Labor considers those over age 45 to be older workers; and the Bureau of Labor Statistics uses age 55 as the point at which a worker becomes old (Work In America Institute, 1980). Thus, reports of retraining projects often deal with an age group considerably younger than the one referred to in other chapters. Persons over age 40 may be affected in their employment by age alone and thus are of interest to us.

However, we must keep in mind that there is a wide range in the age of participants in retraining programs, and a report referring to "older workers" may not signify persons near 65.

Although older workers make up a major part of the work force, the training literature typically ignores their existence and addresses younger employees or those who have social, physical, or cultural handicaps. The benefits to be derived from retraining current older employees have been generally overlooked; in fact, the possibility of retraining has seldom been considered except when labor shortages in specific skill areas have forced employers to use unusual methods to fill the existing positions (Hoos, 1967).

Labor Force Participation

In 1977 there were 97,400,000 people in the U.S. labor force (Work in America Institute, 1980). The rate of participation varied with the age of the worker: Over 94 percent of men aged 25-54 and 58 percent of women that age were employed. With increased age, the level of work force participation declined. Seventy-four percent of men and 41 percent of women aged 55-64 were working. After age 65, 20 percent of men and 8 percent of women were employed (Work in America Institute, 1980).

During this century, there have been two major trends in labor force participation. First, the percentage of women in the work force has increased substantially, especially women aged 45-64. In 1950, 38 percent of women aged 45-54 were employed; by 1977 this proportion had increased to almost 56 percent. For women aged 55-64, the increase from 1950 to 1977 was from 27 to 41 percent. The trend of increasing employment, however, does not hold for women over the age of 65. Between 1950 and 1977, the percentage of 65+ women working declined from 9.7 to 8.1.

The second trend involved the early retirement of increasing numbers of men. In 1950, 87 percent of men aged 55-64 were employed; by 1977 the percentage had dropped to 74. The same is true for men over age 65. In 1950, 46 percent were still employed, but by 1977, only 20 percent were (Work in America Institute, 1980). Today, 59 percent of all males who receive Social Security leave the work force before the age of 65 (Rappaport, 1979). During periods of high unemployment, such as we have experienced during the 1970s and into the 1980s, early retirement is a preferred way to limit the size of the work force. However, the future will see many fewer younger persons entering the job market, and so continuation of this trend may become disadvantageous. For instance, a straight-line projection of employment participation would suggest that by 1990 only 15 percent of men over age 65 would be in the labor force. This would mean that while the labor force was growing from 97 million workers in 1977 to 119 million in 1990, the number of men over 65 who were employed would decrease from 1.8 million to 1.7 million (Work in American Institute, 1980). (Older women comprise a smaller number of employees and their rate of employment is not expected to change much.)

The percentage of the work force that is over age 55 may decline in the future because the rapid growth of the older population is apt to slow considerably. This will result because changes in birthrates during this century will make future older cohorts proportionately smaller than recent ones. Between 1900 and 1925, the birthrate was quite high, but after that it dropped considerably. Consequently, a large number of persons will have reached age 60 between 1960 and 1985. For instance, 19.2 percent more people had their sixtieth birthday between 1965 and 1975 than occurred during the preceding decade. In the current decade (1975-1985), 14.2 percent more people will reach age 60, but in the decade 1985-1995, the increase in persons reaching age 60 will be only 3.7 percent (Gillaspy, 1979). Thus, the number of older people who are available for participation in the labor force during the rest of the century will increase in absolute numbers, but the growth will be substantially slowed. When the baby boom of the 1950s and 1960s reaches age 60 in 2010 to 2030, the size of the older population will again increase substantially.

Increases in gross national product, which we have come to expect in order to improve our standard of living, require a continuing increase in the size of the work force. The smaller size of the approaching older cohorts and the increasing rates of early retirement are likely to reduce the number of older workers. It is unlikely that other age groups will move into the labor force sufficiently to provide the needed personnel. The peak of the baby boom is now entering the labor force, and each succeeding year will see a smaller number of people reaching their twenty-first birthday. It is possible that other groups that have traditionally had low levels of employment will pick up the slack. For instance, women could become more heavily involved in work, but their participation has increased greatly in the past few years, and further expansion seems unlikely. Minority groups and immigrants may furnish some of the supply, but future needs are likely to be in professional and skilled areas, fields in which these groups have traditionally been less involved. Consequently, alternative sources of workers will be needed in order to fill the developing management, skilled labor, and service positions in the future.

It would appear that the most likely source of this needed manpower will be the older worker who has been retiring early and who offers substantial resources of experience, skill, and productivity. This would require a reversal in the trend toward early retirement, but that may occur because of the economic and legislative changes.

Several contemporary factors are generally considered to have made retirement more attractive to older workers. These include the increasing availability of Social Security retirement payments and private pension benefits. As these have become more generally available and as the benefit levels have increased, they have provided a much higher level of income replacement and have doubtless encouraged many people to leave the work force. Since 1972, Social Security retirement benefits have been annually adjusted for increases in the cost of living, and this too has encouraged retirement, as the recipient has less to fear from inflationary trends.

Other factors that have pushed people toward retirement include real and perceived health difficulties, mandatory retirement provisions of many companies, increased accumulated

wealth of some retiring persons, and a high rate of unemployment. Taken together, these factors have encouraged early retirement and have caused the decline in labor market participation by older people.

There are several developments, however, that over the
next few years are likely to change this trend or at least slow
the exodus of older workers. Probably the most powerful of
these is the high rate of inflation we have experienced. So long
as there is the threat of renewed inflation, employment will be
preferred to retirement. Private pensions tend not to be adjusted for inflation, and interest on savings and investments has
not kept pace. Consequently, many workers are indicating an
interest in extending their employment rather than assuming
that they will be able to live in the style they desire for the rest
of their expected life if inflation continues.

A second consideration results from the huge amounts of
funds that are required to operate the Social Security and pension programs. It is clear that unless additional sources of funds
are obtained or reductions are made in the benefits, public and
private pension plans will not remain viable. Extensive debate is
currently underway regarding means by which these financial
burdens can be reduced; the likely result is that Social Security
and pension benefits will be curtailed in the future, either by
raising the age for eligibility or by reducing benefit levels. Whichever way this happens, it will make retirement financially less
desirable and encourage some people to remain employed.

Other pushes toward work can be seen in the improving
quality of health of older people and their rising level of education. Poor health is highly associated with early retirement, as is
a lower level of education. In the future, people in their sixties
are expected to be healthier and able to continue working if
they desire to do so. Likewise, people with higher levels of education are likely to remain employed, and as the level of formal
education of the older population rises, they are likely to
choose to work longer, to be able to move into jobs that are less
physically stressful, and to have skills that are valued by employers.

A final trend toward a longer working life may come

from employers, who appear to be changing their attitude toward maintaining older workers on the payroll. If a labor shortage does begin to occur, it is likely that such arrangements as part-time work, job sharing, work sharing, and phased retirement will be made in order to encourage older people to stay in the work force. These modifications of current policy will result in older people being encouraged to work rather than retire.

There is some indication that this is beginning to occur. In 1978, for the first time since 1947, the percentage of men 65+ in the work force increased. The increase was very slight, from 20.1 to 20.5 percent, but it may be the first sign of a reversal of a trend that has been uninterrupted for the past thirty years (Entine, 1979).

Productivity of the Older Worker

Reversing the early retirement trend is useful only if older people are valuable employees of the organizations in which they work. The stereotype is that older people are less productive and less flexible workers. Some employers have consistently attempted to encourage them to retire early and have made it a policy to seek out younger workers. The stereotypes typically deal with four areas—higher rates of illness and absenteeism, increased susceptibility to accidents, lower productivity, and inflexibility. The last of these has been dealt with in the chapters on intelligence and learning and is clearly untrue. It will not be reviewed here, but the other three will be.

Illness in Old Age. The myth of illness in later life has some basis in fact. It is true that people over 65 have more sick days, more hospital stays, and more days of limited activity than younger people (U.S. Department of Health, Education and Welfare, 1978). This is especially accurate for people over 80 years. This correlation between illness and increased age, however, does not mean that old age is the cause of illness. A person's stamina, resistance, and reserve capacity decline with increased age; thus, older people become easier victims of illness.

Those who do become ill are likely to contract chronic conditions that cannot be easily cured and are likely to require medication or therapy over an extended period. Respiratory disorders occur more frequently in older workers; often they are caused or exacerbated by the conditions of the workplace and may result in transfer of the worker to a different job situation. The increase in chronic conditions, however, is somewhat counterbalanced by the decline in acute conditions. Overcoming the restrictions and handicaps of chronic illness is more likely to occur through the development of adaptive mechanisms by the older person. There are many situations in which we are forced or choose to change our behaviors in order to adapt to alterations in our environment or ourselves. Thus, 80 percent of the older population manage to live their lives with little or no restriction placed on their mobility by health conditions (Palmore, 1977).

It is also clear that the relative health condition of the older population is improving, compared with previous generations. The increased accessibility of health care, the pervasiveness of public health protection, and the improved nutrition of recent cohorts have led to reductions in the limitation of activity due to chronic illness, in the limitation of mobility due to chronic conditions, in the number of bed-disability days per older person, and in the number of acute conditions per older person (Palmore, 1976).

Although illness does reduce the older worker's potential, it seldom interferes with activities until the seventies. Because most employment does not use the maximum potential of the older worker, older people are able to compensate for aging changes and illness with adjustments made possible through experience, increased knowledge, and foresight.

Most people continue to function very well until they are in their seventies and need have little fear of precipitous decline. The conditions they experience are generally of late onset, develop somewhat gradually, and can be overcome with the normal adjustments that most people make to their physical and social situations. Thus, illness and health, though posing potential problems for persons over age 70, generally are not considered detrimental when considering the viability of the older worker.

Accidents and Old Age. The myth that older workers are subject to a greater number and severity of accidents would lead an employer to reject the retention or recruitment of older workers because they would be considered an excessive risk. The myth, however, is generally untrue and should not be used as an excuse to avoid considering ways in which older workers can best contribute. In general, older workers have different types of accidents than younger workers, and overall their record is better. Older workers may be more likely to be involved with falls or to be hit by flying objects, but they are less likely to be injured in operating a machine (Sheppard, 1978).

Birren (1964) has concluded that accidents that are preventable by judgment based on experience decrease with greater age, while accidents that could be avoided by quick evasive action to sudden events increase. Thus, older people are more likely to appreciate the demands of the situation, to use their experience to predict situations in which an accident is likely, and consequently to avoid accidents more frequently than younger workers.

Older workers are likely to be more cautious, to take fewer risks, and to value risk taking less; they are likely to select themselves out of areas where they feel uncomfortable or unsafe, and thus they avoid the situations where accidents are likely to occur. Tasks in which judgment and expecting the unexpected are important in accident prevention are ones in which the older worker is especially likely to be superior. However, in a work setting where both task and pace are rigidly structured, older workers will function less effectively and with a higher level of accidents, since they cannot use their experience or develop ways to compensate for age-related changes.

Job Performance. The myth that job performance declines with increased age is not supported by the facts. Overall work productivity does not decrease with age, at least up to age 65. The many studies conducted in this area indicate that there is no consistent pattern of superior productivity by any age group. Variation in worker productivity is much greater within any age group than it is between age groups (Sheppard, 1978; Baugher, 1978). Age comparisons result in the conclusion that either there is a slight increase in productivity with age or there is no relationship at all (Sheppard, 1978).

This conclusion has been borne out in a number of studies. Citing a few of them should provide an indication of the breadth of coverage and the consistency of findings.

- A study of the work records of 6,000 clerical personnel concluded that older workers had a steadier rate of work, equal accuracy, equal attendance, and lower turnover (Kelleher and Quirk, 1973).
- A study of New York State employees showed that performance of those 65 and over was equal or superior to that of younger workers (Sheppard, 1978).
- A survey of Canadian department store salespersons showed that increased age was an asset if a factor at all (Sonnenfeld, 1978).
- A study of manual workers showed steady productivity until age 50. After that point there was some decline, but it resulted in less than a 10 percent drop in productivity. Rates for attendance and separation from the company improved with age (Sonnenfeld, 1978).
- A study of employees in a printing firm indicated that productivity rose through the fifties and then declined slightly, except for proofreaders in their sixties, who outperformed those under age 50 (Baugher, 1978).
- Sonnenfeld (1978) reported on several companies that encouraged the use of older workers. For instance, Ferle, Inc., a company owned by General Foods, had a work force whose average age was 71. The president (who was 87) commented that older workers were steadier and were accustomed to the discipline of work.
- Macy's in New York City has no mandatory retirement age for its sales force. It reported no decline in performance.
- Polaroid reported that its employees who remained with the company after age 65 tended to be better performers and to have exemplary attendance records.
- Banker's Life and Casualty has maintained a policy of open-ended employment that has resulted in nearly 4 percent of

employees being over age 65. This company reported that older workers showed more wisdom, were more helpful and thorough, and had fewer personality clashes than younger persons.

Impediments to Developing Training for Older Workers

Even though older workers are likely to be healthy, accident-free, and productive, employers remain reluctant to hire persons over age 40 and to train or retrain those already employed. One reason is that employers continue to believe the myths and stereotypes that have circulated in the past. Likewise, older workers are reluctant to volunteer for retraining because they often have feelings of inadequacy about their ability to successfully complete the training program.

Employer Reluctance. A recent survey of corporate managers by the *Harvard Business Review* indicated the depth and strength of stereotypes about the elderly (Rosen and Jerdee, 1977). The questionnaire was in the form of a managerial decision-making exercise in which the respondent was to assume the role of a "trouble shooter" and asked to make decisions about organizational and personnel problems. There were two versions of the questionnaire, which were used equally often. In one, a 32-year-old was the key person in the problem situation; in the other, a 61-year-old was. Otherwise, the two questionnaires were identical. Thus, managerial decisions based on the age of the employee could be identified.

Although the respondents to the survey stated that they valued younger and older workers, their recommended solutions to the problem situations did not indicate an unbiased position. For instance, the respondents—

- Saw more difficulty in changing the behavior of older employees.
- Suggested that items be routed around the older employee rather than dealing with him directly.
- Did not attribute positive motives to older workers desiring retraining.

- Favored career development for younger workers but not for older workers.
- Saw the older worker as less likely to be promoted than younger workers.

In this study, age stereotypes clearly influenced management decisions, always to the detriment of the older worker.

Companies typically choose to replace older workers with younger ones who are already skilled or are perceived to be receptive to training. It is usually only in those geographical areas where a labor shortage exists for a particular skill that employers have initiated training programs for staff other than managerial personnel. Many companies are unable or unwilling to forecast changes in product and process so that they can anticipate employee knowledge and skill needs (Hoos, 1967). Consequently, they are not prepared to retrain their current workers and so attempt to handle personnel needs through terminating older workers and hiring younger ones.

Unions have not been particularly aggressive in encouraging retraining of older employees. Although there is wide variation in union policies, Clague, Palli, and Kramer (1971) noted that a Bureau of Labor Statistics report in 1969 examined 1,823 major collective bargaining agreements and found that only 20 percent contained training or retraining provisions. Six industries—transportation, communications, machinery, primary metals, utilities, and food—contained in their contracts half of all training clauses discovered. Management has not received much pressure from unions to retrain older workers and to use their skills to the utmost.

Current Condition of Older Employees. Currently employed older people have difficulty gaining retraining and promotions, and they have a major difficulty finding a new job when they become unemployed. Nelson (1979) has pointed out that older workers are marginal in several respects. They have less education, less vocational training, and less willingness to change locations in order to gain a promotion. Consequently, collectively they have achieved lower job and economic status than younger workers. Older people also have lower ascribed status. In general, they are less likely to be held in esteem and to be viewed as valuable by management and other workers. Finally, older workers are perceived by employers as being less physically able and more likely to suffer from disabilities and loss of time on the job. Thus, in three areas older people are likely to be viewed as marginal by management.

Older people are also more likely than younger people to be found in marginal occupations. Because they are typically less willing to move to another region of the country in order to obtain a job or improve their situation, they are frequently found in the Northeast, Middle Atlantic, and North Central sections of the United States, where population growth and economic prosperity are in decline. They are generally overrepresented in occupations that are considered marginal (farmers and farm managers, farm laborers, service workers, private household workers, and sales workers) and are underrepresented in occupational groupings that are not marginal (for instance, professional fields, managers and administrators, craftspersons, transport operatives, clerical workers, and other machine operatives). Thus, older workers are likely to be found in those occupational groupings that are least likely to be growing and prosperous and in those parts of the country that are experiencing the greatest economic difficulties.

Older Workers' Perceptions. The values of retraining are not always obvious to older employees. Older workers are not likely to be the first to volunteer for this activity and, in fact, may be very hesitant to become involved. Pacaud (1965) points out that retraining, especially that outside the workday, may be resisted by older workers' families. The spouse typically prefers the worker to be home in the evenings rather than attending an educational session. The worker is often tired after a day at work and so is less likely to participate in instruction.

There are psychological barriers to any type of retraining. Since many older workers have not participated in educational activities for many years, they typically have anxieties about their abilities and competence. They often fear that they will be unable to successfully complete the work and that their inadequacies will be observed by others.

A final deterrent to participation comes in the outcome of the training. In many cases, increased training results in the employee's being promoted into a situation with increased responsibility. This is likely to include greater job-related stress and pressure. Some older workers are seeking ways to reduce rather than increase the pressures of the job, and so they avoid activities that are likely to lead to more responsibility. Thus, retraining for a new position may be the opposite of what an older worker wants at this stage of life. Too often, however, this attitude is also held by those who need the training, not for promotions but in order to retain the job they have.

Values of Retraining Older Workers

Although most educators assume that training and education are valuable to almost everyone in any situation, there are some fairly specific values in training older workers. These depend partly on the situation of the older person and partly on the organization that is offering the instruction. Six types of training for older persons have been identified (Organisation for Economic Co-operation and Development, 1965):

1. Training existing employees for new jobs that the company has or for modifications in current job activities.
2. Training new employees who will be joining the company and who need some orientation or skills in order to carry out their responsibilities.
3. Retraining groups of workers who have lost their jobs because of plant closures or other major layoffs.
4. Special training schemes for persons in particular fields or areas.
5. Training older people who have been unemployed for a long time and are attempting to reenter the job market in a new capacity.
6. Training for reentry into older persons' former occupations through updating of skills and development of new competencies.

Training is valuable in each of these areas. However, most of the programs developed for older people have been for current employees, with only occasional examples of those dealing with persons who are to be employed after they have completed the training. One example of this type of program can be found in the employment and training strategy of ACS America, a company developing computer software, which has taught retirees in Florida to be computer programmers. ACS America found that older persons were interested in part-time work, were anxious to find jobs that would allow them to work at home and on their own schedule, and could be trained to do the work without previous experience. Although the company has now gone out of business, older workers were not the cause, and other corporations are likely to expand use of this group.

In most training programs, however, current employees make up the primary audience. In these settings, the older worker is already familiar with the work environment and is not expected to adjust to the new plant, new colleagues, and the regimen of employment in addition to the development and application of new skills and techniques.

In-Company Training. Four specific values for employers can be seen in training current older employees. The first of these is remediation of the lower levels of formal education that the older worker typically brings to the work situation. Since older people have less and less-recent education, they are unlikely to have the breadth of knowledge and adaptive learning skills needed in a work environment in which change is the norm. Any upgrading will require the acquisition of learning skills; consequently, basic education and orientation to continuing learning are frequently needed as a prerequisite for specific roles and responsibilities.

The second value of retraining older workers is in the prevention or reversal of obsolescence. Most employers are concerned with remaining competitive by frequently revising their production, sales, and management systems. This requires personnel who are able to function at the state of the art in both technical and managerial areas. Skill upgrading is especially needed for the older worker since he or she is furthest from the years of formal education and most likely to need the updating. Older workers have also been shown to be those least likely to volunteer for instruction, and so need management's encouragement to increase participation (Smith, 1973).

A third value of retraining is to increase the motivation of middle-aged and older workers. Litwin (1970) suggested that the major problems involving the worker over age 40 related to the loss of motivation and the resulting decrease in value to the employer when this occurs. This reduced motivation may be seen in decreased self-assertiveness, avoidance of challenge, withdrawal from social interaction, and reduction of risk taking. Although these characteristics certainly do not affect all middle-aged and older workers, in work situations involving repetitive tasks and physical labor or in situations with limited possibilities for advancement there may be motivational decline; retraining can retard this decline and raise the level of enthusiasm through collective agreement on new goals for the individual and the unit.

Retraining can also be viewed as a social responsibility of the employer. Since the older worker has devoted many years of service to the company, some employers believe that they have a responsibility to maintain the productivity of this group through retraining. In the United States this attitude has not been prevalent in the past, but in other nations (especially Japan) companies adjust their whole enterprise to fit the changes of their work force. Older workers typically have a greater commitment to the employer (Kelleher and Quirk, 1973) and are likely to remain with the company longer (Newsham, 1969); they have acquired an extensive understanding of the company and the work environment, and many employers will consequently find it better to retrain them than to replace them with new and younger employees.

Career Planning. Although many situations will require that older workers be retrained for new roles or for specific changes in the work setting, it is preferable to think of retraining as a lifelong process that should be encouraged at every age. One way of approaching this policy is to offer employees several months off for involvement in education every few years. Such sabbaticals not only would provide a valuable interlude for the older worker, allowing the development of new skills, but would provide a regular opportunity for redirecting energies, encouraging the changing of roles within the company, over-coming burnout from continued intense work, and offering younger workers additional jobs through using the positions va-cated by older workers on sabbatical (McConnell, 1979).

Some employers are beginning to take this approach, im-plementing career planning programs in which counseling about training opportunities is provided to workers of all ages and pro-fessional development is encouraged through both in-service training and tuition reimbursement at educational institutions. These programs may go so far as to involve individual self-analy-sis of needs, workshops for groups of employees, and the provi-sion of workbooks that allow employees to plan the future on their own (Schein, 1978). Outplacement counseling may also be included (Walker and Gutteridge, 1979). Programs of this type are frequently available to managerial personnel, but some com-panies, such as IBM, make them available to all employees ("How IBM Avoids Layoffs Through Retraining," 1975). In general, personnel managers who operate such programs feel that they enhance job performance, help the employee use the personnel system more effectively, improve the utilization of employee talent, and reduce turnover without placing undue strain on the personnel system (Walker and Gutteridge, 1979).

Job Redesign. Retraining and career planning will not necessarily ameliorate all the issues involved in the revitalization of the older work force. Some situations may require the modi-fication of work roles and assignments in order for older work-ers to be the most productive. Such modifications are likely to include job redesign, job sharing, work sharing, rotating jobs, or lateral transfers that will result in the most favorable environ-ment for the older worker.

Although considerable variation exists within any age co-hort, after age 60 diversity increases rapidly. This occurs in intellectual abilities, perceptual functioning, reaction speed, motivation, energy level, health, stamina, and self-esteem. Consequently, it is inappropriate to suggest that at any age all persons will need adjustments in the work role. However, more people will need special consideration as age increases. Most often, work tasks requiring speed, strength, complex interactions, and keen senses are those that cause older persons great difficulty. In order for older workers to remain productive, some employers will find it necessary to modify the jobs so that these decrements are minimized.

Often, older workers are able to adapt the work role on their own so that they can compensate without the need for a formal role adjustment. When the worker has little control over the speed or physical demands of the task, as on an assembly line, some help is needed from management in order for the accommodation to occur. As the older work force increases and younger workers become more scarce, greater adjustments are likely to occur in an increasing number of jobs.

Methods of Retraining

Retraining of older workers has been directed primarily toward blue-collar employees. Although it has proved successful in a variety of settings, it should not be assumed that this result occurs without planning and careful execution of the instructional plan. Not only do older blue-collar workers have a lower level of formal education, making them less likely to use effective learning strategies, but they are typically not avid readers, and so their limited verbal facility may result in frequent miscommunication.

Coqueret (1965) points out that although older employees have a rich experiential background to call on, it has typically not been adequately evaluated or organized. Thus, the knowledge they bring to the learning setting is likely to be vague and disorganized; it may be nearly impossible for the older worker to communicate it to others. Too often older employees' insights deal with specific incidents rather than a wide range of general situations. Accordingly, instruction may need to be directed toward helping the worker reexamine, articulate, and generalize what has been previously experienced before the new knowledge can be added to it.

Likewise, older workers are less likely than younger people to be curious about their environment. They are likely to be interested mainly in the items and applications that apply to them and their jobs rather than seeking to understand the many interrelationships that could be explored. This means that for instruction to be well received, it needs to be meaningful and able to be applied.

Although there have been a number of retraining programs for older workers, there has been relatively little conceptualization and organization of the knowledge available. Rather, the training has been done by individual companies that are interested in changing employees' knowledge, skill, or behavior in a particular setting, not in improving instructional techniques. Hence, the literature is devoid of organized means of designing retraining except for the work of Meredith Belbin on a process he called "Discovery Learning." Belbin has taken many of the insights from laboratory studies of learning, combined them with some andragogical applications, and applied them to industrial retraining programs for older workers. They have been shown to work effectively in a variety of training settings in Austria, Sweden, the United Kingdom, and the United States (Barkin, 1970).

Through a series of field experiments coordinated by the Organisation for Economic Co-operation and Development (Paris), the Discovery Method has been shown to work well with employees over the age of 40. However, these projects typically did not include workers over 55. There is little reason to believe, however, that the techniques of the Discovery Method would be less satisfactory with persons older than 55, since they are based on insights from research on older persons.

Discovery Method is an instructional approach in which older workers are helped to discover for themselves answers to a series of problems. The problems are relatively small, are generally sequential, but involve a meaningful whole rather than a subpart that does not have meaning by itself. The employee is helped to discriminate between various functions and gain insight into how a task is performed. The instructor does not lecture or even provide much verbal stimulation other than offering some hints or suggestions if the employee experiences difficulty in completing the task without aid. The experience is made as much like a game as possible so that anxiety level will be reduced and motivation will be enhanced.

Belbin's Discovery Method of learning has many elements that are suggested in the laboratory studies of learning (Chapter Five) and in the maxims of andragogy (Chapter Nine). These include meaningful tasks that are as specific and concrete as possible; tasks that require increasing sophistication and continually challenge the learner; provision of cues and hints on the best way to approach a solution to the problem; rapid feedback when mistakes are made in order to minimize incorrect learning; a low profile for the instructor in which supportiveness, encouragement, and planning are the primary activities; avoidance of interference from previous, current, and future sources; time to practice and consolidate learning before undertaking new tasks; and a clear goal (a job) at the end of the training.

These attributes suggest that the retraining of older workers can be undertaken using strategies very similar to those of other instructional settings. The chief difference may be in the initial motivation of the students. In most adult educational settings, the learner chooses to attend because of an internal want or need. In a retraining setting, the learner may be sent by the employer rather than volunteering to attend. Additional time and energy must then be directed to overcoming any initial anxiety, hesitation, or reluctance to participate. The Discovery Method does this by relating the learning closely to the employee's current or expected role, using the demands of the job to encourage participation.

As with other andragogical approaches, the emphasis is placed on the learning of the student and not on the teaching by the instructor. Discovery Learning strongly emphasizes that the older worker must discover for himself or herself rather than having the instructor explain how the new task is to be performed. This reduces short-term forgetting and involves the older worker much more actively in the learning process.

Results of Retraining

Retraining of older workers is an efficient use of corporate resources. Although it may take the older worker somewhat longer to learn the new skill or knowledge, experience has shown that the retrained worker is likely to be more dependable than the younger employee, have a better attendance record, stay on the job longer, and do as much work (U.S. Congress, 1977). Recurrent education of workers is needed to reduce or prevent obsolescence and structural unemployment, but this need must be met throughout the person's entire work history, not only during the later years.

A variety of retraining programs have been conducted in diverse businesses and industries. The results of these programs and the accompanying research support the contention that the older person is capable of being retrained and that the results are satisfying to both the individual and the employer. The following are some selected conclusions that have been drawn from these studies:

- On-the-job training was effective among hard-core unemployed older workers so long as they had no serious handicaps (Jakubauskas and Taylor, 1969).
- Once recruited and registered, older men were more likely than younger men to complete their training (U.S. Congress, 1967).
- Older persons completing a training program were less likely than nontrainees to depend on social welfare payments as a means of support (Somers, 1967).
- Older persons who completed a training program were more likely to improve their wages than nontrainees (Fillenbaum and Willis, 1976).
- Once trained, older workers were likely to plan to remain with their employers longer than younger trainees (Newsham, 1969).
- The Discovery Method was successfully used to prepare older and younger workers for a major technological change in handling air freight (Mullan and Gorman, 1972).
- Long-service design engineers at General Electric Aerospace Electronic Systems Department were successfully retrained to cope with basic technological advances in the field (Jacobson, 1980).
- International Silver Company converted its facility to the

production of jet engine components and retrained workers averaging 56 years of age as tool-and-die makers (Jacobson, 1980).

· IBM has a lifetime commitment to its workers and retrains and reassigns them regularly with outstanding success ("How IBM Avoids Layoffs Through Retraining," 1975).

In general, then, we are fairly safe in concluding that older workers can be retrained. The difficulty is that few public programs are available to help those older persons who are currently not employed and who need retraining and job placement in later life.

Government Retraining Programs

As indicated previously, most retraining of older workers occurs within the work setting and is sponsored by employers. There are, however, two federal government programs that have helped older people find jobs. In some cases, they offer training designed to increase the employability of the older person. These programs serve the long-term unemployed and low-income persons who have been out of the labor force for some time. They are the CETA program and the SCSEP program of the Older Americans Act.

The Comprehensive Employment and Training Act (CETA) replaced the Manpower Development and Training Act as the federal government's primary attack on unemployment. Though not particularly aimed at older people, three sections of the program have assisted older persons. By 1977, CETA programs had helped 98,000 persons over age 55 find jobs, and Secretary of Labor Ray Marshall expected that an increased number of older workers would be served as the level of unemployment declined (U.S. Congress, 1978). Ahrens (1978) indicated, however, that nearly 6 percent of the persons assisted under CETA Titles II and VI (public service employment) were over age 55 while only 3.3 percent of the persons in CETA training programs were over this age. Thus, older workers appear to be treated as though they were unemployable in the private sector and in need of government help through the creation of jobs for them. Although funding for the CETA program has been drastically reduced, federal government participation in job development and retraining is likely to continue in some form in the future.

The Senior Community Service Employment Program (SCSEP) involves even less training. Under contracts with five national organizations (U.S. Forest Service, Green Thumb, National Council on the Aging, National Retired Teachers Association/American Association of Retired Persons, and the National Council of Senior Citizens), part-time public service jobs for workers over 55 who have experienced chronic unemployment and are below federally established poverty levels have been created. This program has been successful in reintroducing nearly 50,000 older persons into the work force, but this has typically been done without training. When instruction was included, it dealt only with job-seeking skills and attitudes about self and work.

Government interest in this topic is not evident at this time. Four days of hearings on retirement, work, and lifelong learning by the U.S. Senate Special Committee on Aging in 1978 involved only very occasional references to learning, training, retraining, education, or any related topic. It seemed to be the tacit assumption of those testifying, including the Secretaries of Health, Education and Welfare and of Labor, that pensions, Social Security, mandatory retirement, and employment programs were of great importance but that training and education were not even worthy of mention.

Thus, the federal government does not appear to be ready to take the lead in developing retraining programs for older people but has chosen, rather, to create public service jobs for small numbers of persons. Some governmental intervention will be needed if people outside the work force are to gain employment. Corporations may choose to retrain more of their current employees, but there is little evidence to suggest that they will hire older workers and then train them for currently available roles. If they have a choice, they will hire younger workers, minority individuals, women, or other groups before accepting the chance that the older worker can become economically prepared to assume these roles.

Conclusions

Changes in the age structure of the population and in the work force are likely to increase future need for labor force participation by older persons. Although this will require a reversal of current trends, it seems reasonable to expect that it will occur, because increased demands for experienced and productive workers cannot be met by new entrants into the labor force. Hence, current older workers are likely to be viewed more favorably in the future, and employers are expected to find additional incentives to use these older workers.

The result is likely to be later retirement, more part-time work, more job sharing, innovative phased retirement plans, and greater job mobility within the corporation. In each case, job redesign may be required in order to adapt to older workers' desires and abilities. However, this should not be an overwhelming challenge, since older workers' weakness is in the ability to handle heavy, rapid work; these jobs are increasingly handled by automated machinery, the human contribution coming from the monitoring and control of operation.

To date, not many companies have devoted extensive concern or resources to updating or reassigning their older workers. Company commitment will be required to encourage retraining of older workers, to provide lateral transfers rather than linear promotions, and to offer extensive counseling to the workers and their supervisors. The likely result will be a greater commitment by the employer to lifelong retraining so that no worker will become obsolete and the work force will be used effectively and well. This approach to conservation of the corporation's human resources will prove to be of benefit to many companies, as IBM has shown.

Retraining is also extremely beneficial to the older employee. As Belbin and Belbin (1966) pointed out, regardless of the level of skill or education, real employment security comes from the individual's ability to move from one job to another.

Lifelong training is the means by which this flexibility is maintained, because it enhances the individual's ability to adjust, provides new and updated skills, and refreshes learning strategies. Alternation of work and training throughout the adult years will allow the older worker to maintain his or her value to current and future employers.

In order for this training to occur, it is recommended that business and industry work closely with educational institutions in the design and provision of instructional programs (Work in America Institute, 1980). Because pre-service and in-service training need to be coordinated, it will be appropriate for both education and industry to cooperate in determining the emphases and techniques for this instruction. By sharing staff and faculty, it may be possible to draw on the knowledge of both institutions and develop a product that is superior to what would be produced by either undertaking the challenge alone.

Thus, the future is likely to see increased retraining activities and greater concern for the welfare and happiness of the older worker. The knowledge of the instructional process that is provided by educational gerontologists should be of major value in this undertaking and should provide a substantial contribution to business and industry.

12

○I○I○I○I○I○I○I○I○I○I○I○I○I○I○I○I○I○I○I○I○I○I○I○I○I○

Retirement Preparation Programs

Preparation for retirement education is one of the most common forms of organized instruction for older adults. Hence, it is appropriate to provide an overview of the area, to describe the values and problems at the current time, and to identify some of the trends and developments that can be expected in the future. The purpose of this chapter is to deal with retirement preparation as one model of educational programming for middle-aged and older people. This is a valuable model to review because there are currently many retirement preparation programs in operation and because they have much in common. Thus, it is possible to compare their components, emphases, and results. This is one of the few areas in which programming has been sufficiently extensive and sustained to have resulted in the design and dissemination of replicable instructional materials, methods, and curricula. Through the review of published articles and reports on the structures and outcomes of retirement programs, it is possible to gain extensive insight into the scope and impact of this type of educational activity.

Retirement preparation is of great interest today because of the continuing growth in the number of older persons, the expansion of retirement into the middle years of life, the pervasiveness of retirement among persons over age 65, the opportunities that exist in the later years, and the problems facing older persons. Educators, employers, researchers, and older people have become interested and have attempted to expand and improve the quality of preparation for entry into the retirement years.

This chapter will review the literature and programs of retirement preparation. In so doing, it will discuss the current and future aspects of retirement in American society; the value of retirement preparation; the history of its development; some of the program methods, content, and outcomes; a few of the prepared "package" programs; the need for training in the area; and the future opportunities and challenges. Heavy reliance will be placed on the contemporary literature of the field, which is both extensive and widely variable in quality. Much of it deals with the need and value of this type of program, but there are some program reports and conceptual approaches that provide the basis for analysis of the potential and current impact of retirement preparation programs.

Retirement

Before dealing with retirement preparation programs, it is necessary to summarize a few points regarding the nature and extent of retirement itself, which is the object of any preparation program. Preparation for retirement is meaningful only as gauged by the results that occur after the person has left the work force. Retirement is a condition in which a person is forced or allowed to leave the work force, is employed less than full-time, and derives his or her income in part from a retirement pension earned through prior years of service as a jobholder (Atchley, 1976). The person is provided economic support from society but is relieved of most obligations to society (Belbin, 1972). This definition is somewhat vague, since it is very difficult to know when a person is retired, as more and more people move into and out of the work force in second, third, and fourth careers.

Retirement can be seen in several contexts. It is a *process* that begins with informal planning for the situation; it is an *event* that is often accompanied by a ceremony and a gift from the employer and peers; it is a social *role* which replaces that of worker and which is suggested by some to have few clear attributes (Burgess, 1960); and it is a *phase of life* that begins with the retirement event and ends when the person becomes dependent and/or institutionalized and unable to carry out the retirement roles (Atchley, 1976). Retirement is all these things and has become a common circumstance in the lives of most older Americans.

At the turn of the century, nearly 70 percent of all men over the age of 65 were still in the work force. During the eighty intervening years, this condition has been totally reversed, so that now 80 percent of the older men are outside the work force. Older women's employment participation rates have remained approximately the same—8 to 10 percent (Work in America Institute, 1980).

The trend toward retirement of all older people has been accentuated by the growing prevalence of early retirement. Although the normal retirement age differs from one occupation to another, most employers have a pension program that provides some means for early retirement (Patton, 1979). Workers are increasingly choosing these early retirement plans and are extending the number of healthy, vigorous years they spend outside the work force. Expected income in retirement appears to be the main determinant of early retirement (Patton, 1979). Other reasons include the desire to develop new interests or expand current avocations, the wish to enjoy an altered life-style, and the preference for leisure rather than work.

Retirement is also closely associated with the health of the older worker. People who perceive themselves to have health problems are likely to retire early (Barfield and Morgan, 1969). Thus, early retirement may involve movement away from work that is too difficult or pressured for persons with declining health, or it may result from the desire to develop a new set of activities that appear preferable to work. Maintaining one's financial situation after the loss of one's salary, however, is often the key determinant. The Social Security system, employee pensions, and the expansion of capital accumulation are the major causes of both early and normal retirement.

The traditional view among academics and the public has been that work is a valuable and rewarding pastime and that retirement is not desirable. Much has been written about the crisis of retirement, the assumption being that most people experience major problems of adjustment when they confront the transition from full-time work to full-time leisure (Sussman, 1972; Miller, 1965). Early retirement preparation programs were based on this premise and were designed to assist the person in compensating for the trauma of job loss. This condition may have existed in the 1950s and 1960s, but improvements in the health and financial situation of retirees have made this a less typical reaction today. Although some persons still experience severe adjustment difficulties, it is now generally accepted that the majority are able to make the transition with only a small amount of dislocation (Patton, 1979; Atchley, 1971). This probably occurs because of the improved economic condition of many retirees, who experience little or no decrement in their financial life-style resulting from retirement (Ash, 1966). Thus, our approach to retirement and retirement preparation should not be based exclusively on a crisis view but is more appropriately oriented toward assessment of future options, positive planning of preferred activities, and continuing growth in the later stages of life.

This is not to suggest that retirement is an unimportant event or that it does not have significant impacts on the other elements of the person's life. For instance, retirement is likely to affect friendships that were maintained through work, prestige in the community, the amount of discretionary time available, involvement in the vital aspects of the community, autonomy of operation, availability of support services and resources of the employer, the value one places on oneself, state of health, and, of course, financial remuneration. Some of these attributes are more likely to be present in the jobs of highly educated and well-paid professionals (for example, prestige, involvement, and autonomy). Thus, lower-status workers may experience fewer losses from retirement other than the wages involved (Eisdorfer, 1972).

Good adjustment to retirement is encouraged by several variables. First, a positive attitude toward retirement is of great importance (Thompson, 1958). This may include positive attitudes about old age, leisure, and the opportunities that may still lie ahead and may result from a lifelong set of attitudes or a special preparation program preceding retirement. Second, having an accurate preconception of retirement will aid successful adjustment (Thompson, 1958). Many people have had little contact with retirees and have little real understanding of the ways time and resources are spent. Most of us have known someone who had unrealistic plans for retirement—continuous travel, total inactivity, or a career that had little hope of success. Third, adjustment to retirement is facilitated by having made realistic plans for retirement (Thompson, 1958; Ash, 1966). This by itself is not sufficient to achieve success, but combined with the two other elements, it is likely to lead to the successful adjustment of most persons.

Other variables also affect adjustment to retirement. Greene and others (1969) have suggested that the major contributing variables are attitude toward health, retirement income, positive beliefs and attitudes toward retirement, number of retirement activities, attitude toward the company, enjoyment of activities, and plans made for retirement. Thus, there is a complex and interactive relationship among several of the conditions, and collectively these are likely to provide insight into adjustment to the nonwork role.

Most people adjust to retirement reasonably well. A national study by Louis Harris and Associates (1975) reported that nearly two thirds of the retired respondents indicated that retirement had fulfilled their expectations. Although adjustment time varies, the longer a person has been retired, the more likely he or she is to view retirement as positive and satisfying (Shanas, 1958). It does not seem to matter whether the person chooses or was forced to retire. Preretirement attitude and preconceptions of retirement are the key variables in determining adjustment during this period of life (Streib and Schneider, 1971).

Many older people admit regrets about their lives. One typical regret is that they did not plan sufficiently for retirement. Harris and Associates (1975) reported that 26 percent of the retirees indicated that if they had known what the present would be like, they would have saved more, acquired more insurance, or invested more. Fourteen percent would have completed more education, and 9 percent would have planned their careers differently. Specifically preparing for retirement would not have overcome all these problems, but it might have assisted some in planning their financial and interpersonal affairs in order to make the transition to retirement somewhat easier and more pleasant. Heidbreder (1972) found that persons who were poorly adjusted to retirement were twice as likely as the well adjusted to have done little previous planning.

This need is often recognized by persons approaching retirement (Fillenbaum, 1971). Swaboda (1974) reported that 98 percent of his respondents indicated that most people need to plan for retirement, and 77 percent believed that the average person's preparation is probably inadequate. Pyron and Manion (1970) reported that nearly two thirds of their respondents had made almost no financial plans and three fourths had made no health plans. Most people appear to believe that retirement preparation is the responsibility of the individual; yet, they make few plans. They do not generally expect the employer, the government, or community agencies to take the initiative to develop and offer retirement preparation programs.

It would appear, then, that retirement is not a time that is dreaded or a crisis in the lives of most older workers. It is more likely a time which is considered infrequently and about which few concrete plans are made. Those who do think about retirement are likely to make definite plans (McPherson and Guppy, 1979) and to look forward to early retirement. These are typically persons who have high levels of income and education. Thus, there is a great need for retirement planning programs, and considerable value may result from them.

Preparation for Retirement

Most people approaching retirement make some preparations. These may be few and informal, or they may be extensive and obtained through a formal educational program, but there normally occurs some activity in which the person anticipates the approaching reality of retirement and attempts to prepare plans that will be useful in adjusting to the change. Often these preparations are undertaken on a chance basis. If an article in the newspaper is found, it may be read with interest; a friend who has recently retired may be questioned about the experience; or one may review one's current financial situation. At present, however, only a small percentage of the older work force has initiated any formal preparation for retirement. This means that the multiple and interacting adjustments that occur with retirement are approached on a trial-and-error basis with little benefit gained from existing knowledge or experience.

Formal retirement preparation can be undertaken in a number of ways. It may occur through the circulation of printed material on the company's retirement benefits, through individual counseling offered by the personnel department, through group sessions on fringe benefits, or through a comprehensive program of retirement education. Each of these approaches has its value, and each fits under the rubric of retirement preparation. It is the more comprehensive programs that hold the most interest in this discussion, since they address several of the elements of retirement adjustment and provide a means of examining education of older people. Monk and Donovan (1978-1979) have suggested that comprehensive retirement preparation programs would be expected to meet six criteria: (1) counseling or group activities (or both) is the method of program delivery, (2) activities are offered at least five years prior to retirement, (3) activities are offered mainly on employers' time, (4) the program includes more than ten hours of content, (5) the employer takes the initiative and offers the program, and (6) content includes at least the following areas—pension and Social Security, personal financial planning, health and personal care, housing, leisure and part-time employment, and legal aspects. It may not be necessary for community or educational programs to meet all these criteria, but they are likely to include most of these attributes. Comprehensive programs are doubtless in the minority of the existing offerings, but their number appears to be growing as employers increase their commitment to this area (Research and Forecasts, 1979).

These programs address the issue of retirement preparation in its most effective form and provide a means for educational intervention that has the highest chance of improving the lives of retirees. In reviewing the objectives and outcomes of retirement preparation programs, it will be necessary to indicate the differences between comprehensive, educational programs and those in which the employer simply offers a brief analysis of the retirement benefits accrued to the person facing retirement.

Retirement Preparation Programs

Retirement preparation programs have grown rapidly over the past thirty years and now are fairly common in business, industry, education, and community organizations. Because there is no generally accepted definition of the components required for these undertakings to be considered programs, it is difficult to determine their extent and impact. However, comprehensive programs offered to groups of preretirees are variously estimated to have provided information and planning for over 100,000 persons (Reich, 1977) and to have reached nearly 10 percent of current retirees (Monk and Donovan, 1978-1979). This is a wide range of estimates, but regardless of the precise number, it is small in comparison with the number of persons who are retired—currently over 25 million.

People who individually opt to plan for retirement are likely to be those with the highest levels of income and education. People who voluntarily attend retirement preparation programs do not necessarily share these characteristics. Fillenbaum (1971) found that persons who were closer to retirement were more likely to express interest in retirement planning and that persons of lower occupational status more often indicated they would attend than persons in the middle and upper occupational status categories. Monk (1971) reported a similar pattern in which administrative and professional men in their sixties were reluctant to participate in retirement planning. Their savings and investments placed them in good financial condition, but this was due more to a middle-class financial pattern than to saving and planning for retirement.

Instructional programs designed to prepare people for retirement have existed for at least thirty years. In a 1953 article, Donahue asserted that it is fortunately no longer necessary to preface a discussion of preparation for retirement with an argument in its defense. That may have been true, but there are limited data to support the contention that retirement preparation is now available to all persons approaching retirement who would like it. Reich (1977) asserts that over 5,000 persons have been trained to be preretirement group leaders and that they represent 2,000 corporations that are involved in the area. However, many of these programs are very limited in content, emphasizing the company's pension and insurance benefits, and are not comprehensive programs in the sense that Monk and Donovan (1978-1979) have used that term.

The sponsorship of retirement preparation programs falls into three categories—business and industry; colleges, universities, and community service groups; and unions. In sheer quantity of programs, corporate offerings may well be the largest. University and community programs are probably the most comprehensive in content and format, and union programs are quite limited, although they may approach the university programs in content breadth.

Several surveys of corporations and businesses have attempted to measure the extent of current activities in the area. Most have received a fairly small response rate, and so percentage figures should be cautiously used because they reflect the activities of only those who responded, most likely those with the greatest interest and involvement in the area. Donahue (1953) reported a survey of the New York City Sales Executive Club, finding that only 13 percent of the responding companies had any retirement preparation programs. In 1969 Pyron reported that, of one hundred firms surveyed, only twelve had fairly well-developed retirement preparation programs. One exception to the poor response rate was reported by Kalt and Kohn (1975) in a study of forty-six pharmaceutical firms. Forty responded, and nine reported having a preretirement counseling program.

A major survey by Research and Forecasts, Inc. (1979), for the Corporate Committee for Retirement Planning contacted personnel officers and corporate executives of the 1,000 largest companies in the United States. The response rates of these two groups—39 and 34 percent, respectively—indicated some lack of concern. It was especially interesting that 69 percent of the chief executive officers said their corporations had retirement preparation programs, while only 37 percent of the personnel directors indicated such programs existed. It would appear that corporate executives do not agree on whether their current benefits include this activity or not.

A survey by the American Society of Personnel Administration (1980) reported that out of 36 percent of the responding organizations slightly more than half have a preretirement planning program that might be considered comprehensive. Many companies are currently changing their retirement benefits, which is leading to some modification of the retirement planning efforts. This appears to indicate that the companies are concerned with the control of the work force and see preretirement planning as one means of increasing or decreasing retirement by older employees. In this as well as several other reports, the term *preretirement counseling* is used, which may mean an individual discussion of the retirement benefits and the considerations in choosing or postponing retirement. It is likely, then, that at least some of these programs are oriented primarily toward control of the work force and are not undertaken to assist the employee.

Retirement preparation programs offered by colleges and universities are more likely to be of the comprehensive type and to be oriented toward the needs of the older worker. The Universities of Michigan and Chicago were the first to offer well-planned instructional programs in this area. Woodrow Hunter developed a model program at Michigan and provided some of the first evaluative research on the results of the instruction. Other university programs include those at Fordham, Massachusetts, Rhode Island, Rutgers, Southern California, Georgia, Drake, and Oregon. Their activities have collectively provided much of the insight into the value and outcomes of the retirement preparation process and have been used as models for the design of commercial and association programs.

Union programs have not become particularly common. This is puzzling, since many unions have set a priority on moving their older members out of the employment role in order to provide access to promotion for their younger members. To date, however, only the United Auto Workers have found it advantageous to include retirement preparation in their negotiated benefits and to establish nationwide programs for their members.

Although most employees are at least mildly interested in participating in some kind of retirement preparation, there is little consensus on what individual or organization is responsible for developing and offering such assistance. Swaboda (1974) reported that 83 percent of his respondents did not expect the employer to provide comprehensive retirement preparation for them. When they were asked who was responsible, their votes were widely split, 28 percent identifying government agencies, 21 percent community service groups, 18 percent universities, and 13 percent business and industry. These opinions did not seem to be strongly held, and no current institution was generally perceived as having responsibility for fulfilling this need.

Fillenbaum (1971) and Pyron and Manion (1970) report findings contrary to Swaboda's. Both found that employees want company assistance in planning for retirement and that companies that offer such programs have responded to the requests of their workers.

Assumptions in Retirement Planning Programs

The design of a retirement preparation program is based on a series of assumptions that the educational planner makes about the nature of the participants, the constituencies being served, the most effective means of teaching, and the most appropriate outcomes of the program. These preconceptions determine the program's orientation and provide insight into the various elements involved in planning such programs.

Participant Motivation. Monk and Donovan (1978–1979) have suggested that programs differ in their philosophical assumptions. They have identified four models of programs, rational-economic, social, humanistic, and complex, which are consistent with Schein's (1970) images of man. Their first model is titled "rational-economic" and assumes that people have economic self-interest as their major motivation. Retirement preparation, then, is best oriented toward rechanneling the achievement motive into second careers, volunteerism, and other activities that will maintain status and income.

The second model, "social perspective," suggests that people's need is to belong and to be accepted by others. Since retirement often results in a shrinkage of the social world, retirement preparation programs should rely primarily on group activities, which will not only provide information but allow for the development of new social contacts and build new support systems for the future. Skill training in developing new social roles and increasing interpersonal competence is a major part of any such program.

"Humanistic existential" is the third model. It assumes that the primary motivation is the striving for meaning in life and that self-esteem is enhanced as creative capacities are developed. This model would support the facilitation of lifelong learning and the continuing growth of the individual throughout the entire life span. Since meaning is likely to vary from one person to another, the learning is often self-directed and based on the person's previous experience, not on some preordained set of understandings.

The fourth model is the "complex systemic," which presumes that people are complex and highly variable. Thus, each person's interests, concerns, and motivational patterns will be unique. Retirement needs will vary, and so case diagnosis, planning, and the provision of information based on the individual's needs will be necessary in program development. Retirement is one stage in a long progression of life stages and should be addressed on a personal basis related to the history and current situation of the individual. These four models offer diverse views of the nature of the client for preretirement education and allow us to consider the outcomes of the programs from several points of view.

Retirement Preparation Constituencies. Another way of

viewing the field of retirement preparation is to consider the constituencies for the programs and suggest some of the differing emphases that may result. Manion (1976) suggested that four interested groups can be considered the primary constituencies in the development and operation of any retirement program. These are the employer, academic researchers, lifelong educators, and the preretiree himself or herself. Each of these groups has a major stake in the design and operation of any retirement preparation program, but each has a different set of objectives and expectations from participation.

The employer may have a number of expectations for any retirement preparation program that is offered during the workday, on company premises, or with the assistance of the personnel or training department. First, such a program may be an expression of the company's social responsibility regarding the welfare of valued employees (an interest in assuring that the later years of persons who are a part of the company "family" are as productive and satisfying as possible) and a way to improve both employee and labor relations. A second consideration may be the positive public relations value that may result from the program. Providing a model fringe benefit of this type may generate praise from others in the corporate sector as well as those in the community at large. The company-sponsored retirement preparation program may thus be a reward for a faithful employee that will cost the company little but generate good will in the community.

Another motivation of the employer may be to control the work more closely. Since many companies must retire some employees in order to hire or promote others, it is necessary to find a mechanism to ensure that the appropriate number of older workers leave the work force on a regular basis. The opposite situation is true for other employers. They find it impossible to hire sufficient numbers of skilled workers, and so they try to reduce the number of retiring employees. Thus, their objective is to control the work force by encouraging valued older employees to postpone retirement. In either case, the basic motivation in conducting a preretirement preparation program is to benefit the company by increasing worker morale and productivity while the worker is on the job; the personal preferences and values of the individual employee are of secondary importance.

Academic researchers, the second constituency of preretirement preparation programs, are interested in this area for very different reasons. They are collectively attempting to understand the psychological and social behavior of a large group of persons who are facing a new life transition—retirement. Retirement preparation programs are a recently developed intervention, and there is a desire to determine the extent of their success in effecting changes in retirement adjustment and satisfaction. Thus, the researcher is most concerned with determining the objectives and the outcomes of such programs and developing instruments that will accurately measure the changes that result.

Adult educators, the third constituency, are involved in retirement preparation because it is one of the components in a lifelong program of education. The orientation is more toward the value of education than toward this particular period of life or the adjustments involved. Retirement is considered to be a time that offers opportunity for educational programming. Thus, the lifelong educator is interested in many types of education and is not limited primarily or exclusively to this area of practice.

Finally, retirement preparation is of interest to the middle-aged and older worker who wants to ensure successful accommodation to the new events and circumstances that will occur with retirement. The preretiree may be motivated to seek information out of curiosity and exhibit little emotional commitment to the coming change. Interest, however, may be much more focused and directed toward the perceived or real difficulties that are likely to face both the worker and the spouse in future years. These are likely to center on financial and health concerns (Holley and Feild, 1974) but may include use of free time, marital relationships, housing, social contacts, and nutrition.

This book is written primarily from the point of view of the academic interested in research and lifelong education, especially education in the later stages of life. Consequently, among Manion's four categories, the middle two are closest to the orientation presented here. The interests of the employer will be considered but are not the primary reference point. The concerns of the individual retiree are the ultimate consideration, but they are often combined with others, so that it is the collective interest rather than that of any individual which is paramount.

Retirement Planning Program Methods

Comprehensive, group-oriented retirement planning programs have been developed through the use of a variety of instructional methods. Some of these rely heavily on an expert to provide information to the preretirees, while others tend to draw more heavily on the existing knowledge and insight of the participants, with the facilitator simply guiding the discussion through various steps. The programs may be viewed as falling along a continuum with traditional, teacher-focused instruction (pedagogy) on one end and student-centered instruction (andragogy) on the other. Lynch (1977) has provided a very helpful discussion of program methods and uses this conceptualization to clarify the instructional emphases of several current and historical program models. He suggests that preretirement programs can be categorized into four groups, the first being the most content-oriented and the last being more related to allowing the participants to learn for themselves.

Presentation/Audience Mode. Many retirement preparation programs focus heavily on the provision of information about retirement. They use a lecture format in which an expert provides an overview of knowledge in the area. This typically means that the audience is not actively involved in the instructional process and that the content is not specifically selected in response to the audience's perceived needs. Communication typically moves in only one direction, the participants being responsible only for sifting out that information which is useful to them.

In order to offer this type of program, the sponsoring

agency need not have an educator or trainer but only needs access to an expert in each of the areas covered. This may make the program easy to organize but does not provide for any control of the information presented or of the biases or stereotypes that may be conveyed by the expert speaker.

Stimulus/Discussion Mode. The second category of instructional method still involves the presentation of some information to the group but allows for considerably more reaction and discussion than the previous mode. The information may be presented through films, case studies, planning, worksheets, or other means of facilitating the initial thinking and discussion process. The discussion is still reactive, since it is generated through the planned presentation, but the participants' active involvement is encouraged throughout the program. Hunter's trigger films, short case studies, and TAT-type pictures are good examples of the ways a structured stimulus can be used to direct a learning discussion (Hunter, 1968a). AIM's Retirement Planning Seminar is another example of this type of program; filmstrips and audiotapes are used to direct the topic of discussion (Action for Independent Maturity, 1978). The University of Georgia has used this approach by broadcasting lectures on educational television. Thorson (1976) reported that the group discussions following the programs were considered by the participants to cause the greatest learning. This method provides a means of conveying some information but at the same time allows the participants to add their own experience and to explore the meaning for their lives.

Workshop Mode. The third mode of presentation involves small groups of persons working together to seek information and insight on those topics that are of interest to them within the area of retirement preparation. In this approach, the participant is the source of the information as well as the recipient of the learning. The content emphasis is typically on attitudes, feelings, and concerns rather than on the dissemination of facts. A leader is not needed for each small group, as general instructions can be provided ahead of time and informational reading can be done outside the group sessions.

Facilitated Interaction Group Mode. A trained facilitator

can work with a small group of participants. This may involve the provision of some information, but the emphasis is more likely to be placed on shared concerns and experience which will encourage the development of a group that is mutually supportive. Self-awareness is encouraged through this process, and problem-solving skills are developed in relation to the issues generated. Manion (1976) has developed this mode over the past ten years and has found good response. It might be called the group counseling format, since it involves the methods of group dynamics to help individuals and couples prepare for retirement.

These modes of presentation cover most of the emphases in current preretirement programming. Obviously, the length of session, format, and leadership vary from one type of program to another. However, it would appear from the literature that most organized programs last from six to twenty hours, generally meeting once a week for one to two hours and lasting six to ten weeks. Some programs are conducted in an intensive format (all day for one or two days), but most appear to have been designed around the assumption that greater amounts of time between sessions allow implementation of the planning and consideration of the new information presented.

Holley and Feild (1974) have described an interesting alternative to this pattern. A privately owned utility firm offers the retirement planning over a five-year period beginning when the worker reaches age 60. That year, the person attends a session dealing with an orientation to retirement, the psychological effects of retirement, and the uses of leisure time. On reaching age 61, the worker is invited to attend a session on health changes in later life. Financial affairs are discussed in the third year and insurance in the fourth, and finally a session is conducted on Medicare. In this manner the employee is brought into contact with the personnel department annually and is helped to examine one topic each year during the five years preceding the normal age of retirement.

Most of the retirement preparation programs described in the literature attempt to include the spouse in the planning program. This is not always possible, since the spouse may also be employed, and about two thirds of employer preparation programs are offered during the workday (Siegel and Rives, 1978). Although participation of the spouse would appear to be a defensible approach, there are few available data to indicate its value or the effect of having diverse or homogeneous groupings. There is some debate on whether it is preferable to include blue-collar and white-collar workers in the same planning session (Reich, 1977). In general, homogeneity seems more appropriate, but mixed groups have been shown to work well, and so there is no consensus on the best grouping of clients.

Outcomes of Retirement Preparation Programs

Preparation for retirement has many potential values for the employer, the community, and the older worker. It is generally accepted that attainment of these values adequately offsets the expense of the programs and makes them defensible to the sponsors.

Five potential positive results of participation in a retirement preparation program can be identified.

Development of a better understanding of the normal changes that occur as a result of aging and retirement. This would involve topics such as health, financial, family, role, social, and housing changes. It might also include differentiation between the normal changes associated with age and those that are pathological. Instruction in this area would likely reduce some of the uncertainty about retirement by correcting prevalent stereotypes and misconceptions.

Development of planning and interpersonal communication skills and the understanding that the person can control some part of his or her future. Results in this area would include the ability to carry out a self-diagnosis, to identify options, to develop problem-solving skills, to become psychologically involved in planning, and to be committed to taking action that will maintain independence.

Development of a personal plan for retirement. Such a plan would include financial, health, housing, leisure, and social aspects; realistic expectations about retirement; awareness of current life-style and values; means of replacing the work role; and the interests and preferences of the spouse. It would lead to continued personal and social growth.

Development of a positive attitude toward retirement and the potential for continued success and growth. This would include an awareness of one's fears and values, a reduction in anxiety about the retirement process, and the adoption of a positive anticipation of the retirement period.

Development of successful adjustment to retirement. With the achievement of successful adjustment, the person would have improved morale, higher life satisfaction, and greater self-actualization during the retirement period.

Questions have been raised, however, about the extent to which these outcomes do occur, and some criticisms have been voiced that there are insufficient data to support the claims that retirement preparation programs have positive results. Kasschau (1974) reviewed the literature and concluded that programs that attempted to facilitate planning for retirement as their goal were more likely to be successful than programs that had a counseling (attitude change) focus. Others (Reich, 1977) have argued that the affective portions of the programs are of greatest value and address the real needs of the older workers; they are the programs that should be expanded and encouraged. It is therefore of crucial importance to review the small amount of research that has measured the results of comprehensive preretirement planning programs and to assess the extent to which these programs have been shown to result in measurable change.

A review of these studies suggests that the researchers have generally presented their findings in such a way that they address the five areas of results. Each of these five areas will be described in order to indicate the extent to which research support for significant improvement is present.

Increase in information possessed. Since many retirement preparation programs are designed to provide information to the middle-aged and older worker, one expected outcome of most programs is an increase in the amount of knowledge about retirement and greater clarity and accuracy regarding the perceptions of what retirement will be. Several studies indicate that this can indeed result. Both Hunter (1968b) and Mack (1958) reported that greater information was one of the major results of their programs with hourly-rated workers. Fisher (1974) indicated that the increased knowledge acquired by his respondents resulted in a reduced number of denigrating perceptions of retirement, and Boyack (1978) found that minority individuals participating in a preretirement program acquired greater information about community resources, finances, and health. Glamser and DeJong (1975) compared the results of a comprehensive preretirement discussion program and an individual counseling session and found that more knowledge was acquired through the discussion format. Charles (1971) reported that participants changed their level of concern regarding several areas (Social Security, Medicare, legal planning, leisure activities) depending on their perceived preparation or lack of it in each area. Thus, traditional content learning has been shown to occur in those programs that measured this result.

Making specific plans for retirement. Since some people tend not to plan ahead and many are loath to contemplate and plan for retirement, a second important effect of retirement preparation programs is that they can result in a greater number of realistic plans being made for retirement. Glamser and DeJong (1975) reported that persons completing their program were better prepared for retirement, had reduced the level of anxiety about retirement, and had a clearer perception of what to expect after leaving the work force. Christrup and Thurman (1973) reported that persons completing a General Services Administration preretirement planning program were noticeably better prepared for retirement, and Hunter (1968a) reported that participants in a planning program made more plans for retirement than nonparticipants. Ash (1966) found that preretirees who expected "no special problems" in retirement and retirees who experienced "no special problems" were more likely to have planned for retirement than others. These studies indicate that the knowledge gained through a preretirement planning program is likely to be translated into personal and family plans and that, as Charles (1971) reported, these individuals are likely to enjoy planning more.

Taking action to implement plans. Several studies have attempted to determine the extent to which middle-aged and older workers have carried out their plans for retirement. This is a crucial test of the program's impact, for without any action the plans are not of real value. Hunter (1968a) reported that his participants did put their plans into practice. Fitzpatrick (1979) indicated that persons completing the National Council on the Aging (NCOA) retirement planning program were able to complete the program's performance objectives, most of which were designed to measure actions taken after the course had been completed. Tiberi, Boyack, and Kerschner (1978) reported behavioral change in health, legal, and economic preparations. Glamser and DeJong (1975) found that their participants took the suggested action steps, and Bowman and others (1970) reported that on any individual topic up to 25 percent of the participants sought out additional information or undertook some directly related action. Thus, it is clear, at least from these reports, that the information and plans are very often translated into action.

Positive attitude toward retirement. Improving the attitude toward retirement has been a consistent objective of retirement preparation programs. Ash (1966) has suggested that positive attitudes toward retirement are related to having made retirement plans. Mack (1958), Tiberi, Boyack, and Kerschner (1978), and Bowman and others (1970) reported positive attitude change in respondents who participated in their planning program. Glamser and DeJong (1975), however, found little improvement in attitudes toward retirement, since their participants entered the program with such positive perceptions that additional improvement was difficult to achieve on the measures they used. Hunter (1968b) reported a similar problem of measurement. Boyack (1977) found positive attitude change among the minority individuals participating in her program. Thus, not all findings have indicated a significant positive change, mainly because the participants had positive attitudes when entering the program, but in each case the tendency was in the positive direction.

Better adjustment to retirement. Since improvement in the adjustment to and satisfaction in retirement is the major goal of retirement preparation programs, measurements in these areas are of utmost importance. Charles (1971) reported an increase in self-perceived personal competence and personal worth, and Fisher (1974) reported that continuing education enhanced retirement life-styles. Bolton (1976) reported an increase in self-perceived personality change. Meyer (1975) addressed the topic slightly differently. He measured the extent to which a retirement preparation program affected the individual's personal development and progress toward self-actualization. He indicated that movement in both areas resulted from the program. Eteng (1972) reported that the retirement preparation program as well as the additional reading and planning that accompanied it were found to increase the retiree's level of satisfaction with retirement and with the associated life changes. Palmore (1982) reported that significantly better adjustment resulted from a preretirement planning program offered by Duke University. Participants showed statistically significant improvements on health, life satisfaction, and social integration measures when compared with a control group. Thus, there appears to be consistent support for better retirement adjustment as a result of retirement planning programs.

It may be concluded from this review that several researchers who have measured the results of participation in a comprehensive retirement preparation program have identified positive consequences resulting from the experience. Beneficial results have generally been assumed to occur in the areas of knowledge gain and development of plans for retirement. They have been less widely recognized to occur in the areas of initiating action steps, improving attitude toward retirement, and adjusting to retirement. It would appear that a program can be designed to result in any of these outcomes, but the best programs can bring results in all five categories.

The findings cited here will not convince all the critics, however. Much yet remains to be learned about the effect of retirement preparation programs. Many of the evaluations are not rigorous studies, and both instruments and methods need refinement. Likewise, few studies have included control groups in order to confirm that the program was in fact the cause of any observed change. More attention also needs to be given to the comparison of results of various programs. Since the instructors, content, and format may be quite different, it is inappropriate to assume that all programs will obtain all the results previously described.

These concerns notwithstanding, it is nonetheless impressive that an educational intervention typically consisting of less than twenty hours is able to achieve consistently positive outcomes at all. This investment of time is considerably less than the number of hours that the average middle-aged adult watches television in a normal week (*Nielsen Report on Television*, 1980), and to suggest that this small intervention will result in lasting, measurable change in information, plans, actions, attitudes, and adjustment to retirement is a significant accomplishment. The literature shows surprisingly strong support for the efficacy of retirement planning programs and lends credence to the value of education for middle-aged and older people.

Content of Retirement Preparation Programs

The length and sponsorship of retirement preparation programs are likely to have a major impact on their content. Short programs such as those typically offered by employers are likely to concentrate almost exclusively on the financial aspects of retirement. In fact, they are likely to deal primarily with the pension, profit-sharing, or insurance benefits available in the company's retirement package. The longer, more comprehensive programs are likely to include other topics, especially legal affairs, health, psychological change, role losses, and living arrangements.

In most programs, the first session provides an overview of the entire course and includes a series of activities designed to help participants reduce their anxiety about the learning situation and retirement generally. This session stimulates interest in the topic, helps the participant get to know the instructor and other learners, and begins a sharing process that will aid realization that each of them is facing similar situations and concerns. The development of interest and involvement is a key objective of the first session because the participant is not required to continue attendance and the development of a sense of commitment and expectancy is likely to maintain participation.

The remaining sessions include a number of topics, which may be organized and ordered in a variety of ways. Since finances are a salient concern, they are often taken up during the second session. Presentations and discussions on this topic usually involve government programs such as Social Security and Supplemental Security Income, annuities, pensions, investments, budgeting, the effect of inflation, financial planning, estate planning, and life insurance. Depending on the length and organization of the program, this topic may require two or more sessions. It may be followed by a session on the legal aspects of retirement. This might include discussion of drawing up a will, creating a trust, gift and estate taxes, sale of the homestead, income tax benefits of old age, and similar topics. Often the session will include some information on the ways an attorney, a tax consultant, a trust officer, or an investment counselor can be useful in planning the financial and legal aspects of later life.

The third major topic generally is health. This is a principal concern for middle-aged and older people because the stereotypical retiree experiences illness, dependency, and disability. In reality, most older people live relatively healthy lives, requiring only modest accommodations to the chronic conditions they experience. This topic often includes several parts: a discussion of the typical physiological changes that occur with aging; an examination of the most common illnesses of later life; awareness of the means of self-diagnosis for specific illnesses; encouragement of preventive health activities such as exercise, good nutrition, reduced stress, and avoidance of smoking, drinking, and obesity; awareness of community agencies and programs providing specific health-related programs; and health insurance, including Medicare and Medicaid. The distinction between illness and old age is stressed, and the potential for healthy, productive years after retirement is emphasized.

The health session(s) often involves the participation of a physician or a nurse and includes ways in which health practitioners can be used to maintain good health into the later years.

A fourth topic is the psychological changes that occur with retirement. The session may be called mental health, adjustment to retirement, attitudes toward retirement, personal growth, or self-development, but the emphasis in each case is on the psychological changes and on how adjustment can be facilitated. A part of this session may deal with interpersonal relationships, changes in husband/wife relations, sexuality in later life, self-image, and trauma that may result from the death of the spouse or other close relatives and friends. Many programs emphasize the need to replace lost relationships with new ones, the importance of staying active, and the ways a retiree can contribute to others as well as being concerned about himself or herself. This emphasis on serving others is familiar to the current cohort of retirees, and they respond well to the suggestion of voluntary service.

A fifth topic usually included in a comprehensive program is role change resulting from retirement. Since the work role is primary in many people's lives, its loss needs to be recognized, discussed, and replaced. This topic would include some discussion of the feelings people have about their jobs, the changes in social relationships that will occur with elimination of the job, the alternative roles that are available in retirement, the effects role change can have on the family, and the process of replacing the work role. This segment may emphasize opportunities for the individual with increased leisure time. If the latter approach is taken, it will usually include discussion of hobbies, part-time work, volunteer possibilities, membership organizations that offer opportunities, educational offerings, travel programs, and other means of profitably using the additional time that is now available.

A final major topic may be the living arrangements available in later life. Since many people choose to leave the family home, some understanding of the options is needed. This would include discussion of the values of one's current housing; renting out a portion of the house; moving to an apartment, condominium, or smaller house; moving to a retirement community or warmer climate; sharing housing with a friend; and living in a retirement home, nursing home, or extended care facility. The options must be dealt with in both financial and psychological terms because a decision that appears advisable to an outsider may be totally unacceptable to the individual. Consequently, both information sharing and exploring the meaning of the home are desired and needed.

There are many ways to organize the content of a retirement preparation program, and there are other topics that could be included or emphasized. However, the preceding list is a fairly typical categorization of content areas, and it covers the basic topics of a comprehensive program.

Existing Retirement Preparation Programs

Retirement preparation programs have been developed in enough places and to such a degree that there are a number of them that may be considered models that can be purchased or replicated. They typically include an instructional plan, materials for the preretirees, audiovisual aids, reading lists, and evaluative exercises. These programs differ in emphasis and length. Several will be described. Table 3 compares their length and the topics covered.

AIM. The Action for Independent Maturity retirement planning program was developed by the American Association of Retired Persons (AARP) with the objective of motivating people aged 50-65 to plan actively for their retirement years. Two types of programs are available. The first type is an eight-part seminar series using a group discussion format, a series of booklets, and accompanying filmstrips. Each session, designed to accommodate 20-25 people, uses advance reading of case histories and follow-up exercises to be completed at home. The second type of program is an eight-part lecture series designed to reach large groups of 50-100 people. One-hour lectures are delivered by specialists, followed by questions and answers. Consultants from AIM and outside experts are used frequently for the presentation of the lectures and seminar series.

Table 3. Retirement Preparation Programs.

Developer	Title	Length of Program	Topics Included
American Association of Retired Persons/ National Retired Teachers Association 215 Long Beach Blvd. Long Beach, Calif. 90801	Action for Independent Maturity (AIM)	16–20 hours	Challenges of Retirement Health and Safety Housing and Locating Legal Affairs Attitudes and Role Adjustment Meaningful Use of Time Sources of Income Financial Planning
National Council on the Aging 1828 L Street, NW Washington, D.C. 20036	Retirement Planning Program	16–20 hours	Life-Style Planning Financial Planning Being Healthy Interpersonal Relationships Living Arrangements Leisure Time New Careers and Community Service
Manpower Education Institute 127 East 35th Street New York, N.Y. 10016	Ready or Not	15 hours	Introduction Financial Planning Consumer Education Health Housing and Living Arrangements Employment Leisure
Leland P. Bradford University Associates 8517 Production Ave. P.O. Box 26240 San Diego, Calif. 92126	Preparing for Retirement: A Program for Survival	15 hours	Facing the Reality of Retirement The Use of Time Family Relationships You and Retirement Seeking Support Services

Organization	Program	Length	Topics
Retirement Planning Services 235 East 57th Street Suite 48 New York, N.Y. 10022	A Preretirement Guide for Singles	Not applicable	Options in Transition Leisure for a Lifetime You're Always Worth Something (employment) Legally There Be It Ever So Humble (housing) Financial Focus
Levi Strauss Levi Plaza 1155 Battery Street San Francisco, Calif. 94106	Discovery Unlimited	14 hours	It Gets Better After 50 To Your Health Make It Legal Home Sweet Home Have the Time of Your Life Budgeting on Retirement The Financial Plan The Benefits of Your Retirement
Xerox Corporation 800 Long Ridge Road Stamford, Conn. 06904	Planning for Successful Retirement	10 hours	Barriers to Planning Myths and Facts About Retirement Sources of Income Social Security Company Pensions Budgeting Estate Planning Physical and Mental Health Leisure Resources Work and Continuing Education Living Arrangements Changing Relationships

(continued on next page)

Table 3. Retirement Preparation Programs, Cont'd.

Developer	Title	Length of Program	Topics Included
Retirement Services, Inc. P.O. Box 5325 Eugene, Oreg. 97405	Plan Now for Your Retirement— Free to Do, Free to Be	20 hours	Retirement: Dreams, Doubts, Strategies Aging: Older Myths Versus New Facts Financial Planning Thinking About Where You Will Live Activities: Free to Do, Free to Be Your Relationships with Other People Personal Health Management Peace of Mind—Achieve the Vital Balance A Fresh Look at Yourself Self-Fulfillment: Lifelong Challenge
United Auto Workers 8731 East Jefferson Ave. Detroit, Mich. 48214	Planning for Successful Living	12 hours	Planning for Tomorrow Begins Today The Costs and Benefits of Social Security Adding Up Your Retirement Dollars Your Good Health and Personal Happiness Protection Under Law and Your Consumer Rights Retirement Living and Your Future

NCOA. The National Council on the Aging developed a structured retirement program designed for employees in their middle years. Performance objectives, content, strategy, and time allocation are outlined for each of eight sessions. The program is essentially self-contained with no need for outside specialists. Preretirement content is provided in a leader's manual, a participant's manual, and a narrated slide presentation.

Ready or Not. The Manpower Education Institute developed and distributes a retirement planning program entitled "Ready or Not," which consists of ten thirty-minute video cassettes and a workbook that supplements the recorded presentations. The workbook contains information on selected retirement topics and questions that increase preretirees' awareness of planning needs. The video cassettes and workbook may be used in combination or as separate learning tools for preretirees. A typical session is composed of a videotape presentation followed by a group discussion, led by a group member.

Preparing for Retirement: A Program for Survival. Leland P. Bradford, founder of the National Training Laboratories, has developed a program that prepares people to meet the emotional and psychological challenges of retirement. It is designed to be used independently or to be integrated into a comprehensive program that anticipates financial, health, legal, and environmental needs. The program consists of five three-hour sessions, with an emphasis on experiential learning in small groups. The program package includes a facilitator's manual and a participant's workbook. The facilitator's manual consists of a lecturette on the psychological content, required materials, and procedure for conducting the session. The participant's workbook includes summaries, guidelines, home study materials, and lists of suggested readings.

A Preretirement Planning Guide for Singles. Developed by Judy Solwen of Retirement Planning Services, this self-help guide is designed for the divorced, separated, widowed, or "always single" person. The guidebook contains exercises to help preretirees determine retirement goals, preferred leisure activities, work opportunities, legal needs and options, housing preferences, and financial status. On completion of the guidebook, preretirees should be able to establish goals in later life, choose options leading to a smooth transition from employment to retirement, and make retirement a beginning rather than an end. The guidebook is useful as an adjunct to a group program or as an independent planning guide.

Levi Strauss. This corporation has designed and implemented a seven-session retirement planning series titled "Discovery Unlimited." Leader's workbooks contain content information about planning and conduct of the sessions, with outside resources and experts being frequently used for financial, legal, and health components. Two-hour meetings include slides, debates, role playing, and retirement games to encourage group participation. The narrated slide presentation features scenes from Levi factories where one can observe the middle-aged or older worker. Cartoon figures are superimposed on actual work settings, thereby personalizing the generic retirement planning information for most Levi employees.

Xerox Corporation. "Planning for Successful Retirement" is a two-day, intensive preretirement education program based on the PREP model developed at the Andrus Gerontology Center, University of Southern California. The program is designed to provide participants with the skills and information necessary to plan effectively for a positive transition into retirement. This objective is accomplished through identification of planning needs, exposure of myths and facts, techniques of problem solving, and concepts of motivation. A leader's manual contains lecturettes, group activities, and work skills. Small-group activities and group sharing are emphasized throughout the program.

Plan Now for Your Retirement—Free to Do, Free to Be. This program, designed as a one- or two-day workshop for employees and spouses, focuses on general retirement and financial planning issues. Participants are encouraged to examine their individual needs, attitudes, values, feelings, and fears that may occur before and during the retirement experience. The program is usually presented as a joint endeavor by Retirement Services, Inc., and the sponsor. However, when requested, qualified "in-house" personnel are trained to present the program. Accompanying materials are a leader's guide, a slide presentation, audio cassettes, and a participant's workbook. Additionally, there are ten retirement planning guidebooks on various retirement subjects.

Plan for Successful Living. In 1978 the United Auto Workers (UAW), with support from the Fund for the Improvement of Postsecondary Education, developed a preretirement planning program for members of the UAW. The major components of the six-part program are slide/tape presentations, participant workbooks, coordinator manuals, and resource material. Participant workbooks contain information on each topic, exercises, checklists, retiree case histories, evaluations, and quotations from UAW leaders. Procedures for promotion and recruitment and a step-by-step guide to conducting each session are presented in the coordinator's manual.

Preretirement Facilitators

People who plan and conduct retirement preparation programs, here referred to as program facilitators, face demanding responsibilities for the planning and operation of retirement programs. Yet currently few colleges or universities are preparing people for this role. The facilitator has a variety of responsibilities—program planning, administration, leading discussions, lecturing, choosing and orienting guest speakers, developing or selecting written and audiovisual materials, recruiting participants, securing financial resources, designing and conducting the evaluation, and coordinating all of the preceding. Facilitation is a major and complex task.

Perhaps the most difficult part of the task is the determination of what elements of the program the facilitator will try to undertake himself or herself and what parts will be assigned to consultants or other specialists. It is nearly impossible for the facilitator to become an expert on all the content areas included in comprehensive programs. However, the extensive use of consultants is expensive, leads to limited content integration, and is prone to the excesses of any speaker's whims. Probably the best compromise is for the facilitator to host each session and to conduct as many as possible—usually those that provide the overview and conclusion and those on psychological adjustment and the use of leisure time. Others may be undertaken as knowledge and experience increase.

Even these "process" portions of the program require the facilitator to have a good grasp of group dynamics, interpersonal communication, and instructional planning; knowledge of the processes of aging; and a firm belief in the learning abilities of middle-aged and older persons. A variety of professional and disciplinary backgrounds may prepare a person for this position, but today most facilitators slide into this role and learn on the job rather than obtaining formal preparation before undertaking this assignment.

Issues in Preretirement Planning

From the point of view of an educator and researcher, the field of preretirement preparation still has several issues facing it that must be addressed in the near future. These are diverse, as is the field, but they are nonetheless important, for they will determine in many ways the direction that the field will take in the future. A few of these will be discussed here; doubtless others will develop as time passes and the area matures further.

First, there remains the need for continuing and replicable research on the outcomes of retirement preparation programs. Although the data reported above suggest some very positive results, the methodology and statistical procedures are not as carefully drawn as would be desirable. It will be important for each major program to be evaluated in an unbiased fashion and for designs to be used that test not only the immediate results of the program but the effect after the person retires. Aside from Hunter's study (1968a), careful longitudinal investigations have been absent.

Second, the area needs some initial planning regarding the control of program quality. Currently, no standards exist for content, facilitators, or materials. Many new individuals and groups are entering the field of retirement preparation, and their background and motives leave much to be desired. If this area is to continue to grow and to gain the respect of the educational, research, and human service communities, some minimal standards will be needed, as will some means of enforcing them. Since this area is both new and growing, it is vulnerable to exploitation by those who see the possibility of reaping financial rewards from both employers and employees.

Third, programs will need to be developed and tested for various types of audiences. Some of the programs have been used with both blue-collar and white-collar workers; a few have been tested with minority audiences; and some have been developed for widows. Program developers appear to assume that a program will work equally well for all audiences. This may be true, but we have no data at present to confirm or refute that contention. Consequently, more information is needed on what kinds of programs achieve best results with differing audiences.

Finally, training programs for program facilitators are needed in order to assure greater skills and insights by the persons who are the key to achieving a successful program. Although a few courses currently exist, they are often brief overviews that do not provide sufficient depth of understanding in the complex array of factors needed for successful facilitation.

13

Providing Access
to Education

Educational programs for older people are offered by numerous organizations, institutions, and agencies. This variety of providers results in diversity in the purposes, methods, format, and level of content offered within these many programs. Although much is unknown about the present delivery system for offering educational experiences to older people, it is useful to gain some perspective on the distribution of these programs.

In a sense, this chapter responds to the question "Who is offering education to older people?" The focus is on describing the extent and kind of instructional offerings, where they are located in the community, what kinds of curricular and format variations are involved, and what accommodations the providers have made to better serve the older client. The chapter will examine the current state of education for older people from an organizational point of view, describing the "system" of instructional networks that exist.

This reference to a system should not be interpreted to mean that any community has a conscious plan for the development and delivery of educational services for older people so that coverage of interests, levels, and geographical areas is complete. This has yet to occur. However, in many communities a variety of educational options are available to older people, and these options provide us with insight into what could be developed if any community had the desire and resources to create a comprehensive program.

The programs described here are purposely limited to those that are most precisely educational in nature and those that are likely to involve people in collective instructional activities. This limitation allows maintenance of focus on instruction of older people, but it does exclude many ancillary activities offered by educational and community agencies and institutions. For instance, some of the programs not included are the conduct of conferences for or about older people, recreation programs, support or therapy groups, the provision of community services (such as nutrition, transportation, or health care), the printing and distribution of materials, the encouragement of volunteer programs, the development of advocacy groups, or the provision of community service through a speakers' bureau or information and referral services. I also omit any discussion of gerontology instruction or the preparation of people (young or old) to work in the field of aging. All these are worthwhile and legitimate programs, but none is basically an educational effort designed to help older people learn, change, function better, or enjoy life more.

Sources of Information

Knowledge of the instructional programs for older people in colleges and universities, community colleges, community organizations, libraries and museums, corporations and businesses, and public and private schools will never be complete or totally current. There are too many organizations, and the programs are created and modified so rapidly that reporting will always lag behind action. Anyone interested in the field of education for older people knows there has been momentous growth over the past thirty years, but it is worthwhile to assess the extent of change we are witnessing and to estimate the outline of the contemporary situation.

The best data available come from a variety of surveys that have attempted to determine the number and type of programs being offered in various organizations or geographical areas. Several of these have been limited surveys, involving a small initial sample reduced still further by nonresponse. A few have been national in scope, providing a more comprehensive view of current program development. Few have collected comparable data, and so caution should be used in generalizing or comparing them, but they are the best information currently available on the extent of educational programs for older people in a variety of agencies and organizations.

The oldest of these studies is a survey of 136 colleges and universities, conducted by Reals in 1954, which indicated that 36 had some programs for older people (Hendrickson and Barnes, 1964). Tuckman (1955) reported that, in an informal survey, he had located 28 colleges that had educational activities in aging, although most of the participants were service providers enrolled in continuing education designed to sensitize them to the needs of the elderly. Hendrickson and Barnes's (1964) survey of Ohio colleges and universities found 13 institutions enrolling older people in educational programs, although two of them accounted for most of the older participants. These early surveys confirmed that as long as thirty years ago some institutions had already realized the need for education of persons in the later years and were making courses and programs available. The extent of this activity was quite limited, and the studies did not distinguish between the training of persons in gerontology and education of older people. However, some preliminary programs were developing.

During the 1970s, programs for older people developed very rapidly. A 1972 survey of educational institutions in Ohio (Ohio Administration on Aging, 1973) generated 106 responses and reported that 75 schools had some programs in aging, with 19 offering instructional programs exclusively for older people. A survey by the American Association of State Colleges and Universities (1974) of its 313 members indicated that nearly half had some programs for older persons. These included increased access to regular course offerings, instruction created exclusively for older people, training of professionals in aging, and other services; most of the programs allowed for the inclusion of older persons in regular instructional programs. A major survey was done by Korim (1974) for the American Association of Community and Junior Colleges. He mailed questionnaires to the 1,137 community colleges in this country and received 965 responses. Of these, 340 reported programs of cultural enrichment for older persons, and 140 offered preretirement and retirement educational services.

A study by DeCrow (n.d.) involved a questionnaire mailed to 40,000 organizations and institutions thought to be involved in instruction of older persons. About 3,500 usable responses were received from libraries, museums, the Cooperative Extension Service, park and recreation departments, businesses, unions, and community and voluntary organizations, indicating a wide variety of programs and rapid growth of the field. Over 50 percent of the respondents reported adding new programs for older persons within the past year, and almost all identified areas into which they hoped to expand.

In 1977 the American Association of Community and Junior Colleges again surveyed its members, mailing a questionnaire to the 1,200 community colleges in the United States. Of the 547 responses, 169 supplied enrollment figures on persons over age 45. These data indicated substantial growth in educational participation, especially among women, who were returning to school in ever-larger numbers. In addition, 237 community colleges indicated that they made available teaching and service roles for older people (DeCrow, 1978).

It would appear that four-year colleges and universities have been slower to establish instruction for older people than community colleges have. A study by the Academy for Educational Development (1974) reported that about one fifth of the 271 colleges and universities responding had programs for older persons. A 1975–76 study, also by the academy (Murphy and Florio, 1978), examined the involvement of older people in teaching roles. This study found that 75 percent of the 3,145 responding institutions did involve older people as "teachers" in one way or another.

Taken together, these studies suggest an increasing awareness among educational institutions, community organizations, and others of the instructional needs and wants of older persons. Although the response rates to these mailed questionnaires were often small and the aggregate data frequently were of less importance to the authors than the description of case examples, evidence of growth in educational programming, especially in community colleges, is abundant.

Program Types

Educational institutions and community organizations tend to offer two types of instructional programs to older people—one in which older people are integrated with younger students and in which there is some accommodation (typically lower tuition) for the older participants and one in which the program is designed especially for older participants and consequently segregates them from persons of other ages. A good deal of controversy exists over which of these approaches is philosophically preferable, but both currently offer substantial services to the older person interested in education.

DeCrow (n.d.) reported that two thirds of the program administrators who responded to his survey agreed that older people feel more comfortable and learn better with their own age group. Many educational programmers accept this position and design the instruction for people past the age of 55, 60, 62, or 65. Elderhostels, emeritus programs, lifelong learning institutes, and retirement education programs are examples of these endeavors serving an older audience exclusively. Program developers assume that learners are likely to prefer to be with persons of their own age and history, that these individuals are experiencing similar developmental tasks, that some gap exists between the generations, and finally, that educational programs are typically age-graded and movement away from this pattern at the end of life is indefensible.

McClusky (1978), however, argued that an age-integrated educational format is preferable because persons from the different generations can teach and learn from each other. Others have proposed that cross-generational instruction will maintain the involvement of older people in the mainstream of society, will avoid intergenerational antagonism, and will break down generational and historical barriers to communication and cooperation (Jensen-Osinski and others, 1981). Both approaches have their value, and both can be identified in current programs.

Intergenerational Programs. Age-integrated programs offer both the most and the least comprehensive instruction for older persons. At the modest end of the continuum are offerings in which colleges and universities open their regular courses and cultural events to older persons. In a sense this is no program at all, since most educational institutions do not specifically prohibit the attendance of persons over any age. The majority, however, offer some incentive to older persons, such as enrollment with reduced or eliminated tuition on a space-available basis. This means that, in those classes or performances where seats would be unused, older persons can attend at a lower cost.

Chelsvig and Timmermann (1979) surveyed 3,055 community colleges, four-year colleges, and universities to determine the extent of tuition reduction or waiver policies for older persons. Of the 2,401 responding institutions, 63 percent of the community colleges and 43 percent of the colleges and universities had such tuition reduction policies. These were concentrated in the public institutions and typically were restricted to auditing courses rather than enrolling for credit. Community colleges were more likely than others to have implemented a reduced tuition policy and to have developed specific instructional programs for older people.

Long and Rossing (1979) surveyed states to determine whether they had legislation or policy that encouraged educational institutions to provide free or reduced tuition. They reported that nineteen states had passed such laws and eight others had developed policies through a higher education governing board. These accommodations were not the same in all states. Some were limited to certain colleges or types of schools, while others covered all public higher education institutions. Most of these had occurred in the past few years, an indication that tuition reduction or waiver is a politically appealing idea and may continue to spread through institutions of higher education.

Reduction or elimination of tuition has not always been made known to the public. In some cases there has been little money to do so, but in other situations government officials and educational administrators are concerned that older people will inundate the institution and that it will not be able to handle the additional demands on student services, health services, instructors, parking facilities, and other special services (Long, 1980). Some administrators feel that older people are participating in education as a hobby while young people are preparing for roles as citizens and productive workers. These administrators and faculty indicate little sympathy for the needs of older persons and prefer to maintain their mission as the educator of youth. Consequently, they have not actively sought out older students.

If economic concerns were the main obstacles to older persons' participation in the classrooms of higher education, tuition waivers would be of significant value. In reality, many schools that have offered this concession have experienced little change in the enrollment of older persons. Credit and degree-oriented courses tend to attract only a small segment of the older population, and constraints on registration, insecurity about openings, and large crowds around cultural events have limited the participation of most older people. Many educational institutions have concluded that older people are not interested in education. Others, thankfully, have not reached this conclusion and have sought to expand the range of available educational options to older persons.

One way of doing this is to involve the older persons more directly in the life of the educational institution. Clackamas Community College in Oregon City, Oregon, has attempted to do this through participation of older persons on each of the college's lay advisory committees (Glickman, Hersey, and Goldenberg, 1975). These committee members help the college examine its curricula and service offerings in light of older persons' interests and needs.

An extension of this approach is observable at Syracuse

University, where a housing project for older persons has been constructed on the campus (Beattie, 1971). Students from the university spend time with the older residents, and many of the senior citizens participate in campus activities. Though not primarily an educational project, the interaction of students and older people through service and learning projects provides an intergenerational experience that is beneficial to both groups.

An additional step has been taken at Huron College in Huron, South Dakota. A small liberal arts college in a rural area, Huron found enrollment declining as outmigration of younger people became more pronounced. The size of the older population was increasing, however, and so the college sold one of its unused dormitory buildings to a local senior group, which refurbished it with assistance from federal grants and loans. The upper floors of the building were converted into apartments, which generate sufficient rent to pay the interest on the loan for the building. The ground floor is used as a senior center. The intent is to have the whole college become "gerontologized" through the involvement of older people in the life of the campus. To a large extent this has occurred, and hundreds of older people now interact with the students. Undergraduate classes in many departments include gerontology content, and events that bring together the old and the young are a frequent occurrence (Weinstock, 1978).

A final example is the well-known Bridge Project at Fairhaven College of Western Washington University (Rich, 1978). Apartments were converted for use by thirty older persons, and educational and cultural programs involved both young and old in a variety of learning and living activities. The program has not only put to use unneeded dormitories but has proved to be an incentive in the recruitment and retention of younger students, a way to provide meaning and growth to older people, and a source of public relations material for the college. Established in 1973, it continues to be a vital program but faces difficulties because of budget constraints recently experienced by the college.

Real intergenerational learning environments seem to be rare today. Many colleges allow older people to enroll in regular courses, but few have gone so far as Syracuse, Huron, and Fairhaven to modify the shape of the institution in order to accommodate the changing demographic conditions of this nation. These programs, however, offer a glimpse of what the future of higher education in the United States may be and continue the tradition of quality education that is responsive to contemporary social conditions.

There are other approaches that also involve older persons in learning activities in an intergenerational context. These include voluntary and paid roles in which the older person acts as the teacher as well as learner. Although the Bridge Project and the Huron College program incorporate some older volunteers as instructors, most of the older persons are seen as students. In other places, colleges and universities have used older persons mostly in instructional roles. Nearly 75 percent of the educational institutions surveyed by the Academy for Educational Development (Murphy and Florio, 1978) involved older people in helping/teaching activities. Roles specifically involving education included lecturers, teachers, tutors, group leaders, educational advisory committee members, teaching aides, curriculum consultants, counselors, administrators, creators of educational games, and educational researchers.

An example of this type of program can be found in the Andrus Volunteers at the Andrus Gerontology Center of the University of Southern California. These 100 retired professionals design and conduct seminars and programs as well as attending those offered by other groups in the center and the university. They regularly offer a lecture series on recent research developments, serve as subjects of ongoing research projects, act as live examples in undergraduate and graduate courses, and offer workshops for other groups throughout the Los Angeles area (Jellison, 1980).

In none of these roles are older people exclusively the recipients of learning; in all of them they have the opportunity to refine, expand, and update the special knowledge they have in order to transmit it to others. By alternating between the learning and teaching role, they increase the purposefulness of the learning and apply it in concrete and useful ways.

Another type of intergenerational learning can be found

in the corporate sector. When the International Silver Company realized that international competition was cutting deeply into its production, the company and union began exploring alternatives. They settled on converting the stainless steel flatware production facility into a tube-bending operation to supply aircraft engines and similar industries. The company offered sixteen-week training programs for workers of all ages in order to assist them in becoming tool-and-die makers. With instruction provided by a master tool-and-die maker, an apprentice instructor, and a retiree, the training was successfully completed and the company was able to redirect its productive capacity (Jacobsen, 1980).

Intergenerational programs of education offer older persons the opportunity to maintain their interaction with younger people while pursuing the education they desire. These programs have proved to be very valuable and offer great hope for the future. They do, however, require more accommodation by the educational institution than is typically provided. The expectation that older people will enroll in the institution's regular courses is doomed to failure. The courses are often diametrically opposed to the field-dependent preferences of older students. They involve vocationally oriented instruction, with great amounts of competition, testing, and pressure; they meet several times a week, making transportation imperative; they require rigorous admission and enrollment procedures that often demand persistence and cleverness; and they use teaching methodologies that do not consider the experience, wants, or slowness of the older learner. Unless accommodations are made (as they have been at Syracuse, Huron, and Fairhaven), it is unlikely that large numbers of older persons will enroll in the regular instructional programs of educational institutions.

Age-Segregated Programs. These are educational endeavors in which the older person is viewed as the exclusive client. The courses/programs are designed specifically for an older audience, and few younger persons are expected to participate. This approach segregates the older learners from those of other ages and makes it possible to design the curriculum and methods to address the needs and wants of older learners. These accommodations have proved very acceptable to older participants, and most elderly persons choose this type of education today. Because this approach is popular, there exists much variety in the types and extent of programs offered. Some consist of only a course or two for older persons offered by a community college or senior center, while others involve an entire curriculum of educational offerings providing opportunities for every taste.

There are many examples of these programs. At the College of Marin (Kentfield, California), an Emeritus College has been created to serve the needs of older learners. Although the Emeritus College allows persons over 55 to enroll in any of the college's courses, it also develops special daytime courses for older people at half the tuition cost. Some of the courses are offered in local senior centers as well as on the campus and are taught by college faculty and special instructors from the community. Emeritus College is represented in the student government, and so it operates like each of the other divisions of the College of Marin (Glickman, Hersey, and Goldenberg, 1975).

Another age-segregated program that has received a great deal of publicity is the Seniors on Campus program of North Hennepin Community College (Minneapolis). It offers an array of specially designed noncredit courses without tuition to persons over 55, in addition to encouraging older people to enroll in the college's regular credit courses. This program was initiated when older people from the area demanded that they be included in planning and program design of any gerontology activity. The administration responded positively and promptly to this request, and the program has maintained the vitality that accompanies community participation (Weinstock, 1978).

Queensborough College (Bayside, New York) is one community college that has cooperated with the National Retired Teachers Association/American Association of Retired Persons in establishing an Institute of Lifetime Learning. It offers a variety of courses, especially in the areas of consumer affairs, defensive driving, and retirement preparation, which have been developed by the institute and made available to programs such as this (Korim, 1974).

The Elderhostel program is another that is national in

scope; it uses the facilities of community colleges, four-year colleges, and universities to offer residential one-week courses during the summer. Beginning in New England, the program has spread rapidly across the county. In 1981 approximately 406 colleges offered course work and living arrangements for older people. Many older persons are finding that the Elderhostel program provides a way of vacationing in many parts of the country, meeting interesting people, learning new things, and living relatively cheaply.

An interesting aspect of Elderhostel is that although persons under 55 are not allowed and most hostelers are over 65, none of the courses offered is allowed to be designed for the elderly. The belief is that liberal arts courses are the most appropriate content and that courses that deal with aging teach people to be old. The emphasis is on the use of the "higher faculties," which will liberate people from their ignorance and misunderstanding (Knowlton, 1977). As would be expected, the Elderhostel program tends to draw persons with higher educational levels, incomes, and community participation rates.

Another example is the Emeritus Institute of Saddleback Community College (Mission Viejo, California). Through both on-campus and community course offerings, the institute currently has nearly 10,000 registrations by older persons per semester. Since the area has a large number of retirees, especially with Leisure World's population now over 20,000, the college offers course work in a huge variety of areas. The courses carry no tuition and provide age-segregated and age-integrated learning opportunities.

Another type of program is the Senior Citizen Celebration Days conducted annually by the Gerontology Program at the University of Nebraska at Omaha. The three-day event brings nearly a thousand older people to the urban campus for minicourses, health screening, entertainment, crafts sales, and agency displays (Horacek and Francke, 1978). The program is primarily educational in its attempt to provide instruction from faculty and community persons in a wide range of areas to people who otherwise would not come to the campus. It serves to preview future educational offerings and involves a year-long planning process by university staff and the senior citizen community.

An interesting twist on recruiting older students has been undertaken by Broward Community College in Fort Lauderdale, Florida. The staff worked out an arrangement with Dawson College in Montreal, Quebec, to bring a group of older persons to Florida for a month in the winter to enroll in courses, live in comfortable apartments, and escape the cold Canadian winters. The thirty participants not only enjoyed the holiday in the sun but indicated that the educational program offered by the college was a vital part of the trip and deserved to be continued as the major focus of the program (Marks, 1979).

A national program in the humanities is currently available from the National Council on the Aging. It consists of a series of study units that are used by discussion groups in senior centers. Each study unit includes an anthology of materials from history, literature, and philosophy—primarily short readings that stimulate participants to relate their reading to their own experience. Units are currently available in such areas as "Exploring Local History," "The American Family in Literature and History," "Images of Aging," "Americans and the Land," "Work and Life," "The Search for Meaning," and "Words and Music" (*Senior Center Humanities Program*, 1982).

Age-segregated instruction of older people is more common today than is intergenerational programming. The reason is probably the concern of the sponsoring institution in modifying the typical program to better address the preferences and skills of the older learner. Because older learners are the primary or exclusive audience of the program developer, their wishes come first. This priority has led to rapid growth in the number and size of programs, a growth that is expected to continue in the years ahead.

Age-segregated programs, however, have a significant weakness. Because they are offered through extension or community service divisions of educational institutions, their development is typically subject to fewer constraints and less oversight; they become vulnerable to the development of courses that do not meet the quality expectations of the rest of the institution. Because they are new and growing, the institution may ignore their development rather than carefully considering the level or quality of programming desired by the institution. This is a potential problem in any new program development but is of special concern here because most older people do not demand rigorous instruction. Age-segregated programs will continue to expand, but the need is for expansion of quality as well as size.

Organizational Arrangements

Educational programs for older people are available from a variety of institutions and agencies, but there is little information on their organizational arrangements, size, budgets, and functioning. Since most of them are age-segregated programs with small staffs and budgets within larger social service or educational institutions, little attention has been devoted to describing their operation. Studies have concentrated more on the programmatic aspects than the organizational ones, and so information is sketchy at best, except for DeCrow's (n.d.) survey of 3,500 programs. This provides the greatest insight into the current administrative and operational arrangements and offers some view of the typical functioning of various types of educational program providers. (For an overview of the operation of these organizations as they serve all adults, see Darkenwald and Merriam, 1982).

Public School Systems. Education for older people offered by public schools typically consists of a small group of age-segregated courses offered by the adult education division. About 600 school districts responded to DeCrow's survey, 60 percent of which served fewer than 50 older adults annually. Most of the schools offered short courses, but many included lectures, film series, field trips, and radio programs. Typically, the courses were held in the school facilities, and tax support allowed the fees charged to be very modest. Two thirds of the programs were operated by one part-time administrator.

Public school systems have not aggressively involved themselves in education for older people. Perhaps school systems and older people both assume that children are the primary clientele, but that certainly could change. As the concept of community education spreads, the use of school facilities for adult groups will become more common, and older persons' participation will grow. A recent publication from the U.S. Office of Education (*Federal Experience Under the Community Schools Act, 1980,* 1981) listed nearly eighty community schools that offered some educational programs for older persons. However, continued expansion through the school districts will occur only if additional staffing and resources can be acquired. DeCrow (n.d.) pointed out that 53 percent of the respondents in his survey indicated lack of financial resources as the major obstacle to program growth and expansion. In addition, 42 percent cited lack of interest by older persons as a hindrance.

Although the public school system is widespread and could be the primary provider of educational services to older people, it does not appear to be approaching that role at this time. The lack of financial resources available to school districts and the almost total concentration on children and youth have not encouraged schools to offer major programs for older persons. Unless some major change occurs in the finances and priorities of the school districts, they are unlikely to become major providers of educational services to older people.

Community Colleges. The two-year college has been the fastest-growing part of higher education in the past decade. Its responsiveness to the local community has facilitated the accommodation of programs and activities to community wants. Community colleges now exist in most areas of the nation, and the transition from the junior college concept has led to success in acquiring financial resources for facilities and staff. The community college is clearly the institution that is developing the most new educational programs for older people, and it seems to be the educational institution preferred by older people. The literature provides numerous examples of large and vital programs currently being conducted by community colleges (Demko, 1982). DeCrow (n.d.) questions his own data that there are thirty-six community colleges that serve over 1,000 older adults annually. This would appear to be a very modest figure today, as programs have grown so rapidly and expansively.

DeCrow reported that the community college programs mostly consisted of short courses that met weekly for four to six weeks but that discussion groups, film series, and workshops were very common. Both on-campus and community sites were used, and the programs drew a fairly broad audience, including those with learning difficulties. Funding typically came from the college or from state and local tax support. Interestingly, funding was seen as an obstacle to growth by more community college administrators than public school personnel, but lack of interest among older people was seen as less of an obstacle.

The community college appears to have great potential for the future. As retirees' level of formal education approaches twelve years, nearly half of the older population will have had some exposure to higher education. This familiarity will lead to greater interest in education provided by those institutions that are easily accessible—community colleges. By both location and mission, the community college is positioned to appeal to older learners.

This potential audience has not been lost on community college administrators. They have realized the changing demographic profile and have moved aggressively to design programming for this growing clientele. Many of the noncredit courses in arts, travel, exercise, humanities, contemporary events, foreign languages, religion, and consumer affairs that the college has traditionally offered appeal to older persons, and so the transition to this new audience has not been extensive. Likewise, the community college has seen community service and continuing education as a primary mission, unlike more prestigious universities, which tend to downplay these roles. Thus, the community college is ideally placed to assess and address the learning needs of older people in the future.

Colleges and Universities. Education for older adults offered by colleges and universities has typically been administered by the university extension division or by the cooperative extension service. These adult education and noncredit programming arms of higher education have traditionally underserved older people, but enrollment is growing. Although university extension offers many evening, weekend, and off-campus programs, it has not yet targeted the older audience, and so involvement has consisted primarily of enrollment by older people in age-segregated offerings.

Cooperative extension has had much greater involvement with older people. As an outgrowth of the agricultural extension movement, groups, programs, and services have been provided in both rural and urban areas under the auspices of each state's land-grant university. Most of the educational programs are informal, involving discussion groups, demonstration programs, service activities, or intergenerational exchanges; they do involve older people, even though not always in an age-segregated instructional format. The opportunities for expansion of these programs are great, and if the urban mission of cooperative extension is completed as successfully as the rural mission has been, major impact should be felt in the future.

A few examples exist in which colleges and universities have developed substantial programs for older persons. One type is evident in the Institute for Retired Professionals of the New School for Social Research (New York City). Using a substantial pool of retired faculty, business executives, and professionals, this institute has created a teaching/learning center that is in great demand by well-educated and sophisticated retirees. These persons pay an annual fee for the privilege of teaching courses and enrolling in those offered by other members. Participants may also enroll in the general courses of the New School, which involves them in age-integrated instruction. The Institute for Retired Professionals provides a model for educational and cultural programming for elite older persons that could be replicated in many colleges and universities.

Universities, aside from the cooperative extension service and specialized programs like the Institute for Retired Professionals, are unlikely to become major educational providers for older people in the near future. They are more focused on the traditional roles of undergraduate and graduate instruction, research, and publication. Although they will fill a most useful role in sponsoring stimulating learning/teaching environments for the elite elderly—the highly educated, financially secure individuals—through programs such as those operated by the Fromm Institute or the Institute for Retired Professionals, there is little indication that they will develop special programs for older persons. They are likely to encourage the enrollment of older learners in their regular credit courses, but beyond tuition reduction, few other accommodations seem likely.

Business and Industry. As the preceding chapter has dealt with retraining of older persons, mainly in the corporate sector, that aspect of organizational arrangements will not be dealt with here to any extent. However, it should be kept in mind that the employer is a valuable source of education for many older workers and job-related learning remains of high interest to many middle-aged and older persons. Whether it is education in preparation for reentering the work force, skill upgrading, learning the newest technological developments, or preparing for phased or full retirement, the employer is in a position to offer a variety of learning opportunities.

Business and industry have been hesitant to devote extensive resources to retraining older persons because it was assumed that their shorter remaining work life would reduce the payoff from the investment. This attitude is changing as employers realize that the major portion of their employee turnover comes from younger workers. By avoiding obsolescence and declining productivity, the corporation can optimize the potential contributions of the middle-aged and older worker and can reduce the potential negative impact of an aging work force.

Public Libraries. Although traditionally seen as collecting and distributing print media to local patrons, libraries have expanded their services to include films, tapes, and many special programs. Older people are major users of the library, both in independently pursuing learning and as clients for its group programs. Travel, cultural affairs, literature, and current events are popular topics that are typically presented at libraries by volunteers in an informal and occasional manner. Courses are not as likely as lecture or film series, and participation varies with the topic and its interest to the older persons.

The library is not expected to be an expanding service delivery unit in the coming years. Taxpayers' revolts such as Proposition 13 have reduced local and state government resources, thus limiting appropriations to libraries and other community service agencies. Although libraries are respected service providers, they have been unable to generate sufficient political protest to restore the reductions and cannot be expected to develop new program emphases with government funding in the future. Since libraries have no tradition of charging for services, it seems unlikely that they will expand through tuition income.

Churches and Synagogues. Under a broad enough definition of *education,* the religious institution is the largest provider of educational services to the older person. Sunday school classes, discussion groups, Bible study, family and personal development, cultural events, and social concerns form the bases of programs that draw many older people. Local churches and synagogues far outnumber other types of community organizations. The United Methodist Church, for example, points out that it has local facilities in more communities than any other organization except one—the United States Postal Service. This kind of geographical coverage provides a natural foundation for the establishment of a comprehensive instructional program. About 62 percent of all Americans are church members, and nearly 40 percent of the U.S. population attends church regularly. Three quarters of all adult education programs are offered by churches, and over 5 million people participate in church programs annually (Peterson, 1979). Nearly two thirds of these participants are women, and the average age is substantially above the mean age of the U.S. population.

The Harris study (1975) reported that 90 percent of the older respondents rated the church or synagogue as a "convenient" place to go, second only to the home of a neighbor. Seventy-seven percent of the older respondents indicated that they had been to a church or synagogue in the past year, substantially more than the number who had been to a library (22 percent), theater (17 percent), or community center (17 percent). The Harris data showed that, with increased age, church attendance increased until the sixties, when health and mobility obstacles reduced it slightly. Future generations of Americans may be less inclined toward church and synagogue participation, but for today, the religious institution offers tremendous opportunities for the development and conduct of education for older persons.

There are several examples of multifunctional programs for older people offered by a religious institution. Perhaps the best known is the Shepherd's Center in Kansas City, Missouri. Established in 1972, the center has as its goal sustaining the independence of older persons in the service area. Although this involves social, health, and nutrition services, from the beginning it has included educational programs on a wide range of topics. These typically are offered once a week, often with an older person as instructor. Topics have included travel, psychology, current events, dancing, and financial concerns (Maves, 1982).

Another example can be found at the Chatsworth Adult Center at the Point Loma Community Presbyterian Church, San Diego, California. The education program there has been developed around "Twelve Rejuvenating Techniques," a set of activities that provide a comprehensive program of education and services to the community. It has worked well and has proved to be effective in meeting the educational needs of older persons in the community (McClellan, 1977).

Church participation by older people is higher than in other age groups, and so it is appropriate to consider the church one of the major providers of instruction for persons over 55. As members of local congregations, older people are likely to respond positively to the programs developed and offered by the church or synagogue and to volunteer their time and expertise to teach or assist in programs. To date, the potential of the church has not been fully developed, and older people interested in education have been forced to look elsewhere for comprehensive educational opportunities. There is some indication that religious bodies are becoming more aware of the needs of older people and that the future may include more educational programs for the elderly by churches.

Community Centers. Most communities now have some senior citizens' center or club that provides for the social and activity needs of older persons. Administrators and boards of these facilities typically view education as a lower priority than social service delivery, health promotion and screening, recreation, nutrition and meals programs, travel, and social programs. However, many of these activities have a potential for educational development that is likely to be implemented in the future as more of the participants have higher levels of formal education.

Many of these community agencies have a relationship with some national organization, such as the American Association of Retired Persons (AARP), the National Council on the Aging, or the National Council of Senior Citizens, which offers materials and direction on instruction that will lead to volunteer roles. For instance, the AARP trains widows as peer counselors so that they can help others who are experiencing the trauma of a spouse's death. It also offers a Tax-Aide program, which trains tax counselors who help older peers complete and file their federal and state income tax forms (Timmermann, 1981). These programs place the older person in the position of contributing to the welfare of the community immediately after completing the training.

Community agencies and groups will continue to offer educational programs in the future, but they too are likely to see only modest expansion. Since education is a secondary priority for most of them, it seems unlikely that they will invest the resources or staff necessary to develop major programs. The exception will be those agencies interested in a particular problem or disease—the American Cancer Society or the Heart Association—which can be expected to seek out more older persons for their programs in the future.

Access to Available Educational Services

The diversity of this set of educational providers causes difficulties for many older adults seeking instructional opportunities. There is no single place where a person can discover the extent or quality of offerings in any community. Although most people will choose to participate in programs sponsored by organizations with which they are familiar, others have a particular need or interest and seek out educational providers who can respond to this need. There is currently no singular way to enter the "educational system" and discover all the available alternatives.

This is especially detrimental for older people, because they need assistance not only in identifying the existing programs but in determining their appropriateness, accessibility, and receptivity to participation. They need a single source of information on educational and training opportunities. This simply is not available in most communities. Although the federal government has authorized at least fifty separate authorities for developing and conducting educational and occupational information services, none of them relates directly to education for older persons, and there is so much fragmentation that these services need coordination and information sharing among themselves (Hoffman, 1980).

It is inaccurate, then, to suggest that we currently have an educational service delivery system. In most areas, individual agencies, institutions, or organizations offer instructional opportunities with little concern for the pattern that develops or the comprehensiveness of the coverage. Since programming is recent and limited, this is neither surprising nor particularly deleterious. Individual older persons enroll in educational programs offered by those organizations with which they are familiar and which seem most accessible to them. Since interest and need vary from one older person to the next, some variety in the organizational sponsors is useful. However, such uncoordinated programming does not offer much structure on which to build a "system" of education for older people. Individuals or groups interested in determining unmet needs or assisting underserved populations have little access to or influence on organizations providing the instructional services.

In general, most communities do not have a comprehensive array of educational offerings for older people. Most programs are aimed at middle-class, active, motivated persons. These are the persons who volunteer for educational participation, and they are the easiest participants to recruit. Some instruction is also available for persons in institutions such as nursing homes or hospitals, but this is often unknown to other older persons in the geographic area. Ideally, the future will see some organization in each community taking the leadership to assess the local needs and programs and to encourage providers to move into instructional and client areas not addressed by other providers.

The Area Agency on Aging (AAA) has taken this role for the design and provision of social and health services. With such planning and coordinating agencies currently functioning in nearly 600 communities, the mechanism exists for increasing the communication and encouraging the coordination of educational programs within the locale. However, the AAAs have not accepted this responsibility in most places, and although they are likely to be supportive of educational activities, they have not seen it as one of their primary roles. It is hoped that they will realize the potential inherent in encouraging such coordinated program development and will become more assertive in the future.

Some other organization, most likely the community college, is a more likely community educational coordinator for older persons. Community colleges are already offering many educational services for older people, and they could accept the role of identifying gaps in local offerings, providing information and referral to all members of the community, serving as a training resource for other organizations and agencies, and encouraging communication among all educational services providers.

Some organization—the AAA, community college, or another organization—is needed to serve as the communication link and advocate for older people within the local community. Until this occurs, there will be no centralized information source for older persons who are exploring options, no place where educational and job-related counseling can occur, and no mechanism to bring together all the educational service providers so that a rational plan can be cooperatively developed.

14

OIOIOIOIOIOIOIOIOIOIOIOIOIOIOIOIOIOIOIOIO

Planning and Implementing Effective Educational Programs

"How do I establish an educational program for older adults?" That is a question frequently asked by persons who have the responsibility for implementing a new educational program in a community college, public school system, corporation, multipurpose center, or voluntary organization. The answer is both simple and complex. It is simple because all it involves is deciding what you want to do, finding out what is needed, and then going ahead and creating the program. It is more complex, however, because there are many temporal and organizational considerations that complicate any program development process.

The steps in educational program development for older people can vary substantially with the program developer and the sponsoring organization. Some sponsors have extensive experience, and their staff may be able to design and implement new programs with little apparent effort. They have acquired the insight that allows many decisions to be made almost subconsciously. Organizations with less involvement may find the task much more difficult, because they will be forced to consider the ramifications of each decision and follow a lengthy procedure to ensure that the desired result occurs. Whatever the background of the organization and staff, however, the planning process is basically the same; the difference is in how overtly a protocol is followed.

In large part, the approach taken to program development depends on the orientation and function of the organization. Staffs of some agencies are likely to choose a community organization approach in which the client is involved in the needs assessment, planning, and conduct of the program. Client involvement, both within and outside the classroom, is viewed as a positive good, and the development of a constructive relationship between the community and the sponsoring agency may become as important as the content itself. Other program developers start with the purposes and mission of the organization and use them to determine the priorities in program content. In this case, the clients who fit best with this mission are recruited or directed into the programs, but the organizational mission takes precedence.

The emphasis of the program may also vary in terms of the clientele chosen for involvement. In some cases, administrators consciously define the clientele very specifically—for example, those who have high income and education levels, extensive backgrounds in the area, or particular problems. Other planners hope to create a comprehensive program that will reach every person possible, regardless of his or her socioeconomic, experiential, or need level. Obviously, rural programs will vary from urban ones, large programs will differ from small ones, and educational institutions serving the whole community will operate differently than a corporation training its employees. Whatever the differences, however, there are some program development phases that are applicable to most learning settings.

This chapter will describe fifteen phases of educational program development. This number is arbitrary, for it would be possible to divide the process into eight or ten or twenty phases (see Knox and Associates, 1980), but the fifteen do include the steps normally undertaken in the design and implementation of an educational program for older people. The phases are generally sequential; that is, they are presented in the order in which they are typically undertaken. However, circumstances may require some reshuffling of the order, and at some points it will be necessary to move back and forth between various phases. Likewise, there will be situations in which some of the steps can be ignored because of decisions made in previous projects, corporate priorities, or knowledge that is already available (such as knowledge of other resources) from some complementary project. Overall, however, these phases are suggested as appropriate topics to consider in the design and implementation of any educational program for older people.

Throughout this discussion, reference will be made to a program planner or program developer. It is assumed that one person is responsible for the planning process. This might be the instructor, an administrator, or a training specialist. It might also be a group of persons who are sharing the task, but someone has to be responsible for the process, and that person is referred to here as the program developer. (For a statement of the decision processes in program planning, see Knox, 1982.)

Phase One: Assessing the Institutional Context

Educational programs for older people vary for several reasons. One of the most important of these is the organizational context within which the program is planned and conducted. Since organizations have different purposes, goals, and missions, the sponsor will largely determine the program emphasis. For instance, a community college may be more likely to offer academically oriented courses to older people; a multipurpose senior center might concentrate on recreational activities; a church might emphasize activities relating to social action or religious instruction; and an employer might seek to prepare individuals for leadership roles.

The first step in initiating planning of any educational program is to assess the constraints and priorities of the host organization. Most institutions and agencies have a statement of goals or purposes that offers the educational planner insight into the most desired educational outcomes. Less likely to be available in written form is a statement of constraints or prohibitions that the organization places on its programs. These might include budget restrictions, staff limitations, geographical service prohibitions, clienteles that will not be served, or content areas that are traditionally of little interest to the administration and governing board. Whether they are written or not, the program planner needs to be aware of them.

A second set of considerations within the institutional context relates to the current state of expansion or contraction of the organization. Proposing an educational program to retain older workers at a time when the corporation is losing money and trying to reduce staff is unlikely to generate either moral or financial support. However, at those points in an organization's development when funding is sufficient and growth is rapid, it may be possible to secure organizational resources for whole new program areas.

A third area of consideration involves the current needs of the organization. If the sponsor is in need of greater community visibility, if it is seeking public service opportunities, if it is attempting to recruit a new type of clientele, or if there is some other organizational need that may be met by some new educational programs, substantial institutional support will likely materialize. The timing, however, is important in determining when to initiate new program activities, but regardless, it will be important to identify the current priorities and constraints that the host organization presently faces.

Program developers generally assume that their priorities and those of their clients constitute the moving forces that will lead to programmatic development; often this is not so. The state of the organization generally sets the tone, defines the parameters, and places the constraints on the development of any new program. Too many program developers overlook this organizational context and subsequently experience lack of administrative support in the developmental process.

Phase Two: Identifying Current Organizational Activities

Concurrent with the exploration of the institutional context, it is helpful to identify current activities underway by the host organization that have some relation to education for older people. If the organization is small and limited in its activities, this may be a very modest undertaking; however, if the host institution is a community college, a religious organization, a national volunteer association, a major corporation, or a university, many current activities may be tangentially related to education and aging. It is imperative that these undertakings be recognized and that the major ones be accommodated in the plan developed.

One example of this approach is seen in the involvement of personnel who are conducting similar programming. Perhaps the greatest constraint placed on any program developer occurs in the form of a person or group of persons who consciously oppose the development of a new program area. Individuals who see their "turf" threatened are the most likely opposition to new instructional activities. To minimize the likelihood of this kind of opposition, the program developer should be aware of such persons' current activities and try to integrate them into the planning process. When successfully completed, this process should help them feel a part of the new developmental efforts and should reduce the likelihood that they will choose to oppose an effort that they have helped plan.

A second reason for determining current organizational activity is to use the knowledge and experience base that is available from the previous programming. It is wasteful to replicate planning and development strategies which have been used in the past and which may provide insight into client needs, organizational issues, or instructional resources. If the organization has some experience in a particular area, it is most important to use this experience in order to avoid the mistakes and omissions that have occurred in the past.

It is simply good policy to build on one's strength. This occurs when instruction for older people is built on the insights resulting from education and training programs for other age groups. An organization is generally well advised to do what it knows best rather than to initiate new areas of programming in which there has been little or no past involvement. By building on the strength of past programming, the program developer is likely to avoid internal roadblocks and to maximize the benefits of existing organizational resources.

Phase Three: Gaining Familiarity with
Comparable Programs

Familiarity with other educational programs for middle-aged and older people will be very helpful to the program developer. Awareness of current programs offered by other organizations allows the program developer to avoid duplication of these existing activities, to seek the support of personnel from other projects, and to draw on their experience in order to avoid mistakes. The program developer can learn from the experiences of others, especially those local personnel who have recently undertaken the same planning steps and can provide insight into the unique characteristics of the area and clientele. One may draw on needs-assessment studies that have been done or examine others' instructional areas in order to anticipate the response to new content and format. Others may also have sought out local resources, such as faculty, audiovisual materials, available teaching space, or funding, and may offer good advice on what the local prospects are.

By familiarizing oneself with other education and training activities in the area, one can ensure that the newly developed educational activity will not compete with existing or planned programs by other organizations. One can thus immediately communicate to other service providers a cooperative stance that may be expected to result in better interinstitutional relationships, exchange of information and resources, and closer ties with existing programs. This will serve the program developer well in the future when difficulties arise and the assistance and support of colleagues are needed.

As in phases one and two, activities in phase three are not designed specifically to create new educational programs; rather, all three provide knowledge of the environment in which the program will be developed. The process and the resulting insight reduce the likelihood of any opposition to the program and enhance the probability of receiving local support. It is always tempting to ignore or minimize these first three stages; however, many program developers have found to their dismay that a false economy results when these coordinative efforts are shortchanged.

Phase Four: Determining Program Emphases

Before specific program planning can occur, the staff must make some initial decisions on the parameters and emphases of the instructional program. These typically result from the mission of the sponsoring organization, the history of activities related to education for older people, and some insight into what is available and needed in the local community. However, the staff may choose to modify some of these parameters and develop programs that are new to the organization or indistinct from other local activities.

It may be surprising to some readers to consider the parameters of the program before doing a needs assessment. Their logic would suggest that the program developer must have a clear picture of needs before the program can be developed. There is some persuasiveness to their logic if the organization is willing to design programs to meet any needs it finds. This is typically not the case. Most organizations are better equipped and disposed to provide certain kinds of programs than others. They need to clarify their own strengths and inclinations before examining the needs that exist.

There are three major decisions to be made at this time. The first deals with the clientele that will be served. Some colleges and universities may opt to serve a higher economic- and educational-level clientele. Community-based agencies may seek clients from all socioeconomic levels, and some centers or service organizations may consciously search out low-income, vulnerable, or undereducated groups. Corporations are likely to settle on their employees or on persons who are potential recruits for employment. There is value in providing education to each of these categories of people, and the decision probably depends on the traditional mission of the organization and needs of the community. Selection of a client group or a mix of groups will to a large extent determine the level and type of content that can be offered.

The second decision involves the type of content that will be emphasized in the instructional program. There are thousands of topics to select from, and priorities depend on the wants and needs of the clientele chosen. Although selection of specific course titles should be postponed until phase seven, it is important at this time to select priority areas or content parameters that will be emphasized in the program. These might include retirement preparation, citizenship instruction, and foreign language courses but exclude travel programs, arts and crafts, and skill training. Topics selected or excluded are important, because they reflect the orientation of the program and greatly affect the type of clientele attracted. Since it is not possible (or probably desirable) to offer all conceivable topics, selections are typically made on the basis of faculty availability, historical precedent, or identified need.

The third decision deals with the format that will be used. Often program developers assume that a classroom setting is the only appropriate means of providing instruction to older people. Although it is a popular and effective approach, others may be preferable on certain occasions. For instance, a one- or two-day conference or training session might prove more effective in building a supportive environment for behavioral change than a course offered one or two hours a day, one day a week. Field trips or visits to institutions or installations may be preferable to a classroom setting in which the topic is discussed rather than experienced. Media approaches might be used—local cable television, printing of materials that could be distributed widely, a "hotline" telephone service, or a sequence of speakers in connection with some social occasions such as regular luncheons.

By making early decisions on the clientele, content, and format, the program developer can provide an outline of the proposed program to the host organization's management or board and can gain some support for the plan before moving to the community discussion phase of the proposed undertaking. In a sense, this phase is the development of goals for the program. Although the specific needs are not yet known, the program staff have determined the general format, clientele, and content of the program. These decisions are based on some understanding of the general wants and needs of the older participant and the mission of the organization. The goals are likely to be very general and nebulous, but they give an indication of the end state toward which the program is directed. They are not necessarily measurable or even totally attainable, but the development process requires that by this time they be generally agreed on by the staff members involved.

Phase Five: Forming an Advisory Committee

Most developers of educational and service programs that relate directly to a particular community find it helpful to organize an advisory committee of providers and consumers that can act as a sounding board for ideas and provide information for coordinating the new program with existing community activities. The advisory committee is especially useful in the design of educational programs for older people, because it provides a means of involving influential and knowledgeable persons who may offer assistance in identifying needs and recruiting participants.

The advisory committee probably functions best if it numbers between twelve and eighteen persons. It should include representatives of other organizations or agencies that offer educational programs for older people as well as a good sample of older persons who have leadership roles in voluntary groups, clubs, centers, or other senior citizen activities. Selection of the "best" people is always difficult, but in general, it is effective to include persons who are likely to be detractors from the program as well as those who are expected to enthusiastically support the planned developments. By providing an open forum for discussion of the new program, the program developer can defuse possible community criticism and build a spirit of cooperation into the design and implementation of the new instructional endeavors.

Since the advisory committee is created to provide advice to the developing program, the program planner should specify as clearly as possible what authority and initiative the advisory committee is to take. Many program planners feel it is generally inappropriate for the advisory committee to be characterized as a policy board that determines the programs of the organization. Rather, it is better to seek advice, counsel, and coordination from the advisory committee, making it clear that although the committee's input is desired and appreciated, decisions will still be made by the staff and the authorized officers of the host organization.

This orientation is not accepted by all educational developers. Some prefer to give an advisory group of older persons primary responsibility for the policies and procedures of the program. This will increase their commitment and will allow the participants to "own" the program. To make this approach successful, a good deal of time and effort is required to orient the advisory group and to ensure that it will direct the program in ways the organization will consider appropriate. The decision on the amount of authority the advisory committee has is a significant one and will determine whether the instructional activities are conducted by or for the older clientele.

An effective advisory committee can be a powerful force in any educational program. Involving visible and knowledgeable persons will create great advocacy potential, because the group can assist in seeking funds, encourage the host organization to commit greater resources, and increase the contacts available in the local community.

For the advisory committee to be effective, its members must meet regularly and be completely familiar with the plans and operations of the educational program. This requires substantial staff time, and the program developer will need to give careful consideration to the expenditure of staff resources in comparison with the resulting value of the advisory committee. Usually the costs seem to be outweighed by the support and coordination that the committee can provide; however, there may be situations in which the costs are too high, and it may be preferable to have no committee at all or one which meets infrequently and which simply lends the names of prestigious persons to the organization. This would represent a much more modest use of organizational resources but may still provide some value to the project.

Phase Six: Assessing Needs

Education for adults is normally designed to meet the needs or interests of its participants. Unlike elementary education, in which an ideal curriculum is prescribed for all young persons, education for older people must generally respond to the individual preferences, priorities, and weaknesses of its clients. Consequently, the assessment of educational needs and wants is of major importance in the design of any instructional program.

Not all the needs of older people are educational needs, nor can education meet all the needs that mature individuals have. If the new instructional program is being designed by an organization that provides health, recreational, and social services, it may be appropriate to do a broad needs assessment and to direct noneducational wants to other units of the organization. However, if the program is being developed by an educational institution, it is probably more appropriate to limit the needs assessment to those areas that may be responsive to educational interventions. In general, it is better not to raise clients' expectations if there is little likelihood of responding to their preferences and needs.

There are a variety of ways to measure educational wants (Pennington, 1980). Perhaps the most frequently used is the questionnaire. Often this involves a listing of course topics that can be prioritized by older respondents. Hiemstra (1972) conducted his needs assessment by listing a large number of potential educational programs and asking the older respondents to choose those of most interest to them. This method has the advantage of being direct, easily applied to large numbers of people, and relatively easy to analyze. However, there are no data to support the assumption that courses checked on such a list by older people are ones that will entice them to enroll. In fact, other researchers (March, Hooper, and Baum, 1977) have found very little relation between responses and actions of older people once the instructional programs are offered.

Another type of paper-and-pencil instrument involves questions designed to address needs rather than specific educational content (Knowles, 1980). A questionnaire of this type might ask such questions as—

· When you see your doctor, do you wish you had additional information about some condition or illness that he or she describes?

- When you are shopping, do you sometimes wonder whether you are making the best use of your money?
- When you watch the news on television, do you sometimes wish you had more information about a particular story or event?
- When you see a painting or hear a song, do you sometimes think you've always wanted to develop your talent in that area?
- When you hear someone complain about old age, do you ever wish you knew what was normal at your age and what changes you should be concerned about?

Questions such as these can be used to identify areas in which older adults feel additional information would be helpful. By translating these into courses or experiential activities, a positive response by older persons is enhanced. However, there remains a possibility that older persons will not act on their indicated needs; so recruiting participants may still be difficult.

A third paper-and-pencil test, which appears to overcome some of these limitations, involves a needs assessment in which the concerns of the older person are directly related to possible instructional activities. This would appear to enhance the chances for a relevant needs assessment and could be used in many instructional settings. The instrument provided in Exhibit 1 was developed by Glickman, Hersey, and Goldenberg in a sourcebook titled *Community Colleges Respond to Elders* (1975). It has been modified here to emphasize instructional programs rather than other services that could be provided by community colleges.

Most of the analysis of this needs-assessment instrument will be obvious from the data collected. However, the activities in the right column can be grouped into four program categories:

Enrichment: Activities numbered 1, 4, 9, 13.
Retirement planning: Activities numbered 2, 6, 11, 14.
Second careers: Activities numbered 3, 7, 10, 16.
Advocacy: Activities numbered 5, 8, 12, 15.

Exhibit 1. Needs-Assessment Instrument

We are interested in finding out what kinds of needs and interests older people have and what kinds of programs and activities they would like to see developed. In order to get this information, your help is needed by filling out this brief form. Below, in the left column, are listed 16 statements describing feelings, both good and bad, that older adults often feel. In the right column are examples of activities, courses, or programs that a community college might develop. Please choose the statements in the left-hand column that best describe your feelings about yourself. Next, draw an arrow from each of these descriptions to the activity or program that you think would make you feel even better about a good feeling or would help to improve a bad feeling. In other words, connect statements describing how you feel with activities you would like to see developed because of those feelings.

Feelings

1. I am often lonely.
2. I don't know where to go to get information on programs.
3. I don't feel that I'm making the most of my talents and knowledge.
4. I feel powerless to change most of the financial and housing problems I face.
5. I like meeting new people.
6. I am confused about what benefits I am eligible for.
7. I miss the routine of work.
8. I feel older people are discriminated against.
9. I enjoy having increased leisure time.
10. I don't know much about options for retirement.
11. I don't think other people understand the problems elders face.
12. I need help in finding where to go for specialized help.
13. I don't have enough to keep me busy.
14. I feel I'm presently dealing quite well with my retirement, but there may be future problems I haven't foreseen.
15. I have to feel useful to be happy.
16. I think there are many laws and policies that should be changed.

Activities

1. Learning a new language.
2. Meeting with a counselor and a small group of elders to discuss how to cope with retirement and/or widowhood.
3. Being trained to help care for young children.
4. Going on field trips to local points of interest.
5. Learning how to deal with and negotiate with local, state, and federal agencies.
6. Learning about the effects and the problems of growing old in this society.
7. Volunteer work several days a week.
8. Learning about my legal rights and the law as it affects older people.
9. Attending a film series.
10. Being trained to assist and inform other elders.
11. Learning about Social Security, health, and other benefits for elders.
12. Learning how to understand and overcome the myths and stereotypes of aging.
13. Taking courses in literature or world events, for example.
14. Learning what local programs exist that are especially for elders.
15. Learning how to organize with other adults to help one another.
16. Being trained to work several hours a week at a part-time job.

Source: Adapted from Glickman, L. L., Hersey, B. S., and Goldenberg, I. I., *Community Colleges Respond to Elders.* Washington, D.C.: U.S. Government Printing Office, 1975.

A fourth approach to needs assessment would be through the use of the advisory committee. Since persons on the committee represent consumers as well as knowledgeable educational providers, it should be possible to have the group identify a variety of topics, client groups, or formats that would be of local interest. This is a much quicker way of determining instructional needs but may reflect the biases of that group rather than particular preferences of the older clientele to be served.

Another approach to needs assessment is to interview knowledgeable persons in the community. Those selected may be leaders of organizations or groups, or they may be simply persons who participate in programs and are assumed to know the preferences of people like themselves. It may also be beneficial to interview providers of educational or other services. For instance, hospital personnel may be aware of the health education needs of older people, and second-careers personnel may have knowledge of the employment needs that can be addressed by retraining.

Additional insight can be found in a review of the literature on educational needs and wants of older people, as described in Chapter Seven. Media stories on activities and problems facing older people may also suggest opportunities for educational programming, as may the general gerontology literature. These sources will provide more depth of understanding than a short survey or interview can. However, they do not give insight into the current problems of a particular group of potential students.

In general, needs assessment is an underutilized mechanism in the design of instructional programs for older people. Because it requires time and resources, it is frequently abbreviated, and the insights gained may prove less effective than desired. The circumstance in which the program is to be developed will determine the extent of needs assessment. If a community college is simply planning to offer one course for older people, it may not be necessary to do a major needs assessment. A few phone calls and interviews with some local leaders may prove sufficient. However, if a community agency is planning to initiate a whole curriculum of courses for older people, it may be a very prudent investment to undertake a variety of assessment activities before moving to the operational stage.

Needs assessment in a corporate setting may take on a different form from those described thus far. Because the employer typically develops and offers the instruction in order to help employees achieve a goal that has been set by management, the needs-assessment process may deal mainly with current skills and knowledge of the middle-aged and older workers rather than with their desires and preferences for learning. Determining their current state makes it possible for the training staff to develop instruction that will move the employees toward the established standard of productivity.

This view of training, traditionally prevalent in the private sector, is now being replaced by increased awareness of the reactions of older employees to the proposed instruction. It is not enough to know what the employee needs to learn; the trainer must also be aware of the extent of the employee's awareness of this need, his or her interest in addressing the need, the types of motivation that can be used to encourage the older learner, and the methods of instruction that the older worker feels will be most effective. Thus, several of the needs-assessment strategies are relevant to the private sector, even though they may be operationalized in somewhat different ways.

Phase Seven: Determining the Program Objectives

Objectives follow closely from the goals that have been established and the needs and wants that have been identified. Objectives are the outcomes of the program, the end results, the changes in needs or wants that result from the program of instruction being offered. Good objectives are hard to develop and write. It is very easy to be diverted to statements that are activities rather than objectives. For instance, a statement that says, "The project will offer six courses for older people in this county," is only a statement of the activities to be undertaken unless the need identified is simply insufficient educational programming. It is more likely that the need is to change the level of knowledge or typical behavior. Usually the objective will be something like "During a field visit to a supermarket, 50 percent of the participants in the consumer education class will compare the per-serving price of brand-name and generic-label canned goods before purchasing a new product."

In general, objectives tell who will be doing (or will be able to do) how much of something at what point in time and how it will be measured. These points are often arranged in a different order, but they are usually all included in the objective statement.

In educational programs, there are typically two levels of objectives. The largest are program objectives, which deal with the results of the whole program. For instance, the program might have as an objective to help twenty women in Retirement Acres reduce their weekly food costs by 10 percent over a six-week period by doing more comparison shopping. The second level of objectives deals with instructional outcomes. These are specific to a particular class or individual learner and are generally quite measurable—for instance, in a sewing class, "All students completing the six-week course will be able to modify a pattern to fit their body measurements without help from the instructor."

In developing an instructional program for older people, the establishment of objectives in terms of the expected outcomes of the program needs to be considered. These are likely to deal with the clientele to be served, the format to be followed, and the areas of need that will be addressed as well as the changes in behavior and knowledge that can result. In most programs there are numerous objectives that could be specified. Although there may be some value in identifying all of them, it is more useful to choose a few and to specify them in a way that will allow them to be measured at the end of the program.

Phase Eight: Developing Instruction

Once the objectives are determined, the next step is to design the particular instructional experience. If the needs assessment has been done well and the objectives are clearly specified, much of the instructional activity will follow easily. However, the program developer must be careful to be responsive to the participants' wishes and to select learning activities that will achieve the objectives and be well received. Criteria for selecting these activities should include such considerations as appropriateness of the activity to the clientele, suitability for the intended learning group, effectiveness of the activity, satisfactory pacing and variety of learning activities, and compatibility with the instructor's teaching style (Szczypkowski, 1980).

Questions need to be raised at this time about the total curriculum to be offered. In many cases, the needs and wants are so diverse that a cafeteria of courses is provided, each of which has no particular relation to the others. The older consumers simply chose from this array a diet that will suit their particular needs or desires. The sponsoring organization makes no attempt to ensure that a "balanced diet" of intellectual activities is attained. This approach will probably prove acceptable so long as the program is small. If a comprehensive array of courses is offered, some thought needs to be given to sequencing and prerequisites for various courses and topics.

Most of us have had the experience of enrolling in a class and then discovering that the instructor had expectations of our background knowledge and experience that were substantially different from reality. Either we were "in over our heads," or we already knew most of the content provided. This problem is frequent in all educational programs and could be addressed through descriptions of the content level or through designing sequences of courses. For instance, language classes are often listed as French I, French II, and French III; it is possible to describe the knowledge level that is expected. Similar sequencing could be done in other course areas, such as the arts, sciences, and humanities.

One consideration is the appropriate mix of courses in the instructional program. If all of them are offered at an advanced level, some people will obviously be excluded; however, if there are no advanced courses available, people are likely to attend for a semester or two and then discover that there are few challenging opportunities left for them. When this occurs, they are likely to seek other educational providers.

This is also the time when decisions should be made about

the format of the instructional program. If it has been decided in phase four that instruction is to take forms other than a classroom setting, then plans for travel, services, social activities, advocacy, or experiential learning should be designed at this time. Although it is easier to create a classroom environment, it is often a good policy to involve both types of activities in order to appeal to a broader audience. People learn in different ways, and to assume a classroom is the only learning setting is to ignore the learning needs of some older persons.

Phase Nine: Recruiting Students

As indicated in Chapter Three, most older people do not participate in instructional activities. Consequently, the program developer will find it beneficial to invest some resources in the process of marketing the instructional program that is developed. A substantial beginning will have been made if the program emphases are clear (phase four) so that the desired clientele are already identified. Likewise, an advisory committee (phase five) will be an initial conduit to various elements in the community. However, additional activities will also need to be undertaken.

These include advertising or direct mailing, communication with complementary organizations, and involvement of past participants. As every program planner knows, the best advertising is a satisfied customer. Therefore, in the long run, the most effective approach to recruiting new students will be word-of-mouth sharing by former students. This can be maximized by ensuring that the previous participants are aware of the total extent of the program, the future offerings, and the schedules planned. They should be informed by mailed brochures, but personal contact should be maintained insofar as possible.

Other community organizations that have complementary missions are also valuable recruitment avenues. Printed materials sent to them will reach likely participants in senior centers, study groups, women's clubs, churches, and civic organizations. These provide an inexpensive and effective means of program information sharing.

Each program will also need a means of information distribution to the community generally. This can be accomplished through news releases on interesting offerings, paid advertisements, public service announcements on radio and television, and direct mailings to older persons and the general community. These procedures apply to all adult education programs and are described in Bock's (1980) chapter on participation and marketing. This topic is of major importance to fledgling programs but never becomes unimportant, since participant turnover and societal change require continuing public awareness of the program offerings.

Phase Ten: Evaluation

Program evaluation is generally considered the last step in carrying out an instructional endeavor. Although it may be necessary for the program to be completed before the final evaluation can be done, postponing the evaluation planning until late in the program development process is inappropriate. The quality of the evaluation is determined by the clarity and preciseness with which the needs are identified, the objectives are specified, and the activities are completed. The whole planning process affects the evaluation, and so measurement of outcomes is an early consideration in planning.

Evaluations can have two main purposes—to determine how well the plan is being carried out (activities accomplished) and how well the problem is being resolved (objectives achieved). The first purpose leads us to process evaluation, which is typically the principal kind undertaken. It is formative in nature, helping staff members determine whether they are adequately carrying through the plan and whether the plan is moving them toward achievement of the objectives. This evaluation process allows the program developer to plan, implement, evaluate, and then decide what changes should be made in the next round of activities. It is an ongoing process that is started early and carried through to the end of the project. It is generally of most interest to the staff and administration and of less importance to funders and board members.

The second type of evaluation—product, or impact, evaluation—is a process that is used to determine the extent to which the program or instructional objectives were achieved. Its success depends not only on how well the instruction is completed but on how clear and measurable the objectives were. It is of interest to the funding agencies and the board members, because it is the measure of how much the problems or needs were affected by the instructional effort (Knox, 1979).

There are generally four steps in product evaluation. First, the objectives must be operationally defined. For instance, if the objective was to have participants be able to discuss intelligently the various characters in a particular book that has been read, it will be necessary to define what intelligent discussion means and how many characters will be discussed. Second, plans need to be developed for measuring the elements to be observed. In the example above, it may be appropriate for an outside observer to listen to the discussion to determine whether certain participants did take part in the discussion of particular characters.

A third step is to compare the achieved state with some standard. This may be the group's performance before the instruction, some comparison group that has not received the instruction, or some absolute standard that has been set. In the example, the observer might be given a set of criteria regarding intelligent points for the several characters being discussed. Finally, the evaluation results need to be reported to the staff, funders, and others who may be interested. It is important that the evaluators know what each group is looking for so that they can provide relevant information to that group rather than reporting everything that is known about every possible objective.

Evaluation can be a time-consuming task, but it is important and necessary in order to determine the efficiency and effectiveness of the program. It is not possible to describe the procedure extensively here, but the reader is encouraged to review discussions such as that provided by Grotelueschen (1980) for greater detail.

Phase Eleven: Choosing Instructional Locations

Most organizations or agencies sponsoring educational activities are likely to conduct those activities within the facility that houses the sponsoring unit. However, there may be advantages to seeking alternative locations for courses and activities rather than conducting them all in-house. Certainly, the size of the program, the location of the organization, and the availability of classroom or seminar space are most important in this decision; however, even if sufficient space and equipment are available, alternative sites should be considered.

The purpose and mission of the sponsoring organization become important at this point. If the organization is seeking to increase visibility for the whole organization, it may be most appropriate to use the current facilities. If it is trying to create an image of cooperation with other community groups, however, using other sites may be much more appropriate. Another factor in the decision is the scheduling of course offerings. Instructional programs for older people are generally preferred in the daytime, and scheduling courses in the evenings or on weekends may prove detrimental to enrollment. The organization may not have sufficient daytime space, however, and consequently using other settings, such as a church, a bank or savings and loan association, a community agency, a public school, or a conference center, may prove preferable to locating all activities within the sponsoring organization.

Decentralized location of courses can have some negative effects. Because there is no one location where administration and service provision are located, it may be difficult for people in the community to see the whole organization and develop an image of its programs and activities. Use of several locations is likely to dilute the organization's image and impact; people tend to think in concrete terms, and a program without a visible facility is harder to understand than one that stands on the corner and has a sign in the front yard. In considering the use of multiple locations, the program developer would be wise to seek out cooperative relationships with other programs and agencies so that communication can be directed through them and thus the image of the instructional program can be enhanced.

Phase Twelve: Staffing

The instructional staff is the key to an effective educational program. Selection of teachers is the most important activity and should be given highest priority. Because many programs offering education to older people have small budgets, instructors are often paid minimal amounts or contribute their teaching time. This makes it extremely difficult for the program developer to require extensive backgrounds or to force particular procedures on the instructors involved. However, maintaining a high-quality program requires the best teachers possible.

In some states, licenses or certificates are required for instructors teaching at certain institutions. This should be ascertained before instructors are hired so that requirements can be met. For instance, in some states teachers at the community college level are required to have a master's degree, or teachers in adult education programs of the public school system are expected to have at least a bachelor's. However, in most cases it is possible to waive this requirement and to acquire a special certificate for well-qualified but noncredentialed instructors.

More critical than credentialing, however, is the individual instructor's knowledge of the content and skill in teaching. There is probably no way to determine these qualifications without observing the instructor in a teaching role. However, an interview to discuss the content to be provided should offer some insight into the instructor's current level of knowledge, and a discussion of teaching philosophy and style may elicit some understanding of his or her preferences and biases.

Instructors who have taught at the elementary, secondary, or college level are likely to assume that a lecture format is the most appropriate approach. This methodology is not always well received by older learners, and instructors who are flexible in their approach are more likely to discover the style that works best with any particular group of students.

Other staff members will also play an important part in the development and conduct of the instructional programs. Depending on the setting and size of the total educational program, it may be necessary to have hosts or hostesses available at the facility to help people locate the correct room, to provide a cordial and supportive atmosphere, and to handle arrangements such as the provision of motion-picture projectors, maps, blackboards, or furniture. Hosts can also be helpful in creating a social

setting before and after classes by making coffee and light refreshments available and serving as greeters and support persons
during the period when class is not in session.

Other administrative personnel may be needed to assist
with registration, fee collection, advising, and evaluation. Frequently educational programs for older people have no one in
charge of educational counseling. This role may not be needed
if only a few courses are offered, but for programs of substantial proportions with courses involving prerequisites and background expectations, it will be necessary to have someone familiar with the curriculum provide advice to persons selecting
courses. The need for other staff members will be determined
by the scope and focus of the program. If low-income or handicapped persons are a major client group, transportation services
may be required. This obviously will involve additional staff and
will substantially increase the cost of the program. However, to
recruit and serve this client group, such supplementary services
may be very necessary.

A final staff consideration relates to recruitment and outreach activities. As pointed out in Chapter Three, older people
tend to be limited consumers of education. Consequently, new
programs may need to invest heavily in outreach and recruitment for initial groups of participants. Whether the recruitment
staff member is limited to sending out public relations announcements and posting signs in community centers or whether a door-to-door campaign is waged will depend on the emphasis and resources of the program. However, unless a close liaison
has been formed with an existing senior citizens' group or the
sponsoring organization already has access to large numbers of
older people, it will be necessary to conduct some recruitment
activities.

Phase Thirteen: Program Structural and Organizational Placement

If the instructional program being developed is a very
substantial one, it will require some decisions about its internal
structure and its placement within the host organization. This

may seem a trival concern during the initial phases of program development and planning, but it can have crucial effects on the long-run success and health of the instructional unit.

The first issue deals with the placement of the instructional unit within the host organization. In many cases, the unit reports to the administrator responsible for community services or adult education. In a community college this may be a dean of community services; in a public school it is likely to be the adult education director. In a community agency the administrator of the education program is likely to report to a director of community services or to the administrator of the organization. In a business or industry placement is typically within a training division, generally within the human resources development area. Whatever the logical placement, the program developer should attempt to report to the highest-level administrator possible. Access to a dean, vice-president, or organizational manager is likely to result in increased visibility and expanded resources during the course of the program's development. Reporting at a lower level may lead to competition with other operating units and lack of visibility at the upper reaches of the host organization.

A second consideration relates to the internal organization of the instructional program. If few staff members are involved, they probably should each report to the program planner or administrator. If there are several, however, some internal structure may be required; this is especially true if volunteers are used. Generally, a volunteer should report to a particular staff member rather than floating freely within the organization or reporting to the administrator, who may have insufficient time to supervise the volunteer's activities. All staff members and volunteers need written job descriptions to help them and others understand their role and to maintain coordination within the operating structure.

A third consideration involves the selection of staff and volunteers for the program. Many organizations that serve older people have found that the clients prefer to have older persons as staff members. Others have rejected this idea and have simply recruited staff and volunteers on the basis of competence rather than age. Experience would suggest that people of any age can successfully perform instructional or administrative functions. However, some consideration should be given to the mix of older and younger persons on the staff so that the organization is not viewed primarily as younger people doing good things for older people or as older people operating programs without well-trained staff. It seems unnecessary to recruit an entire staff of either older people or younger people simply because persons in later life will be the clientele of the instructional programs.

A final consideration involves the naming of the unit that will be created. Many colleges have chosen the term *Emeritus Center* for their educational programs. This has some status attached to it and is likely to be positively received by several groups. However, its meaning is likely to be unclear to people who have had little association with institutions of higher education. Therefore, other titles might be considered, such as the French term *University of the Third Age, Elder School, Senior College, Senior Education,* or *Lifelong Learning Institute.* Whatever the choice, the advisory committee should be involved in discussing the topic and may provide valuable insight into the local variations and meanings of alternative titles.

Phase Fourteen: Determining Needed Resources

When we think of resources, financial needs immediately come to mind. These would include funds for salaries, supplies, advertising, utilities, and rental of space if necessary. Many educational programs for older people operate on a very minimal budget. It might cover a part-time salary for an administrator, small stipends to instructors, and a few dollars for printing and telephone. Others operate on a more realistic basis with a staff of several people and adequate budgets for materials acquisition, equipment rental, and field experiences.

Securing increased funds is a continuing difficulty for educational programmers. The first source of funds, of course, is the host organization or institution. Generally, some commitment can be acquired in order to start a program. What is often difficult, however, is to gain increased budget as the program expands. This is the case in many California community colleges today. Programs have been instituted and have subsequently grown very large. Additional funding, however, has not been forthcoming. Program developers and staff are therefore cursed by their success, since the bigger the program becomes, the more inadequate are the financial resources they have.

This situation is one in which the advisory committee can be very helpful. The committee can become an advocate for the program within the host institution far more actively and forcefully than paid staff members can. It can also identify outside resources, such as federal or foundation funds that may be acquired on a grant basis. Community colleges and public schools in some states can acquire reimbursement for expenses based on enrollment. Senior citizens who enroll in credit courses or courses that meet the priorities set by state or federal government may prove to be a major source of income for some educational providers.

Grant funds for educational programs are more likely to be acquired from federal agencies or from private foundations. At present it is difficult to obtain government funds, because all human service support is declining and because education of older people has not been perceived to be a high-priority area for government funding. Foundations, however, have been more supportive of educational programming, and many programs have been funded through local foundation sources or by the national foundations that have evidenced an interest in this area.

In the future, it would appear that local businesses and industries may be more supportive of educational programs for older people. As they see the aging of their work force and realize the changing demographic structure of the nation, they may undertake greater involvement in and contribution to educational agencies attempting to maintain the quality of life and health for older people.

Business and industry provide much education and training to their employees. They are involving themselves more in services and programs that are not exclusively related to their business, ones that will improve the quality of life of their employees and the community. Thus, they may be seen as potential supporters of educational programs for older people in the future. It would seem prudent for program developers to begin making contacts with business and industry leaders in order to assess the probability of some resources being made available from that source.

Phase Fifteen: Timing and Sequencing

As pointed out previously, the phases indicated do not necessarily occur in absolute sequence; there may need to be some shifting back and forth between the stages. Occasionally, some of the stages may be totally unnecessary. In general, however, the background activity of clarifying institutional mission and assessing current activity should take place first. Determining emphases and making community contacts through an advisory committee should follow, and needs assessment and specific program planning would then occur.

For most programs, the goal of a major comprehensive educational effort is not immediately achievable. Consequently, some sequencing of developmental activities is required. In general, it seems to be good advice to begin programs that are close to those already in existence. This will probably mean that the new programs are very consistent with the organizational goals and historical activities of the host organization. As growth occurs, the educational programs for older people can create new organizational goals as additional needs and receptive audiences are identified. Movement from core programs to extension programs offered in other locations, to travel or holiday programs, to television or other media offerings, and to community organization or advocacy is likely to be a long-term development. It will depend partly on the needs of the community and partly on the energy and resources of the staff and advisory council.

It would seem preferable to begin small, to operate a high-quality program, and to grow incrementally into new areas as opportunities and resources become available. Frequently, programs begin without sufficient financial support to continue them, leading to difficulties in long-range survival. It is good advice to do some things well rather than doing everything half well. The needs and opportunities are great, but experience and a reputation for quality instruction should precede major program development and diversity.

Although the analogy may be extreme, when President Lowell of Harvard was asked what made that university great, he answered, "Three hundred years." The maturation of a "great" program usually takes time.

Conclusions

The design of educational programs for older people is encouraged and constrained by the environment in which it occurs. The contemporary situation is ideal because of the growth of the older population and the increasing educational attainment of the older cohort. It is a less than ideal time because of the reduction of financial resources from the federal government. Like most periods, it has its advantages and its disadvantages, which must be accommodated by the program planner. However, by following the fifteen phases described in this chapter, a program developer should be able to avoid the greatest obstacles to successful educational program development and should optimize the opportunities for immediate and long-range success.

15

ଠଠଠଠଠଠଠଠଠଠଠଠଠଠଠଠଠଠଠଠଠଠଠଠଠଠ

Future Issues
in Education
for Older Learners

Over the past three decades, educators and program planners interested in the elderly have had the task of finding older
people and attracting them to instructional programs. To a large
extent this task has been successfully accomplished. "Our colleges are slowly but surely beginning to set up a wide variety of
courses, institutes, and research studies aimed at the ultimate
goal of making man's later years his golden years." That statement was made in 1949 by the New York State Joint Legislative Committee on Problems of the Aging (Donahue, 1952, p.
119). If it was true then, it is certainly more so thirty years
later. That part of the task is rapidly being completed, for
awareness and programmatic adaptation are quickly expanding.

The future can expect to see major increases in the number of older people involved in educational pursuits of all types,
because each cohort of persons reaching age 55 will be larger
and will have higher levels of formal education, higher socioeconomic status, and better health (Palmore, 1976). Each of these

qualities is positively associated with educational participation in later life, and so the demand for instruction from our older citizens should continue to expand.

Likewise, there is reason to believe that our educational institutions, corporations, and community service agencies will be more willing to devote increased energy and resources to educational experiences for older people in the future. The number of younger people is declining, and organizations that hope to continue their growth will need to appeal to new audiences. This is obvious in higher education, where the number of traditional-aged students (ages 18–24) will decline substantially during the 1980s. Many colleges and universities are seeking new clienteles—minorities, women, handicapped, and the elderly—rather than carrying out faculty and program retrenchment. The same will be true of corporations. As they recognize the changing age mix of the population, they will begin to market products meant to appeal to the older adult. This is already visible as makers of clothing, makeup, over-the-counter drugs, and foods begin to orient their products toward the older consumer. It will happen in education also.

Much of the struggle to eradicate the myths about later life and the negative attitudes toward the potentials of older people remains, but this too should be accomplished in the not too distant future. As the extensive knowledge about aging is widely disseminated, it will become harder for program developers to ignore older people in any educational enterprise. Institutions will welcome them and make provision for special services, while trained instructors will be prepared for the unique circumstances of teaching this age group.

This circumstance does not universally exist today, however, even among institutions that offer programs primarily for older people. Some institutional programmers, such as the national Elderhostel, refuse to offer courses that deal with the topic of aging. They prefer to concentrate on the liberal arts and sciences, which exclude any emphasis on the physical, psychological, or social changes that occur across the life span. Reluctance to admit that the later years involve any uniqueness or interest contributes to the stereotypes that old age is to be avoided, ignored, or denied and leads to an attempt to be middle-aged forever. A preferable strategy would be to admit that one is serving older clients, to provide both age-segregated and age-integrated instruction, and to treat old age as a period that includes both unique problems and unique opportunities.

Learning Activities over the Life Span

In earlier portions of this century, the life span could be thought of as comprising four parts: a period of infancy and early childhood; youth, in which the person spent a great proportion of the available time in an educational setting; the majority of the life span, in which the person was employed or raised a family; and the last period of life, in which leisure time and chronic illness were the major considerations. Because persons born at the beginning of the twentieth century could expect to live only forty-seven years, the period of time spent in retirement was fairly short and not particularly enjoyable (Cutler and Harootyan, 1975). By 1940, the length of the work life had been extended, as had the period of retirement, since life expectancy was over sixty years. Today, the initial period of education is longer, and the period of retirement is much longer, with many people experiencing twenty years in this leisure condition.

We can observe social changes, however, that suggest that while life expectancy will continue to increase, substantial changes will occur in the distribution of education, work, and leisure across the life span. People are continuing to be involved in education throughout the life span, and they are moving into and out of the work force with greater frequency. This means that the learning society is becoming a reality and that most adults will find themselves in formal learning situations regardless of their age. Figure 4 shows some of these changes and indicates that education can be selected by middle-aged and older adults at a variety of times throughout their lives, depending on need and motivation.

This conceptualization of life-span activity implicitly suggests that people are involved in one major type of activity at

Figure 4. Life-Span Distribution of Education, Work, and Leisure.

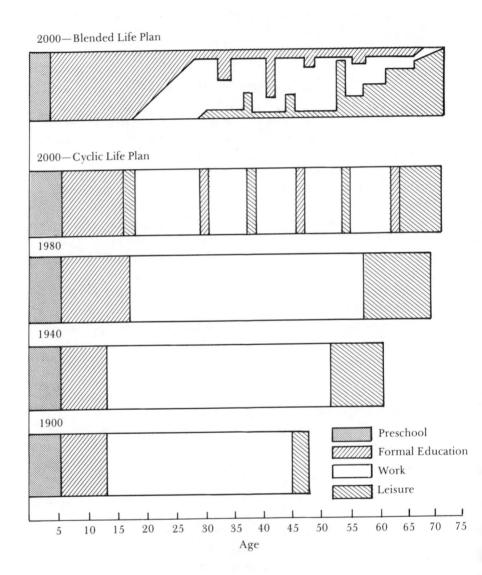

Source: Adapted from Work in America Institute, The Future of Older
Workers in America. Scarsdale, N.Y.: Work in America Institute, 1980.

any time—education, work, or leisure. As most of us are aware, this is not necessarily an accurate description of current reality. Many adults are involved in two or three of these activities simultaneously. Thus, it is not unusual to meet persons who are employed part-time and are attending college or university courses part-time. Others attend training programs on a part-time basis while vacationing or remaining unemployed the rest of the time. Some are employed part-time and care for a family the rest of their time. Thus, the current situation is much different from the sequential life plan that has been suggested. Cross (1981) describes this new situation as a "blended life plan"—one in which the person is involved in two or more major activities simultaneously.

As this pattern becomes common, it will be much more likely that each of these activities will be continued throughout the life span, rather than assuming that any of them will be relegated to a particular period of life. Thus, recurrent education is likely to continue throughout middle age and well into later life. This suggests that the model of education that continuing and adult education programs have successfully carried on over the past decades—part-time recurrent learning—will continue to be a viable approach into the future.

As Aslanian and Brickell (1980) have pointed out, the transition between one primary activity and another is often facilitated by formal learning. As these transitions become more frequent and as one transition phases into another, it should be expected that adults will engage in education nearly continuously, although on a part-time basis, in order to acquire the skills and knowledge needed to identify the transitions they are approaching, to learn what is needed for optimum adjustment, and to make the best decisions based on their goals and obligations.

Priority of Educational Programming. Education is interventionist by nature; that is, it is undertaken to bring about change, ideally change for the better. We have not reached general agreement on which changes are most needed, which programs are of greatest importance, and which outcomes are most

prized. The possible results from education are almost limit-
less. Birren and Woodruff (1973) suggested three—elimination
of illiteracy, skill development for problem solving, and prevention of future problems. McClusky (1971) added the development of contributive skills and those needed to influence society. The Academy for Educational Development (1974)
suggested new roles both in employment and in volunteerism.
Moody (1976) urged self-actualization through liberal study.

We must assume that a great deal of variety will be maintained in educational programming for older adults, since both
the older population and the educational delivery system are
very diverse. However, developing consensus on priorities seems
likely. In the past, program emphases have been determined primarily by client responsiveness to various program offerings and
to the availability of funding. Leisure pursuits, religious instruction, and consumer education have attracted the largest audiences and so have been the mainstay of instructional programs.
However, federal support of Adult Basic Education and volunteer training has led to major program thrusts in these areas.

The future is likely to include some other priorities as the
social and economic pressures generated by the growing older
population continue to be felt. The need for older people in the
work force will create pressures for retraining and obsolescence
avoidance. Changes in mandatory retirement, increased longevity,
improved health, and the need for skilled workers are likely to
encourage many people to remain in the work force longer, to
seek part-time employment, and to move into and out of retirement. Volunteer roles will become increasingly prevalent and
demanding; older persons will fill more of them and will be expected to function at a high level of competence. Because of the
growing pattern of lifelong education, older workers are likely
to be willing to accept instruction when it is offered.

Similarly, employers who once limited their instructional
activities for older people to retirement preparation are now retraining older workers, training persons who supervise them,
and upgrading personnel staff who will work with them. As employers realize the need for the skills that older employees have,
they can be expected both to expand in-house training pro-

grams and to fund participation in local colleges, public schools, and voluntary associations. This will provide a major impetus to the expansion of instructional programs and will provide a source of funding that has not been present in any major way in the past.

To date, all educational offerings have been viewed as being of equal importance; little priority has been placed on any single area of instruction. In the future, this is not likely to be the case. Some areas are likely to be seen as important to keep older people contributing to the economic welfare of themselves and society and to prevent a premature decline in health and physical functioning that would demand costly services. These types of employment and preventive education are likely to receive high commitments of public dollars, while other content areas, such as personal development, consumerism, and advocacy, will be viewed as a lower priority, resulting in little public funding. Course work in these latter areas will still be offered, but the participant will be expected to defray its costs rather than receive the instruction as part of the nation's commitment to education.

Financing Educational Programs. Generation of financial resources to support the planning and operation of educational programs for older persons will be crucial to program stability in the future. The federal government has invested as much as $14 billion annually in 270 programs of lifelong learning (Christoffel, 1978), but little of this is directed toward older people. Foundations have also contributed to individual projects, but for the most part, financial support has come from local sources or from volunteer contributions by faculty, staff, and laypersons to specific programs. The availability of hard dollars is not likely to expand in the future. Foundations are currently overwhelmed by requests from all kinds of human service programs, and the federal government is reducing its commitment both in education and in services. Volunteers have proved to be a major resource, but total reliance on the willingness of planners or instructors to contribute their time is not a viable strategy for the long run.

State government has historically carried the responsibility for educating children and young people. As the number of persons in the 6-to-22 age cohort declines, state departments of education could begin to direct additional dollars to the programs for adults and older persons. This would be responsive to demographic change and would indicate a commitment on the part of state government to expand public education throughout the life span. In reality, however, most states are in no financial position to expand funding in any discretionary area. They are seeking every means of reducing appropriations, and public schools and higher education are likely to receive some of the cuts. Consequently, it does not seem likely that state funding will expand rapidly, except for those students who participate in the regular degree programs of state educational institutions.

At the local level, financial support could become available. Local millage and federal block grants may allow for some additional funding, but local considerations are likely to result in substantial competition from many other service areas. Administrators and policy makers will have to be convinced that there is a substantial payoff if scarce dollars are to be spent on education for older persons. One rationale for this type of expenditure is that by providing educational services to older people, the institution is more likely to receive their support. This is very important in K–12 or community college districts in which the citizenry is asked to vote for higher taxes in order to support educational institutions. Older people are frequently believed to oppose increased education millage and are often blamed for the rejection of special tax levies. The community school, as exemplified by the Flint, Michigan, schools, has shown that providing attractive and relevant social and educational activities can result in consistent passage of millage issues. If other educational institutions were to act on the insight provided by Flint, it might prove to be a major source of financial support in the future.

Fees and tuition paid by participants are currently a major source of support for educational programs. The Academy for Educational Development (1974) reported that fees were used by 70 percent of all institutions offering programs for older people—substantially more than received government or philanthropic funding. The drawback is that fees charged are often minimal and do not cover the real costs of instruction. Most of us realize that we must pay for the services we receive, either directly or through taxes. If educational offerings are perceived to lead to renewed job opportunities or to facilitate volunteer functioning, some older persons are likely to pay for the educational service. This will be feasible for those in the highest socioeconomic circumstances, but the majority of older people will need some assistance.

Employers may be expected to bear the costs of retraining their older workers to reduce the impact of technological obsolescence on their work force. However, older persons who desire to reenter the work force will typically be expected to have acquired their training before accepting the job rather than after. Government sponsored job training programs are not high priority at this time, but we may be forced to revise and reinstitute them in the future if the productive capacity of the older population is to be effectively tapped.

The financial future of education for older people, then, is quite unclear. There exists no substantial source of funding that may be used for all types of programs, and funders who have supported particular programs in the past are unlikely to expand funding significantly in the future. The result will be continuing struggle by local educational providers to find resources. The best that can be expected is access to a variety of funding sources, each with different priorities, which will encourage variety in program development. In the long run, however, it will be necessary for educational providers to convince the older population of the value of education and to begin charging more realistic fees for the courses and programs offered.

Individualization of the Population

Another development that will substantially affect the learning participation of older people is the greater individualization of the American population. This can be seen in the great diversity of magazines, books, movies, television channels, specialty shops, organizations, and products on the market. Although we still think of America as a mass society, it is becoming a large number of minisocieties in which preferences, goals, and procedures differ substantially. Toffler (1980) refers to this development as the third wave, a sequel to the agrarian and industrial societies of the past, in which the general patterns of life in our mass culture are replaced by greater individualism.

Toffler makes a strong case that we are in the early stages of this "demassifying" process. If he is correct, then we can expect a need for greater variety in the educational and training offerings that are available and greater differences in the learning methods selected by middle-aged and older adults. This is evident as a few older persons choose to participate in the regular offerings of colleges and universities, some are involved in community programs, church and membership groups offer more courses, and business and industry involve some older persons. However, the majority of older learners are involved in learning activities outside formal instruction that are directed by the learner himself or herself (Tough, 1971). These learning experiences are undertaken through self-study, television courses, learning from friends or neighbors, and other informal opportunities available to each of us.

Toffler suggested that these will be expanded even more rapidly as interactive cable television and home microcomputers become more common. The numerous permutations of these communication and information-processing developments will allow adults to learn a variety of topics at home with little expense, at their own pace, and with great convenience. If educational providers are to continue to reach this audience, they will need to expand their delivery systems so that a variety of approaches in addition to classroom instruction are made available. The result will doubtless be an even greater array of organizations and companies involved in the provision of educational services. This is probably an appropriate development, since there is no centralized means of meeting the learning needs of all people, and the learners' backgrounds and inclinations are so different that many approaches will be needed in the future.

Educational Providers. Which organizations/institutions will become the major providers of educational services to older people remains somewhat in doubt. Informal organizations such as churches, clubs, and associations currently offer the greatest amount of instruction, but public schools, higher education, and the media can be expected to attract a larger audience in the future. There is little likelihood that any one provider will become dominant, as a growth trend can be seen in all areas (Farmer and Knox, 1977).

Expanded use of the media by older people can be expected. Since mobility and lack of energy prevent some older persons from traveling to a classroom location, the media may become much larger providers of information and instruction. There are several television programs designed exclusively for middle-aged and older people that now have gained some experience. These include *Over Easy, Old Friends/New Friends,* and *Winslow House* (Davis, 1980). The impact of these programs on the older segment of our population remains unknown, but they carry the potential of raising the level of consciousness as well as increasing knowledge about the many aspects of aging. The media bring instruction to the home where many older people are alone. Their needs for social interaction are not currently met through this approach, and increased dispersion of developing technology will be needed before most older viewers will become "participants" through interactive opportunities. However, the media are almost universally available and will continue to play a big role in the lives of older persons.

As the older audience is seen as a market for consumer products, it is possible that corporations will invest funds through commercials to support this type of programming. Some programs that appeal mainly to older persons—for instance, *The Lawrence Welk Show*—are sponsored by products that are of most interest to this group. Efforts in this direction still have a long way to go before they become sufficient to sponsor many programs for older learners, however.

Other potential providers of educational services to older people include profit-making corporations, which may enter those aspects of the area in which a profit can be made. Such

areas would include retirement preparation, health maintenance, second-career planning, financial planning, and others
that have the potential of attracting selected individuals or
groups who perceive benefit in learning new skills or knowledge.

To date, little marketing of this type has occurred. Older
people have been seen as small consumers of education, with
limited resources; consequently, they were not targeted for
sales. However, as the disposable income of the older cohort
grows and as their health improves, innovative marketing will
occur. Parallels in the large numbers of travel packages designed
for older persons, the savings plans for the "second half of life,"
and the restaurants with senior citizen specials show the potential of private-sector marketing to the older consumer.

Age-Integrated or Age-Segregated Instruction. An issue to
be addressed in the future is whether older students should be
included in course work for younger learners, whether older
learners are so distinct as to justify programs designed exclusively for them, or whether there should be some new form of
course work that is designed for age-integrated audiences. The
first two types of programming currently exist, and sentiment
supports each.

Inclusion of older people in regular courses for younger
learners has proven to be an appealing alternative for a minority of older learners. This type of instruction typically involves
admission restrictions, tests, rigorous assignments, and credentialing, all of which create a competitive environment that is
contrary to the desires of most older people. Some persons, especially those with relatively high levels of formal education,
those with strong self-images, those who desire a credential, and
those having a field-independent cognitive style, find these programs to their liking and move easily into the formal education
system. This approach is supported by many older persons and
program planners who believe that intergenerational learning is
preferable to that which is segmented by age.

However, age-segregated education has become the most
common form of instruction offered to older persons, because
of its low cost, the informal/social nature of the classroom, and
the relevance of the content to participants' interests. Frequently

programs are sponsored by senior citizen programmers and involve membership as well as content motivations. They have grown rapidly over the past few years and are likely to remain a major portion of the field. Although some deal with coping skills and job preparation, many are social in their orientation and appeal to enrollees as a leisure-time pursuit rather than as a way to expand their skills.

The third type of programming, some new form that is age-integrated but incorporates what is known about the learning desires and styles of older people, has yet to be developed. Although there may be examples in local areas, there is no national model of this type of instruction. It is important that this be developed. We cannot limit age-integrated opportunities to field-independent persons who wish to participate in pedagogical learning. Likewise, we cannot exclude younger people from informal, volunteer learning opportunities with older people simply because they are still seeking credentialing. Some as yet unknown pattern of instruction is needed that involves all age groups and offers opportunities for intergenerational exchange and interaction. It will need to involve both a conscious awareness of the unique abilities and interests of older people and some way to integrate them in a setting that is appealing to them and to younger people. This will not be an easy task, but it can be done in educational institutions as well as community agencies if careful planning and consensus gathering are appropriately undertaken.

Quality of Programming. Determination of the quality of educational programming for older persons will become a serious issue in the future. As limited resources affect more and more programs, it will be necessary for program planners to accept the accountability that comes with the public trust and to show that they are providing a valued and valuable service. As indicated previously, reports on instruction of older people are largely anecdotal, providing little in the way of clear evaluative outcomes that can be replicated in other settings. We have limited insight into why certain programs fail while others succeed; there are many questions that need systematic study. These include the long-term effect on a program of involvement by top administration; the importance of a charismatic leader; the effect of outside funding being available and later being phased out; the value of advisory committees; the best mix of personal development, liberal education, and coping skills classes; the effects of educational participation on the lives of older participants; the effect of a senior citizen program on voting behavior in local millage elections; the most effective types of instruction for various groups of learners; and the effect on younger students of learning in an intergenerational environment.

Today we have only fragmentary data on any of these and dozens of other questions about the development and conduct of instructional programs for older people. Over the past thirty years, the many programs established have met local needs and have been attuned to local organization guidelines. Reporting of developmental steps has been infrequent, and little insight is available on the extent to which unique local circumstances and activities affect results. Few research projects have examined either project outcomes or procedures, and none has compared the approaches of several administrators or instructors.

Likewise, there is currently no government or private group that regularly collects data on the extent, type, and budget of existing programs. The surveys done by the National Center for Education Statistics in 1969, 1972, and 1975 provide some insight into the changing enrollment of older people in adult education, but this is the only panel study that has attempted to indicate trends. Various studies such as those by Johnstone and Rivera (1965) and Harris and Associates (1975) can be examined, but differing samples, instruments, and analyses make comparability difficult. What is needed is a continuing data-collection process that reports participation of older people in various types of educational programs and allows for comparisons across time, sponsor, and program type.

It is unreasonable to expect that all program developers will have the resources or interest to rigorously evaluate each instructional program. However, it is reasonable to predict that increasing evaluation will take place in programs receiving outside funding and that some efforts will be made to determine the variables that cause local programs to succeed or fail. Although we have extensive knowledge of how to help older people learn in the laboratory, we have little reported experience on how to achieve maximum benefits in a classroom setting. Evaluation of outcomes and measures needs to be a priority in the future; one hopes that university-based regional or national centers will develop that have this aim.

Instructor quality is a part of this issue. Currently, instructors of older people have minimal background about the older person as a learner and the instructional processes that are most likely to result in effective learning. They are likely to be trained as teachers of children or to have content knowledge with little preparation in methodology and instructional design. Hence, teacher preparation will be required in the future. It is not likely that college degrees in teaching the older adult will become common for instructors, but continuing education offerings are likely to increase in number and quality, so that ignorance of the basics of instruction and older people will become a thing of the past.

Conclusions

Fries and Crapo (1981) have suggested that the national mortality profile of the United States is changing from a curve to a rectangle, with ever-greater numbers of people avoiding health difficulties and decline until later in life, so that their longevity extends into the late eighties. This projection indicates that fewer persons will die in their sixties and seventies, thus making the death rate very low until age 85 or so is reached.

It is important that this optimistic projection of physical vitality in old age be complemented by an equally optimistic expectation for social and psychological well-being. Education in the later years has a significant role to play in ensuring that this occurs. The provision of a variety of instructional activities from diverse providers can maximize the potential for retarding decline and encouraging growth.

For this to occur, instructional and learning opportunities

for older persons must be universally available. Educational institutions, community organizations, membership groups, and employers must all determine the extent to which they can serve older people and develop their offerings in accordance with the best precepts of instructional methodology. It would appear that this is in fact occurring. They are becoming beacons for society rather than mirrors of current expectations (Okun, 1982b). The development of programs is rapidly expanding, concern for assurance of quality is taking hold, and training of faculty is beginning to be more common.

The future, then, is bright. It is expected to be a time when persons of any age can continue their intellectual development and satisfy their learning wants in any part of the nation. The result will be the achievement of the learning society and the opportunity for people of any age to reach toward their full potential.

References

Academy for Educational Development. *Never Too Old to Learn*. New York: Academy for Educational Development, 1974.

Action for Independent Maturity. *Retirement Preparation Program*. Washington, D.C.: American Association of Retired Persons, 1978.

Adventures in Learning. Providence: University of Rhode Island, 1969.

Ahrens, R. "Testimony to the U.S. Senate Special Committee on Aging." In *Hearings on Retirement, Work, and Life Long Learning, Sept. 8, 1978*. Washington, D.C.: U.S. Government Printing Office, 1978.

American Association of State Colleges and Universities. *Alternatives for Later Life and Learning: Some Programs Designed for Older Persons at State Colleges and Universities*. Washington, D.C.: American Association of State Colleges and Universities, 1974.

American Society of Personnel Administration. "ASPA-BNA Survey No. 39: Retirement Policies and Programs." *ASPA Bulletin to Management,* January 24, 1980, pp. 1–12.

Anderson, R. E., and Darkenwald, G. G. *Participation and Persistence in American Adult Education*. New York: College Entrance Examination Board, 1979.

Arenberg, D. "Concept Problem Solving in Young and Old Adults." *Journal of Gerontology,* 1968, *23,* 279-282.

Arenberg, D., and Robertson, E. A. "The Older Individual as a Learner." In S. M. Grabowski and W. D. Mason (Eds.), *Education for the Aging.* Syracuse, N.Y.: ERIC Clearinghouse on Adult Education, n.d.

Arenberg, D., and Robertson-Tchabo, E. A. "Learning and Aging." In J. E. Birren and K. W. Schaie (Eds.), *Handbook of the Psychology of Aging.* New York: Van Nostrand Reinhold, 1977.

Ash, P. "Pre-Retirement Counseling." *Gerontologist,* 1966, *6,* 97-99.

Aslanian, C. B., and Brickell, H. M. *Americans in Transition.* New York: College Entrance Examination Board, 1980.

Atchley, R. C. "Retirement and Leisure Participation: Continuity or Crisis?" *Gerontologist,* 1971, *11,* 13-17.

Atchley, R. C. *The Sociology of Retirement.* New York: Wiley, 1976.

Axelrod, S., and Cohen, L. B. "Senescence and Embedded-Figure Performance in Vision and Touch." *Perceptual and Motor Skills,* 1961, *12,* 283-288.

Baltes, P. B., and others. "On the Dilemma of Regression Effects in Examining Ability-Level-Related Differentials in Ontogenetic Patterns of Intelligence." *Developmental Psychology,* 1972, *6,* 78-84.

Barfield, R., and Morgan, J. *Early Retirement.* Ann Arbor: University of Michigan, 1969.

Barkin, S. "Retraining and Job Redesign: Positive Approaches to the Continued Employment of Older Persons." In H. L. Sheppard (Ed.), *Toward an Industrial Gerontology.* Cambridge, Mass.: Schenkman, 1970.

Bauer, B. M. "A Model of Continuing Education for Older Adults." Unpublished doctoral dissertation, University of Minnesota, 1975.

Baugher, D. "Is the Older Worker Inherently Incompetent?" *Aging and Work,* 1978, *1,* 243-250.

Bayley, N., and Oden, M. H. "The Maintenance of Intellectual Ability in Gifted Adults." *Journal of Gerontology,* 1955, *10,* 91-107.

Beattie, W. M., Jr. "Preface." *Gerontologist,* 1971, *11,* iii–iv.

Belbin, E., and Belbin, R. M. "New Careers in Middle Age." In *Proceedings: 7th International Congress of Gerontology.* Paris: Organisation for Economic Co-operation and Development, 1966.

Belbin, E., and Belbin, R. M. *Problems in Adult Retraining.* London: Heinemann Educational Books, 1972.

Belbin, R. M. "Retirement Strategy in an Evolving Society." In F. M. Carp (Ed.), *Retirement.* New York: Behavioral Publications, 1972.

Bergman, M. "Changes in Hearing with Age." *Gerontologist,* 1971, *11,* 148–151.

Birren, J. E. *The Psychology of Aging.* Englewood Cliffs, N.J.: Prentice-Hall, 1964.

Birren, J. E., and Morrison, D. F. "Analysis of the WAIS Subtests in Relation to Age and Education." *Journal of Gerontology,* 1961, *16,* 363–369.

Birren, J. E., and Woodruff, D. S. "Human Development over the Life Span Through Education." In P. Baltes and K. W. Schaie (Eds.), *Life Span Developmental Psychology.* New York: Academic Press, 1973.

Bock, L. K. "Participation." In A. B. Knox and Associates, *Developing, Administering, and Evaluating Adult Education.* San Francisco: Jossey-Bass, 1980.

Bolton, C. R. *Planning and the Third Age: Retirement Education for Nebraskans.* Omaha: University of Nebraska at Omaha, 1975.

Bolton, C. R. "Humanistic Instructional Strategies and Retirement Education Programming." *Gerontologist,* 1976, *16,* 550–555.

Bolton, C. R. "Alternative Instructional Strategies for Older Learners." In R. H. Sherron and D. B. Lumsden (Eds.), *Introduction to Educational Gerontology.* Washington, D.C.: Hemisphere, 1978.

Bolton, E. B. "Cognitive and Non-Cognitive Factors That Affect Learning in Older Adults and Their Implications for Instruction." *Educational Gerontology,* 1978, *3,* 331–334.

Boshier, R. W., and Riddell, G. "Education Participation Scale

Factor Structure for Older Adults." *Adult Education,* 1978, *28,* 165-175.

Botwinick, J. "Intellectual Abilities." In J. E. Birren and K. W. Schaie (Eds.), *Handbook of the Psychology of Aging.* New York: Van Nostrand Reinhold, 1977.

Botwinick, J. *Aging and Behavior.* New York: Springer, 1978.

Botwinick, J., and Birren, J. E. "Cognitive Processes: Mental Abilities and Psychomotor Responses in Healthy Aged Men." In J. E. Birren and others (Eds.), *Human Aging: A Biological and Behavioral Study.* Washington, D.C.: U.S. Government Printing Office, 1963.

Bowman, D. L., and others. *How Pre-Retirement Planning Works.* Des Moines, Iowa: Drake University, 1970.

Boyack, V. L. "A Research and Training Model for Pre-Retirement Education Programs for Minority Populations." Paper presented at the Gerontological Society Scientific Meeting, San Francisco, November 1977.

Boyack, V. L. "Preparing for Retirement: Crisis or Challenge?" Testimony to the House Select Committee on Aging, June 19, 1978.

Brahce, C. I., and Hunter, W. W. "Leadership Training for Retirement Education." In R. H. Sherron and D. B. Lumsden (Eds.), *Introduction to Educational Gerontology.* Washington, D.C.: Hemisphere, 1978.

Buehler, C. "Genetic Aspects of the Self." *Annals of the New York Academy of Sciences,* 1962, *96,* 730-764.

Burgess, E. *Aging in Western Societies.* Chicago: University of Chicago Press, 1960.

Burkey, F. T. "Educational Interest of Older Adult Members of the Brethren Church in Ohio." Unpublished doctoral dissertation, Ohio State University, 1975.

Butler, R. N. *Why Survive? Being Old in America.* New York: Harper & Row, 1975.

Butler, R. N., and Lewis, M. I. *Aging and Mental Health.* St. Louis, Mo.: Mosby, 1977.

Butts, R. F., and Cremin, L. A. *A History of Education in American Culture.* New York: Holt, Rinehart and Winston, 1953.

Bynum, J. E., Cooper, B. L., and Acuff, A. G. "Retirement Reorientation: Senior Adult Education." *Journal of Gerontology,* 1978, *33,* 253-261.

Calhoun, R. O., and Gounard, B. R. "Meaningfulness, Presentation Rate, List Length, and Age in Elderly Adults' Paired Associate Learning." *Educational Gerontology,* 1979, *4,* 49-56.

Califano, J. A. "The Aging of America: Questions for the Four Generation Society." In *Annals of the American Academy of Political and Social Science,* 1978, *438,* 96-107.

Canestrari, R. E., Jr. "Paced and Self-Paced Learning in Young and Elderly Adults." *Journal of Gerontology,* 1963, *18,* 165-168.

Canestrari, R. E., Jr. "Age Changes in Acquisition." In G. A. Talland (Ed.), *Human Aging and Behavior.* New York: Academic Press, 1968.

Cattell, R. B. "Theory of Fluid and Crystallized Intelligence: A Clinical Experiment." *Journal of Educational Psychology,* 1963, *54,* 1-22.

Central Bureau for the Jewish Aged. *Extending Educational and Cultural Opportunities for Old People.* New York: Central Bureau for the Jewish Aged, 1971.

Charles, D. C. "Effect of Participation in a Pre-Retirement Program." *Gerontologist,* 1971, *11,* 24-28.

Chelsvig, K. A., and Timmermann, S. "Tuition Policies of Higher Educational Institutions and State Governments and the Older Learner." *Educational Gerontology,* 1979, *4,* 147-159.

Chickering, A. W., and Associates. *The Modern American College: Responding to the New Realities of Diverse Students and a Changing Society.* San Francisco: Jossey-Bass, 1981.

Christoffel, P. H. "Current Federal Programs for Lifelong Learning: A $14 Billion Effort." *School Review,* 1978, *86,* 348-359.

Christrup, H., and Thurman, C. "A Preretirement Program That Works." *Journal of Home Economics,* 1973, *65,* 20-22.

Claeys, R. R. *Utilization of College Resources in Gerontology: A Program Guide.* Upper Montclair, N.J.: Montclair State College, 1976.

Clague, E., Palli, B., and Kramer, L. *The Aging Worker and the Union.* New York: Praeger, 1971.

Comalli, P. E., Jr. "Cognitive Functioning in a Group of 80-90 Year Old Men." *Journal of Gerontology,* 1965, *20,* 14-17.

Comalli, P. E., Jr., Krus, D. M., and Wapner, S. "Cognitive Functioning in Two Groups of Aged; One Institutionalized, the Other Living in the Community." *Journal of Gerontology,* 1965, *20,* 9-13.

Coqueret, A. "Methods of Vocational Training for Older Workers in the French National Railways." In *Job-Redesign and Occupational Training for Older Workers.* Paris: Organisation for Economic Co-operation and Development, 1965.

Corso, J. F. "Auditory Perception and Communication." In J. E. Birren and K. W. Schaie (Eds.), *Handbook of the Psychology of Aging.* New York: Van Nostrand Reinhold, 1977.

Covey, H. C. "An Exploratory Study of the Acquisition of a College Student Role by Older People." *Gerontologist,* 1980, *20,* 173-181.

Craik, F. I. M. "Age Differences in Human Memory." In J. E. Birren and K. W. Schaie (Eds.), *Handbook of the Psychology of Aging.* New York: Van Nostrand Reinhold, 1977.

Crawford, J. "Interactions of Learner Characteristics with the Difficulty Level of Instruction." *Journal of Educational Psychology,* 1978, *70,* 523-531.

Cross, K. P. "Learning Society." *College Board Review,* 1974, *91,* 1-6.

Cross, K. P. *The Missing Link: Connecting Adult Learners to Learning Resources.* New York: College Entrance Examination Board, 1978.

Cross, K. P. "Adult Learners: Characteristics, Needs, and Interests." In R. E. Peterson and Associates, *Lifelong Learning in America: An Overview of Current Practices, Available Resources, and Future Prospects.* San Francisco: Jossey-Bass, 1979.

Cross, K. P. *Adults as Learners: Increasing Participation and Facilitating Learning.* San Francisco: Jossey-Bass, 1981.

Cross, W., and Florio, C. *You Are Never Too Old to Learn.* New York: McGraw-Hill, 1978.

Cutler, N. E., and Harootyan, R. A. "Demography of the Aged."

In D. S. Woodruff and J. E. Birren (Eds.), *Aging: Scientific Perspectives and Social Issues.* New York: D. Van Nostrand, 1975.

Darkenwald, G. G., and Merriam, S. B. *Adult Education: Foundations of Practice.* New York: Harper & Row, 1982.

Davis, R. H. *Television and the Aging Audience.* Los Angeles: Andrus Gerontology Center, 1980.

DeCrow, R. *Older Americans: New Uses of Mature Ability.* Washington, D.C.: American Association of Community and Junior Colleges, 1978.

DeCrow, R. *New Learning for Older Americans.* Washington, D.C.: Adult Education Association of the U.S.A., n.d.

Demko, D. J. "The Aging Education Continuum: A Community College's Response." In M. A. Okun (Ed.), *New Directions for Continuing Education: Programs for Older Adults,* no. 14. San Francisco: Jossey-Bass, 1982.

DiStafano, J. J. "Interpersonal Perceptions of Field-Independent and Field-Dependent Teachers and Students." Unpublished doctoral dissertation, Cornell University, 1969.

Doebler, L. K., and Eicke, F. J. "Effects of Teacher Awareness of the Educational Implications of Field-Dependent/Field-Independent Cognitive Style on Selected Classroom Variables." *Journal of Educational Psychology,* 1979, *71,* 226-231.

Donahue, W. T. "Education's Role in Maintaining the Individual's Status." In *Annals of the American Academy of Political and Social Science,* 1952, *283,* 115-125.

Donahue, W. T. "Adjusting Employees to Retirement." *Management Record,* September 1953, pp. 1-3.

Donahue, W. T. (Ed.). *Education for Later Maturity.* New York: Whiteside, 1955.

Downey, G. W. "The Greying of America." *Nation's Schools and Colleges,* 1974, *1,* 36-43.

Edelson, I. *The Role of State University Systems in Opportunities for Senior Citizens.* Albany: State University of New York at Albany, 1976.

Eisdorfer, C. "Adaptation to Loss of Work." In F. M. Carp (Ed.), *Retirement.* New York: Behavioral Publications, 1972.

Eisdorfer, C., Busse, E. W., and Cohen, L. D. "The WAIS Performance of an Aged Sample: The Relationship Between Verbal and Performance I.Q.s." *Journal of Gerontology,* 1959, *14,* 197-201.

Eisdorfer, C., Nowlin, F., and Wilkie, F. "Improvement of Learning in the Aged by Modification of Autonomic Nervous System Activity." *Science,* 1970, *170,* 1327-1329.

Elias, M. F., and Elias, P. K. "Motivation and Activity." In J. E. Birren and K. W. Schaie (Eds.), *Handbook of the Psychology of Aging.* New York: Van Nostrand Reinhold, 1977.

Entine, A. D. "New Roles for Older Americans." *Generations,* 1979, *3,* 20-21.

Erikson, E. H. *Childhood and Society.* (2nd ed.) New York: Norton, 1963.

Erikson, E. H. *Identity and the Life Cycle.* New York: Norton, 1980.

Eteng, W. I. A. "Adjustment to Retirement and Aging Transitions in Wisconsin." Unpublished doctoral dissertation, University of Wisconsin, 1972.

Farmer, J., and Knox, A. *Alternative Patterns for Strengthening Community Service Programs in Institutions of Higher Education.* Urbana: University of Illinois, 1977.

Federal Experience Under the Community Schools Act, 1980. Washington, D.C.: U.S. Government Printing Office, 1981.

Fillenbaum, G. G. "Retirement Planning Programs: At What Age and for Whom?" *Gerontologist,* 1971, *11,* 33-36.

Fillenbaum, G. G., and Willis, E. "Effects of Training Program." *Industrial Gerontology,* 1976, 213-221.

Fisher, D. L. "A Psychology Experiment: Training Laboratory for Retirement." Unpublished doctoral dissertation, United States International University, 1974.

Fisher, J. C. "Educational Attainment, Anomie, Life Satisfaction and Situational Variables as Predictors of Participation in Educational Activities by Active Older Adults." Unpublished doctoral dissertation, University of Wisconsin, Milwaukee, 1979.

Fitzpatrick, E. W. "Evaluating a New Retirement Planning Program: Results with Hourly Workers." *Aging and Work,* 1979, *2,* 87-94.

Florio, C. *Collegiate Programs for Older Adults: A Summary Report on a 1976 Survey.* New York: Academy for Educational Development, 1978.

Florio, C. "Education and Work Programs for Older Persons." Mimeographed, n.d.

Fozard, J. L., and others. "Visual Perception and Communication." In J. E. Birren and K. W. Schaie (Eds.), *Handbook of the Psychology of Aging.* New York: Van Nostrand Reinhold, 1977.

Frank, L. "Education for Aging." In W. T. Donahue (Ed.), *Education for Later Maturity.* New York: Whiteside, 1955.

Fries, J. F., and Crapo, L. M. *Vitality and Aging.* San Francisco: W. H. Freeman, 1981.

Furry, C. A., and Baltes, P. B. "The Effect of Age Differences in Ability-Extraneous Performance Variables on the Assessment of Intelligence in Children, Adults, and the Elderly." *Journal of Gerontology,* 1973, *28,* 68-72.

Galvin, K., and others. *Educational and Retraining Needs of Older Adults.* Washington, D.C.: Educational Resources Information Center, 1975. (ED 110 132)

Gillaspy, R. T. "Labor Force Participation of the Older Population: Toward 1990—a Demographic Approach." In P. K. Ragan (Ed.), *Work and Retirement: Policy Issues.* Los Angeles: Andrus Gerontology Center, 1979.

Glamser, F. D., and DeJong, G. F. "The Efficacy of Preretirement Preparation Programs for Industrial Workers." *Journal of Gerontology,* 1975, *30,* 595-600.

Glickman, L. L., Hersey, B. S., and Goldenberg, I. I. *Community Colleges Respond to Elders.* Washington, D.C.: U.S. Government Printing Office, 1975.

Gonda, J. "History by Training Interactions and Cognitive Performance in the Elderly." Paper presented at the annual meeting of the American Psychological Association, San Francisco, September 1977.

Goodrow, B. A. "The Learning Needs and Interests of the Elderly in Knox County, Tennessee." Unpublished doctoral dissertation, University of Tennessee, 1975a.

Goodrow, B. A. "Limiting Factors in Reducing Participation in

Older Adult Learning Opportunities." *Gerontologist,* 1975b, *15,* 418-422.

Grabowski, S. M., and Mason, W. D. (Eds.). *Education for the Aging.* Syracuse, N.Y.: ERIC Clearinghouse on Adult Education, n.d.

Graney, M. J., and Hays, W. C. "Senior Students: Higher Education After Age 62." *Educational Gerontology,* 1976, *1,* 343-360.

Granick, S., Kleben, M. H., and Weiss, A. D. "Relationships Between Hearing Loss and Cognition in Normally Hearing Aged Persons." *Journal of Gerontology,* 1976, *31,* 434-440.

Grattan, C. H. *In Quest of Knowledge.* New York: Associated Press, 1955.

Greene, M. R., and others. *Preretirement Counseling, Retirement Adjustment, and the Older Employee.* Eugene: University of Oregon, 1969.

Gross, R., Hebert, T., and Tough, A. "Independent, Self-Directed Learners in American Life: The Other 80% of Learning." Paper presented at George Washington University, 1977.

Grotelueschen, A. D. "Program Evaluation." In A. B. Knox and Associates, *Developing, Administering, and Evaluating Adult Education.* San Francisco: Jossey-Bass, 1980.

Hall, G. S. *Senescence: The Last Half of Life.* New York: D. Appleton, 1922.

Harris, L., and Associates. *The Myth and Reality of Aging in America.* Washington, D.C.: National Council on the Aging, 1975.

Havighurst, R. J. *Developmental Tasks and Education.* New York: McKay, 1952.

Havighurst, R. J. "Education Through the Adult Life Span." *Educational Gerontology,* 1976, *1,* 41-52.

Heidbreder, E. M. "Factors in Retirement Adjustment: White Collar/Blue Collar Experience." *Industrial Gerontology,* Winter 1972, 69-79.

Heisel, M. A., Darkenwald, G. G., and Anderson, R. E. "Participation in Organized Educational Activities Among Adults Age 60 and Over." *Educational Gerontology,* 1981, *6,* 227-240.

Hendrickson, A. (Ed.). *A Manual on Planning Educational Pro-*

grams for Older Adults. Tallahassee: Florida State University, 1973.

Hendrickson, A., and Aker, G. F. *Education for Senior Adults.* Tallahassee: Florida State University, 1969.

Hendrickson, A., and Aker, G. F. *Report on Education for Older Citizens: Proceedings of Leadership Development Institute.* Tallahassee: Florida State University, 1971.

Hendrickson, A., and Barnes, R. E. *The Role of Colleges and Universities in the Education of the Aged.* Columbus: Ohio State University, 1964.

Hiemstra, R. P. "Continuing Education for the Aged: A Survey of Needs and Interests of Older People." *Adult Education,* 1972, *22,* 100-109.

Hiemstra, R. P. "Educational Planning for Older Adults: A Survey of 'Expressive' vs. 'Instrumental' Preferences." *International Journal of Aging and Human Development,* 1973, *4,* 147-156.

Hiemstra, R. P. *The Older Adult and Learning.* Lincoln: University of Nebraska—Lincoln, 1975.

Hiemstra, R. P., and Long, R. A. "A Survey of 'Felt' Versus 'Real' Needs of Physical Therapists." *Adult Education,* 1974, *24, 270-279.

Hixson, L. E. *Formula for Success: A Step by Step Procedure for Organizing a Local Institute of Lifetime Learning.* Washington, D.C.: Educational Resources Information Center, 1968. (ED 028 366)

Hoffman, D. H. "Arts Programming for the Elderly." *Educational Gerontology,* 1978, *3,* 17-33.

Hoffman, E. *The Federal Role in Lifelong Learning.* New York: College Entrance Examination Board, 1980.

Holley, W. H., Jr., and Feild, H. S., Jr. "The Design of a Retirement Preparation Program: A Case History." *Personnel Journal,* 1974, *53,* 527-530.

Hooper, J. O., and March, G. B. "A Study of Older Students Attending University Classes." *Educational Gerontology,* 1978, *3,* 321-330.

Hoos, I. R. *Retraining the Work Force: An Analysis of Current Experience.* Berkeley: University of California Press, 1967.

Horacek, B. J., and Francke, S. N. "Senior Citizen Celebration

Days: A University-Based Education Program." *Educational Gerontology*, 1978, *3*, 61-70.

Hornblum, J. N., and Overton, W. F. "Area and Volume Conservation Among the Elderly: Assessment and Training." *Developmental Psychology*, 1976, *12*, 68-74.

Houle, C. O. *The Inquiring Mind.* Madison: University of Wisconsin Press, 1961.

Houle, C. O. *The Design of Education.* San Francisco: Jossey-Bass, 1972.

"How IBM Avoids Layoffs Through Retraining." *Business Week*, November 10, 1975, pp. 110-112.

Hulicka, I. M. "Age Differences in Retention as a Function of Interference." *Journal of Gerontology*, 1967, *22*, 180-184.

Hultsch, D. "Adult Age Differences in the Organization of Free Recall." *Developmental Psychology*, 1969, *1*, 673-678.

Hunter, S. E. "A Comparison of the Perceived and Assessed Learning Needs of Senior Citizens in Weld County, Colorado." Unpublished doctoral dissertation, University of Northern Colorado, 1977.

Hunter, W. W. *A Longitudinal Study of Retirement Preparation.* Ann Arbor: University of Michigan Institute of Gerontology, 1968a.

Hunter, W. W. *Preretirement Education for Hourly-Rated Employees.* Washington, D.C.: Bureau of Research, Office of Education, U.S. Department of Health, Education and Welfare, 1968b.

Institute of Law and Aging. *Survey of National Law School Programs and Materials in Law and Aging.* Washington, D.C.: National Law Center, George Washington University, 1978.

Jacobs, A. L., Mason, W. D., and Kauffman, E. (Eds.). *Education for Aging: A Review of Recent Literature.* Washington, D.C.: Adult Education Association of the U.S.A., 1970.

Jacobson, B. *Young Programs for Older Workers: Case Studies in Progressive Personnel Policies.* New York: Van Nostrand Reinhold, 1980.

Jakubauskas, E. B., and Taylor, V. "On-the-Job Training and Reemployment of the Older Worker." *Industrial Gerontology*, June 1969, 10-18.

Jarvik, L. F., Kallman, F. J., and Falek, A. "Intellectual Changes in Aged Twins." *Journal of Gerontology,* 1962, *17,* 289-294.

Jellison, H. *Higher Education and the Older Volunteer: A Place for Everyone.* Washington, D.C.: American Association of Community and Junior Colleges, 1980.

Jensen-Osinski, B. H., and others. *The Graying of the College Classroom: Impact of Older People as Peers in the Classroom on Attitudes and on Performance of Undergraduates.* Bethlehem, Pa.: Lehigh University, 1981.

Johnstone, J. W. C., and Rivera, R. J. *Volunteers for Learning.* Chicago: Aldine Press, 1965.

Kalt, N. C., and Kohn, M. H. "Pre-Retirement Counseling: Characteristics of Programs and Preferences of Retirees." *Gerontologist,* 1975, *15,* 179-181.

Kaplan, M. "The Uses of Leisure." In C. Tibbitts (Ed.), *Handbook of Social Gerontology.* Chicago: University of Chicago Press, 1960.

Kasschau, P. L. "Reevaluating the Need for Retirement Preparation Programs." *Industrial Gertonology,* Winter 1974, 42-59.

Kelleher, C. H., and Quirk, D. A. "Age, Functional Capacity and Work: An Annotated Bibliography." *Industrial Gerontology,* Fall 1973, 80-98.

Klodin, V. M. "Verbal Facilitation of Perceptual-Integrative Performance in Relation to Age." Unpublished doctoral dissertation, Washington University, St. Louis, 1975.

Knowles, M. S. *The Modern Practice of Adult Education.* Chicago: Association Press, 1980.

Knowlton, M. P. "Liberal Arts: The Elderhostel Plan for Survival." *Educational Gerontology,* 1977, *2,* 87-94.

Knox, A. B. *Adult Development and Learning: A Handbook on Individual Growth and Competence in the Adult Years for Education and the Helping Professions.* San Francisco: Jossey-Bass, 1977.

Knox, A. B. (Ed.). *New Directions for Continuing Education: Assessing the Impact of Continuing Education,* no. 3. San Francisco: Jossey-Bass, 1979.

Knox, A. B. (Ed.). *New Directions for Continuing Education:*

Leadership Strategies for Meeting New Challenges, no. 13. San Francisco: Jossey-Bass, 1982.

Knox, A. B., and Associates. *Developing, Administering, and Evaluating Adult Education.* San Francisco: Jossey-Bass, 1980.

Korim, A. S. *Older Americans and Community Colleges: An Overview.* Washington, D.C.: American Association of Community and Junior Colleges, 1974.

Labouvie-Vief, G. "Models of Cognitive Functioning in the Older Adult: Research Needs in Educational Gerontology." In R. H. Sherron and D. B. Lumsden (Eds.), *Introduction to Educational Gerontology.* Washington, D.C.: Hemisphere, 1978.

Lee, J. A., and Pollack, R. H. "The Effects of Age on Perceptual Problem-Solving Strategies." *Experimental Aging Research,* 1978, *4,* 37–54.

Leech, S., and Witte, K. L. "Paired-Associate Learning in Elderly Adults as Related to Pacing and Incentive Conditions." *Developmental Psychology,* 1971, *5,* 180.

Levinson, D. J. *The Seasons of a Man's Life.* New York: Knopf, 1978.

Linton, T. E., and Spence, D. L. "The Aged: A Challenge to Education." *Adult Leadership,* 1964, *12,* 261–280.

Litwin, G. H. "Achievement Motivation and the Older Worker." In H. L. Sheppard (Ed.), *Toward an Industrial Gerontology.* Cambridge, Mass.: Schenkman, 1970.

Londoner, C. A. "Instrumental and Expressive Education: A Basis for Needs Assessment and Planning." In R. H. Sherron and D. B. Lumsden (Eds.), *Introduction to Educational Gerontology.* Washington, D.C.: Hemisphere, 1978.

Long, H. B. "Characteristics of Senior Citizens. Educational Tuition Waivers in Twenty-One States: A Follow-Up Study." *Educational Gerontology,* 1980, *5,* 139–150.

Long, H. B., and Rossing, B. E. "Tuition Waiver Plans for Older Americans in Post-secondary Public Education Institutions." *Educational Gerontology,* 1979, *4,* 161–174.

Lusterman, S. *Education in Industry.* New York: Conference Board, 1977.

Lynch, J. H. "Pre-retirement Education: Issues in Nomenclature and Methodology." Paper presented at annual meeting of the Western Gerontological Society, Denver, November 1977.

McClellan, R. W. *Claiming a Frontier: Ministry and Older People.* Los Angeles: University of Southern California Press, 1977.

McClusky, H. Y. *Education: Background and Issues.* Washington, D.C.: White House Conference on Aging, 1971.

McClusky, H. Y. "The Community of Generations: A Goal and a Context for the Education of Persons in the Later Years." In R. H. Sherron and D. B. Lumsden (Eds.), *Introduction to Educational Gerontology.* New York: Hemisphere, 1978.

McClusky, H. Y. "Education for Aging: The Scope of the Field and Perspectives for the Future." In S. M. Grabowski and W. D. Mason (Eds.), *Education for the Aging.* Syracuse, N.Y.: ERIC Clearinghouse on Adult Education, n.d.

McConnell, S. R. "Alternative Work Patterns for an Aging Work Force." In P. K. Ragan (Ed.), *Work and Retirement: Policy Issues.* Los Angeles: Andrus Gerontology Center, 1979.

McConnell, S. R., and others. *Alternative Work Options for Older Workers: A Feasibility Study.* Los Angeles: Andrus Gerontology Center, 1979.

McGhie, A., Chapman, J., and Lawson, J. S. "Changes in Immediate Memory with Age." *British Journal of Psychology,* 1965, *56,* 69–75.

Mack, M. J. "An Evaluation of a Retirement-Planning Program." *Journal of Gerontology,* 1958, *13,* 198–202.

McPherson, B., and Guppy, N. "Pre-retirement Life-Style and the Degree of Planning for Retirement." *Journal of Gerontology,* 1979, *34,* 254–263.

Manion, U. V. "Preretirement Counseling: The Need for a New Approach." *Personnel and Guidance Journal,* 1976, *55,* 119–121.

March, G. B., Hooper, J. O., and Baum, J. "Life Span Education and the Older Adult: Living Is Learning." *Educational Gerontology,* 1977, *2,* 163–172.

Marcus, E. E. "Effects of Age, Sex and Status on Perception of the Utility of Educational Participation." *Educational Geron-tology*, 1978, *3*, 295-319.

Marcus, E. E., and Havighurst, R. J. "Education for the Aging." In E. J. Boone, R. W. Shearon, E. E. White, and Associates, *Serving Personal and Community Needs Through Adult Education*. San Francisco: Jossey-Bass, 1980.

Marks, C. "Learning in the Sun: A Winter Retreat." *Educational Gerontology*, 1979, *4*, 143-146.

Maves, P. B. "Programming for Older Adults: A Church's Response." In M. A. Okun (Ed.), *New Directions for Continuing Education: Programs for Older Adults*, no. 14. San Francisco: Jossey-Bass, 1982.

Meyer, S. L. "A Study of the Effects of a Pre-retirement Workshop on the Measured Level of Self-Actualization of University Civil Service Employees." Unpublished doctoral dissertation, Oregon State University, Corvallis, 1975.

Meyer, S. L. "Andragogy and the Adult Learner." *Educational Gerontology*, 1977, *2*, 115-122.

Miller, S. J. "The Social Dilemma of the Aging Leisure Participant." In A. M. Rose and W. A. Peterson (Eds.), *Older People and Their Social World*. Philadelphia: F. A. Davis, 1965.

Moberg, D. O. "Life Enrichment Educational Needs of Older People." *Adult Leadership*, 1962, *2*, 162-164.

Monge, R., and Hultsch, D. "Paired-Associate Learning as a Function of Adult Age and the Length of the Anticipation and Inspection Intervals." *Journal of Gerontology*, 1971, *26*, 157-162.

Monk, A. "Factors in the Preparation for Retirement by Middle Aged Adults." *Gerontologist*, 1971, *11*, 348-351.

Monk, A., and Donovan, R. "Pre-retirement Preparation Programs: A Review of the Recent Literature." *Aged Care and Services Review*, 1978-1979, *1*, 1-7.

Moody, H. R. "Philosophical Presuppositions of Education for Old Age." *Educational Gerontology*, 1976, *1*, 1-16.

Moody, H. R. "Education and the Life-Cycle: A Philosophy of Aging." In R. H. Sherron and D. B. Lumsden (Eds.), *Introduction to Educational Gerontology*. Washington, D.C.: Hemisphere, 1978.

Mullan, C., and Gorman, L. "Facilitating Adaptation to Change: A Case Study in Retraining Middle-Age and Older Workers at Aer Lingus." *Industrial Gerontology,* Fall 1972, 20-39.

Murphy, J., and Florio, C. *Never Too Old to Teach.* New York: Academy for Educational Development, 1978.

Myhr, P. J. *The Older Adult's Training Program: A Report on the 1975-76 Developmental Year.* Seattle: University of Washington, 1976.

Nagle, R. M. "Personality Differences Between Graduate Students in Clinical and Experimental Psychology at Varying Experience Levels." Unpublished doctoral dissertation, Michigan State University, 1967.

National Center for Education Statistics. *Participation in Adult Education: Final Report—1975.* Washington, D.C.: U.S. Government Printing Office, 1978.

National Retired Teachers Association/American Association of Retired Persons. *A Survey of Opinions of Older Americans.* Washington, D.C.: National Retired Teachers Association/ American Association of Retired Persons, 1980.

Nelson, T. C. "The Age Structure of Occupations." In P. K. Ragan (Ed.), *Work and Retirement: Policy Issues.* Los Angeles: Andrus Gerontology Center, 1979.

Newsham, D. B. "The Challenge of Change to the Older Trainee." *Industrial Gerontology,* October 1969, 32-33.

Nielsen Report on Television, 1980. Northbrook, Ill.: A. C. Nielsen Co., 1980.

Norton, P. G. *Consideration of How Levels of Achievement and Anxiety Toward Education Affect Older People's Participation in Adult Education Programs.* Boston: Boston University, 1970.

Ohio Administration on Aging. *The Older American and Higher Education in Ohio.* Columbus, Ohio: Administration on Aging, 1973.

Okun, M. A. (Ed.). *New Directions for Continuing Education: Programs for Older Adults,* no. 14. San Francisco: Jossey-Bass, 1982a.

Okun, M. A. "Reflections on Programs for Older Adults." In M. A. Okun (Ed.), *New Directions for Continuing Education:*

Programs for Older Adults, no. 14. San Francisco: Jossey-Bass, 1982b.

Okun, M. A., and Siegler, I. C. "The Perception of Outcome-Effort Covariation in Younger and Older Men." *Educational Gerontology,* 1977, *2,* 27–32.

Oltman, P. K., Raskin, E., and Witkin, H. A. *Group Embedded Figures Test.* Palo Alto, Calif.: Consulting Psychologists Press, 1971.

Organisation for Economic Co-operation and Development. *Job Design and Occupational Training for Older Workers.* Paris: Organisation for Economic Co-operation and Development, 1965.

Owens, W. A., Jr. "Age and Mental Abilities: A Longitudinal Study." *Genetic Psychology Monographs,* 1953, *48,* 3–54.

Owens, W. A., Jr. "Is Age Kinder to the Initially More Able?" *Journal of Gerontology,* 1959, *14,* 334–337.

Pacaud, S. "Some Concrete Examples of the Advantages and Disadvantages of Age Encountered in the Occupational Training of Older Workers." *Job-Redesign and Occupational Training for Older Workers.* Paris: Organisation for Economic Co-operation and Development, 1965.

Palmore, E. "The Future Status of the Aged." *Gerontologist,* 1976, *16,* 297–302.

Palmore, E. "Facts on Aging Quiz." *Gerontologist,* 1977, *17,* 315–320.

Palmore, E. "Preparation for Retirement: The Impact of Pre-retirement Programs on Retirement and Leisure." Paper presented at annual meeting of the Association for Gerontology in Higher Education, Washington, D.C., February 1982.

Panek, P. E., and Associates. "Age Differences in Perceptual Style, Selective Attention, and Perceptual-Motor Reaction Time." *Experimental Aging Research,* 1978, *4,* 337–387.

Parnes, H. S., and others. *From the Middle to the Later Years: Longitudinal Studies of Retirement and Postretirement Experiences of Men.* Columbus: Center for Human Resources Research, Ohio State University, 1979.

Patton, C. V. *Academia in Transition: Mid-career Change or Early Retirement.* Cambridge, Mass.: Abt Books, 1979.

Pennington, F. C. (Ed.). *New Directions for Continuing Educa-*

tion: Assessing Educational Needs of Adults, no. 7. San Francisco: Jossey-Bass, 1980.

Peterson, D. A. "Toward a Definition of Educational Gerontology." In R. H. Sherron and D. B. Lumsden (Eds.), *Introduction to Educational Gerontology.* Washington, D.C.: Hemisphere, 1978.

Peterson, R. E. "Present Sources of Education and Learning." In R. E. Peterson and Associates, *Lifelong Learning in America: An Overview of Current Practices, Available Resources, and Future Prospects.* San Francisco: Jossey-Bass, 1979.

Plopper, M. "Mental Health in the Elderly." In R. H. Davis (Ed.), *Aging: Prospects and Issues.* Los Angeles: University of Southern California Press, 1981.

Powell, A. H., Jr., Eisdorfer, C., and Bogdonoff, M. D. "Physiologic Response Patterns Observed in a Learning Task." *Archives of General Psychiatry,* 1964, *10,* 192-195.

Pyron, H. C. "Preparing Employees for Retirement." *Personnel Journal,* 1969, *48,* 722-727.

Pyron, H. C., and Manion, U. V. "The Company, the Individual, and the Decision to Retire." *Industrial Gerontology,* Winter 1970, 1-11.

Rappaport, F. S. A. "Retirement Ages, Issues, and Trends." Paper prepared for the President's Commission on Pension Policy, 1979.

Rappole, G. H. "An Overview of Community College Programs for Elderly Texans." *Educational Gerontology,* 1978, *3,* 35-59.

Rehermann, O., and Brun, B. "Embedded Figures Test Compared with Clinical Tests of Abstraction and Memory in Intellectual Impairment." *Scandinavian Journal of Psychology,* 1978, *19,* 495-504.

Reich, M. H. "Group Preretirement Education Program: Whither the Proliferation?" *Industrial Gerontology,* 1977, 29-43.

Research and Forecasts, Inc. *Retirement Preparation: Growing Corporate Involvement.* New York: Corporate Committee for Retirement Planning, 1979.

Rich, D. D. "Campus Offers Intergenerational Bridge." *Generations,* 1978, *3,* 32-33.

Richardson, P. "Teaching-Learning Styles and Older Learners."

Presentation to the Adult Education Association of the U.S.A., Anaheim, Calif., November 1981.

Riegel, K. F., and Riegel, R. M. "Development, Drop, and Death." *Developmental Psychology,* 1972, *6,* 306-319.

Riley, M. W., and Foner, A. *Aging and Society: An Inventory of Research Findings.* New York: Russell Sage Foundation, 1968.

Rindskopf, K., and Charles, D. C. "Instructor Age and the Older Learner." *Gerontologist,* 1974, *14,* 479-482.

Robinson, P. B., Jr. "Socio-cultural Characteristics of Senior Citizen Participants in Adult Education." *Adult Leadership,* 1972, *20,* 234-235ff.

Rockstein, M., Chesky, J., and Sussman, M. "Comparative Biology and Evolution of Aging." In C. E. Finch and L. Hayflick (Eds.), *Handbook of the Biology of Aging.* New York: Van Nostrand Reinhold, 1977.

Rosen, B., and Jerdee, T. H. "Too Old or Not Too Old." *Harvard Business Review,* 1977, *55,* 97-106.

Rosow, I. *Housing and Social Interaction of the Aged.* New York: Free Press, 1967.

Ross, E. "Effect of Challenging and Supportive Instructions in Verbal Learning in Older Persons." *Journal of Educational Psychology,* 1968, *59,* 261-266.

Sarno, M. R. *Activities in the Field of Aging as Reported by Representatives of Colleges and Universities in Ohio.* Columbus, Ohio: Columbus Technical Institute, 1975.

Scanlon, J. *How to Plan a College Program for Older People.* New York: Academy for Educational Development, 1978.

Schaie, K. W. "Age Changes in Adult Intelligence." In D. S. Woodruff and J. E. Birren (Eds.), *Aging: Scientific Perspectives and Social Issues.* New York: Van Nostrand Reinhold, 1975.

Schaie, K. W. "Age Changes in Intelligence." In R. L. Sprott (Ed.), *Age, Learning Ability and Intelligence.* New York: Van Nostrand Reinhold, 1980.

Schaie, K. W., and Parr, J. "Intelligence." In A. W. Chickering and Associates, *The Modern American College: Responding to the New Realities of Diverse Students and a Changing Society.* San Francisco: Jossey-Bass, 1981.

Schein, E. H. *Organizational Psychology*. Englewood Cliffs, N.J.: Prentice-Hall, 1970.

Schein, E. H. *Career Dynamics: Matching Individual and Organizational Needs*. Reading, Mass.: Addison-Wesley, 1978.

Schow, R. L., and others. *Communication Disorders of the Aged: A Guide for Health Professionals*. Baltimore: University Park Press, 1978.

Schultz, N. R., and Hoyer, W. J. "Feedback Effects on Spatial Egocentrism in Old Age." *Journal of Gerontology*, 1976, *31*, 72-75.

Schwartz, D. W., and Karp, S. A. "Field Dependence in a Geriatric Population." *Perceptual and Motor Skills*, 1967, *24*, 495-504.

Senior Center Humanities Program. Washington, D.C.: National Council on the Aging, 1982.

Shanas, E. "Facts Versus Stereotypes: Cornell Study of Occupational Retirement." *Journal of Social Issues*, 1958, *14*, 61-62.

Sheppard, H. L. *Research and Development Strategy on Employment-Related Problems of Older Workers*. Washington, D.C.: American Institutes for Research, 1978.

Sherron, R. H., and Lumsden, D. B. (Eds.). *Introduction to Educational Gerontology*. Washington, D.C.: Hemisphere, 1978.

Shooter, A. M. N., and others. "Some Field Data on the Training of Older People." *Occupational Psychology*, 1956, *30*, 1-12.

Siegel, S. R., and Rives, J. M. "Characteristics of Existing and Planned Preretirement Programs." *Aging and Work*, 1978, *1*, 93-99.

Smith, J. M. "Aging and Retraining." *Occupational Psychology*, 1973, *47*, 141-147.

Somers, G. *Evaluation of Work Experience and Training of Older Workers*. Washington, D.C.: National Council on the Aging, 1967.

Sonnenfeld, J. "Dealing with the Aging Work Force." *Harvard Business Review*, 1978, *56*, 81-92.

Spencer, B. "Overcoming the Age Bias of Continuing Education." In G. G. Darkenwald and G. A. Larson (Eds.), *New Di-*

rections for Continuing Education: Reaching Hard-to-Reach Adults, no. 8. San Francisco: Jossey-Bass, 1980.

Sprague, N. "Industrial Gerontology." In H. Sheppard (Ed.), *Toward an Industrial Gerontology.* Cambridge, Mass.: Schenkman, 1970.

Sprouse, B. M. (Ed.). *National Directory of Educational Programs in Gerontology.* Washington, D.C.: U.S. Government Printing Office, 1976.

Sprouse, B. M. *Community-Based Learning Centers for Older Adults: Research Report.* Madison: Faye McBeath Institute on Aging and Adult Life, University of Wisconsin—Madison, 1981.

Storandt, M. "Age, Ability Level, and Method of Administering and Scoring the WAIS." *Journal of Gerontology,* 1977, *32,* 177-178.

Streib, G. F., and Schneider, C. J. *Retirement in American Society: Impact and Process.* Ithaca, N.Y.: Cornell University Press, 1971.

Sussman, M. B. "An Analytic Model for the Sociological Study of Retirement." In F. M. Carp (Ed.), *Retirement.* New York: Behavioral Publications, 1972.

Swaboda, D. W. "A Survey of the Perceptions of Pre-retired Older Workers in Selected Businesses Toward Various Aspects of Retirement with Implications for Pre-retirement Education." Unpublished doctoral dissertation, University of Nebraska—Lincoln, 1974.

Szczypkowski, R. "Objectives and Activities." In A. B. Knox and Associates, *Developing, Administering, and Evaluating Adult Education.* San Francisco: Jossey-Bass, 1980.

Tager, R. M. "Physical Health Realities—a Medical View." In R. H. Davis (Ed.), *Aging: Prospects and Issues.* Los Angeles: University of Southern California Press, 1981.

Taub, H. A. "Mode of Presentation, Age, and Short Term Memory." *Journal of Gerontology,* 1975, *30,* 56-59.

Thompson, W. E. "Pre-retirement Anticipation and Adjustment in Retirement." *Journal of Social Issues,* 1958, *14,* 35-45.

Thorson, J. A. "A Media Approach to Pre-retirement Education." *Adult Leadership,* 1976, *24,* 344-346.

Thorson, J. A. "Future Trends in Education for Older Adults." In R. H. Sherron and D. B. Lumsden (Eds.), *Introduction to Educational Gerontology*. Washington, D.C.: Hemisphere, 1978.

Tiberi, D. M., Boyack, V. L., and Kerschner, P. A. "A Comparative Analysis of Four Preretirement Education Models." *Educational Gerontology*, 1978, *3*, 355-374.

Timmermann, S. "Education for Older Persons in the USA." Paper presented at the 12th International Congress of Gerontology, Hamburg, Germany, July 1981.

Toffler, A. *The Third Wave*. New York: Bantam, 1980.

Tough, A. *The Adult's Learning Projects*. Austin, Texas: Learning Concepts, 1971.

Tough, A. *Major Learning Efforts: Recent Research and Future Directions*. Toronto: Ontario Institute for Studies in Education, 1977.

Tramer, R. R., and Schludermann, E. H. "Cognitive Differentiation in a Geriatric Population." *Perceptual and Motor Skills*, 1974, *39*, 1071-1075.

Tuckman, J. "Educational Programing." In W. T. Donahue (Ed.), *Education for Later Maturity*. New York: Whiteside, 1955.

U.S. Bureau of the Census. *Statistical Abstract of the United States, 1979*. Washington, D.C.: U.S. Government Printing Office, 1979.

U.S. Bureau of the Census. *Educational Attainment in the United States, March 1978 and 1979*. Washington, D.C.: U.S. Government Printing Office, 1980.

U.S. Congress, Senate Committee on Human Resources. *Findings on Age, Capacity, and Productivity*. Washington, D.C.: U.S. Government Printing Office, 1977.

U.S. Congress, Senate Special Committee on Aging. *Hearings on Retirement, Work and Lifelong Learning, Sept. 8, 1978*. Washington, D.C.: U.S. Government Printing Office, 1978.

U.S. Congress, Senate Subcommittee on Manpower, Employment and Labor. *Examination of the War on Poverty*. Vol. 2. Washington, D.C.: U.S. Government Printing Office, 1967.

U.S. Department of Health, Education and Welfare, Public

Health Service, National Institute on Aging. "Our Future Selves—a Research Plan Toward Understanding Aging. Report of the Panel on Research on Human Services and Delivery Systems." Washington, D.C.: U.S. Government Printing Office, 1978.

User's Guide: Age Related Vision and Hearing Changes—an Empathic Approach. Ann Arbor: University of Michigan, 1976.

Van Dusen, W. D., Miller, R. H., and Pokorny, D. M. *Planning for a Statewide Educational Information Center Network.* New York: College Entrance Examination Board, 1978.

Walker, J. W., and Gutteridge, T. G. *Career Planning Practices: An AMA Survey Report.* New York: American Management Association, 1979.

Wasserman, I. M. "The Educational Interests of the Elderly: A Case Study." *Educational Gerontology,* 1976, *1,* 323-330.

Watkins, B. T. "Renaissance at Chautauqua." *Chronicle of Higher Education,* September 23, 1981, pp. 4-5.

Weinstock, R. *The Graying of the Campus.* New York: Educational Facilities Laboratories, 1978.

Whatley, L. F. "Expressive and Instrumental Educational Interests of Older Adults as Perceived by Adult Educators, Gerontologists, and Older Adults." Unpublished master's thesis, University of Georgia, 1974.

Willis, S. "Introductory Remarks: Contemporary Approaches to Learning in Later Adulthood—a Symposium." *Educational Gerontology,* 1977, *2,* iii.

Witkin, H. A. "Cognitive Style in Academic Peer Performance and in Teacher-Student Relations." In S. Messick and Associates, *Individuality in Learning: Implications of Cognitive Styles and Creativity for Human Development.* San Francisco: Jossey-Bass, 1976.

Woodruff, D. S., and Walsh, D. A. "Research in Adult Learning: The Individual." *Gerontologist,* 1975, *15,* 424-430.

Work in America Institute. *The Future of Older Workers in America.* Scarsdale, N.Y.: Work in America Institute, 1980.

Index

331